THINGS TO COME

HERMAN KAHN
B. BRUCE-BRIGGS

THINGS

THINKING ABOUT
THE SEVENTIES
AND EIGHTIES

TO

COME

THE MACMILLAN COMPANY, New York, New York

901.94
K12t
1972

The Macmillan Company
866 Third Avenue, New York, N.Y. 10022
Collier-Macmillan Canada Ltd., Toronto, Ontario

Library of Congress Catalog Card Number: 74-182449

THIRD PRINTING 1972

Printed in the United States of America

Acknowledgments

A glance at the copyright page of this book will reveal that *Things to Come* was copyrighted by The Hudson Institute. Even in an age when the submergence of the individual into the organization is a commonplace phenomenon, the institutionalization of a book is still rare. Authorship, like most other intellectual pursuits, still remains largely individualistic. In this book we the authors, as is proper, must necessarily take full blame for any of the flaws in the work; however, it is basically an organizational product. All of the staff at Hudson have contributed in some way to this work, as have the thousands of people with whom we have discussed these issues at meetings, seminars, and briefings at the Institute and other locations around the world. We should like to especially acknowledge: the economic projections of Gus Weiss, Jr.; the foreign policy studies of Edmund Stillman and William Pfaff; the studies on Asia and American public opinion of Frank Armbruster; the contributions of Barry Smernoff to the chapter on technological forecasting; the assistance of William Kristol with the editing; and the supervision of the typing by Carolann (Mrs. Louis) Roussel, Robert Panero, Anthony J. Wiener, and Garrett N. Scalera deserve special mention for their invaluable contributions to so many of the concepts herein.

> ... the success,
> Although particular, shall give a scantling
> Of good or bad unto the general;
> And in such indexes, although small pricks
> To their subsequent volumes, there is seen
> The baby figure of the giant mass
> Of things to come at large.
>
> *Troilus and Cressida*

Contents

INTRODUCTION   1

I

The Multifold Trend in the Seventies and
Eighties—The Macro-historical Perspective   7

II

La Belle Epoque—The Metaphorical Use of
Historical Analogy   ⁊0

III

A Surprise-Free Projection—The World of the
Seventies and Eighties   39

IV

Counterculture or Counterreformation—
Countervailing Forces   88

V

Sources of Stability and Instability in the
International System—Where we are and
where we are going   114

VI

Alternate U.S. Futures—Scenarios and
Branch Points   162

VII

Military-Technological Possibilities in the Seventies
and Eighties—Technological Forecasting   186

VIII

The 1985 Technological Crisis—The Social
Effects of Technology   205

IX

The Emerging Post-Industrial Society—
Evolutionary and Revolutionary Change   220

X

The Rise of Japan—A Case Study in Methodology   232

XI

The Ideology of Tomorrow   244

INDEX   251

Introduction

In the last decade, studying the long-range future has become both a serious intellectual pursuit and a very pervasive fad. Studies of the future are being conducted in the United States, Japan, and parts of Europe. Some of these future studies can be distinguished from earlier works by their use of a sustained, cooperative, and relatively systematic approach; others by being part of some semi-religious, semi-political cult. Still others are basically faddish journalism—sometimes good, sometimes bad—but still journalism. And, of course, discussing the future is necessarily an art and not a science in the usual sense, though many disciplines are enlisted in a common, integrated effort of analysis and speculation. Despite their proliferation, it is unlikely that these efforts will replace the works of writers such as Jules Verne, H. G. Wells, or Aldous Huxley; their visionary fantasies have made deeper impressions and have been more widely accepted than the more systematic and professional attempts of long-range forecasters. However, from our perspective—that of influencing relatively specific private and public decisions—a properly integrated project is more likely to incorporate relevant insights from a broad range of academic and technical disciplines and has a better chance of identifying the policy issues of the future.

A competent interdisciplinary study will not necessarily arouse the interest and concern of citizens and decision makers, but it should, at least, contain discussions on which subsequent research and debate can build. Hudson Institute, originally founded in 1961 to engage in policy analysis, particularly on American national security issues, has in recent years been more and more engaged in the infant but growing field of future studies, or *futurology*.* This interest was continually prompted by a

* This is an ugly word, smacking of pseudoscience, but we seem to be stuck with it

growing recognition that policy planning requires some idea of what the world is going to be like when these policies come to fruition. The acceleration of change is such that decision makers can no longer make plans and other choices on the basis of a historically workable "status quo" or "business-as-usual" premise. Very little can be known for certain about future changes, but the changes will be there and appropriate discussion can shed useful light on the possibilities. Thinking about the future can tell us a lot about the present.

Perhaps this is as good a time as any to lay to rest the idea that anyone can predict the future. To the best of our knowledge, no professional futurologists claim infallibility. But, that said, it must be qualified, maintaining that the future can be predicted, much as it is when you buy an airplane ticket on the basis of the airline's prediction that it will reach San Francisco at 9:00 P.M. or when you bend your finger expecting that the Winchester in your arms will propel a few grams of lead into a fleeing deer. Of course, your plans may go awry, your plane may be diverted or crash, or your rifle may misfire. But in each case you have acted with a pretty good idea of what the future would bring. You also take action on the basis of future events which have a very low probability of happening—you buy double indemnity life insurance and carry a spare tire. Essentially, these are the same sorts of things that are done in studying the future.

It is impossible to delineate the future with absolute certainty or in detail, but a range of likelihood can be established: in 1985 there will still be an Atlantic Ocean; in 1985 there will still be a French state; in 1985 people will still drive automobiles; in 1985 the Communists will still rule Russia. None of the above statements is true in that it can be proved, but certainly all are more true (i.e., more probable) than statements like: in 1985 America will be Communist; in 1985 France will be part of the Fourth Reich; in 1985 Americans will enjoy universal promiscuity. Some future events are improbable, others are almost certain, with a wide range in between. The purpose of this book is to get some idea of the possibilities and probabilities of the future. Even though the future does not yet exist, it can be studied.*

---

* For a detailed theoretical justification of future studies see Bertrand de Jouvenel's *The Art of Conjecture* (New York, 1966).

Since the mid-1960s, Hudson has been engaged in a continuing study of the future of the United States and of the world. We expect to continue this research at least through the mid-1970s. Over this decade, we expect to perform a unique study of the future of mankind. Much of this study has been funded by research grants and contracts from various government agencies that are concerned with the future of their particular areas of concern and responsibility; some has been funded by grants from foundations and contracts from private nonprofit and profitmaking organizations. Recently, primary support for Hudson's future study has come from about one hundred American and foreign (mostly multi-national) corporations, with which we are conducting our current study of "The Corporate Environment, 1975–1985."

Things To Come is a working document of our continuing study of the future, reflecting partial and tentative conclusions. We sometimes joke that nothing is ever really finished at Hudson: we merely pause from time to time to write up what we have so far. This book can be viewed as such a temporary pause for reflection. The reader may be aware of two previous documents— Herman Kahn and Anthony J. Wiener's, *The Year 2000* (1967), and Kahn's, *The Emerging Japanese Superstate* (1970). Both of these were products of the study. Readers familiar with *The Year 2000* will recognize some of the ideas contained here since *The Year 2000* represents an earlier document of our ongoing future studies. In many ways this book overlaps and continues the argument of *The Year 2000*. In fact, we are very pleased that *The Year 2000* holds up remarkably well six years after it was written. As a result, any discussion of the 1970s and 1980s by us will, on the whole, elaborate and develop the discussion of that book rather than contradict it. We hope that this relatively short and introductory work will also serve as a popularizer of many of the ideas discussed at great length in *The Year 2000*. Also, *Things To Come* has a somewhat different emphasis. Whereas *The Year 2000* is concerned with the long-range prospects of mankind, *Things To Come* looks toward the 1970s and 1980s, or in what we would call the "short-" and "middle-range" prospects of mankind. Some things which we feel are very important in the long run will not have any great impact in the short run. On the other hand, some short-range events may be very striking and vital, but essentially transitory. *The Year 2000* also contained an extended theoretical justification of futurology, while this book tries to present examples of futurist methodology in use. If *The Year 2000* can be thought of as strategic, *Things To Come* can be thought of as tactical.

Like Hudson's previous works, this book has several purposes. By circulating it through commercial channels, we hope to enlighten the concerned and interested public about the issues of the future. We also hope that by organizing this book around a methodological framework and giving a short introduction to the techniques and assumptions of futurology and policy research,* as well as to the terminology used in the work at Hudson, that people who deal with us directly or indirectly can better understand what we are about and how we are organized. One of the most trying problems of our time is the lack of a shared language among the educated public.

We hope that circulating this volume will help to construct a shared language for serious and intellectual discussions. Historically the educated classes have always had a common frame of reference in which they could conduct public discussions and attempt to further the public interest. For example, the Founding Fathers of the American Republic had read the Bible, Plutarch, Shakespeare, Adam Smith, John Locke, and Edward Gibbon. When they came together at Philadelphia in 1787, they had a common set of references which they could use to express their ideas. Such a common set of references is noticeably lacking today. Even for issues that affect everyone, there is no available shared literature—no storehouse of well-understood concepts, no standard types. For this reason we have developed our own. The use of jargon is obviously less appealing than the use of, for example, references to the great books of history, but few of these are read today. We think our terminology is preferable to the alternatives—either endless streams of paper elaborating various aspects of the subject, or the relatively clumsy or diffuse formulations and insights which are evident in much public explication of societal issues today.

Hudson has also found helpful the use of charts, that is, lists,

* Shortly, we intend to publish a technical guide to methodology of principal interest to specialists.

graphs, quotations, and tables concisely providing large amounts of information quickly and succinctly on as many key issues of a given topic as possible. We have prepared thousands of charts, some of which are included here. These charts are normally gathered into "chartpages" (examples of which can be found in Chapters V and VII) or "chartbooks." Such a chartpage or chartbook can be described as a topical or thematic overview and checklist. We are pleased to see that in the last few years the chartbook format has been adopted by U.S. Government agencies and other institutions.

By 1976, the year of the bicentennial celebration of the American Republic, Hudson hopes to have accomplished an important milestone in our study of the future. In cooperation with other organizations, we hope to have a relatively elaborate in-depth discussion of U.S. issues; perhaps looking back two hundred years to 1776 to discuss how these arose and looking ahead to the year 2000 to conjecture on how they might further develop. Such a review of how far we have come and where we are headed should be most useful and extremely interesting. If the project is really successful, it may put many things in proper perspective and thus change many current attitudes. We hope that this book, if not precisely "The baby figure of the giant mass/Of things to come at large," at least helps to indicate some of the problems we will be dealing with and the opportunities we will have in the next ten to twenty years.

I

The Multifold Trend in the Seventies and Eighties— The Macro-historical Perspective

THE long-term multifold trend in Western culture began approximately a thousand years ago, but not all the aspects of it can be traced back that far. Some can be first detected only a few hundred years ago; others go back almost the full millennium. The existence of these secular trends is based upon empirical observation rather than theoretical construction and is independent of any particular perspective on—or theory of—macro-history.

A macro-historian (sometimes called a universal historian) is one who seeks to understand and explain all of human history. St. Augustine, Karl Marx, Oswald Spengler, and Arnold J. Toynbee are among the best known. Many academic historians have a low opinion of such efforts and most of their technical and professional criticisms have some validity. However, the academics offer no alternative solutions to the important issues tackled by macro-historians. Indeed, some academics deny that the issues are relevant and say that useful discussion is impossible. We would argue that critics who dispute the very notion of macro-history (rather than any particular scheme) may be like a man who uses a microscope to examine a river flowing to the sea and then claims it is impossible to determine the direction of flow. He is so close to the subject that minor details mask its general movement. These critics may also be similar to the man who is too close to the mouth of the river where the river flow is dominated by the ebbs and flows of the tide. The tidal phenomenon is such that he cannot tell the direction of flow by just watching this portion of river—it seems to flow backward about as often as forward. He has to know about the *whole* river to make a correct decision. We would judge that the overwhelming majority of historians recognize the unproven existence of the multifold trend— and that those who do not may be either too close to the subject or confused by the ebb and flow phenomenon.

All of the macro-historians who have seriously discussed the rise and fall of cultures in the last century have noticed some aspects of the multifold trend and have attributed enormous significance to them—even if they disagree with each other about details, terminology, and implications. The idea of a long-term multifold trend as an important organizational concept is used in this book, as it was in *The Year 2000*. This is a useful source of conjectures as well as a context and framework. Some of these conjectures overlap with the constructs of the macro-historians, but they do not accept any particular theory of macro-history as being proven.

The Long-term Multifold Trend of Western Culture

1. Increasingly sensate (empirical, this-worldly, secular, humanistic, pragmatic, manipulative, explicitly rational, utilitarian, contractual, epicurean, hedonistic, etc.) cultures
2. Bourgeois, bureaucratic, and meritocratic elites
3. Centralization and concentration of economic and political power
4. Accumulation of scientific and technical knowledge
5. Institutionalization of technological change, especially research, development, innovation, and diffusion
6. Increasing military capability

7. Westernization, modernization, and industrialization
8. Increasing affluence and (recently) leisure
9. Population growth
10. Urbanization, recently suburbanization and "urban sprawl" —soon the growth of megalopoli
11. Decreasing importance of primary and (recently) secondary and tertiary occupations; increasing importance of tertiary and (recently) quarternary occupations
12. Increasing literacy and education and (recently) the "knowledge industry" and increasing role of intellectuals
13. Innovative and manipulative social engineering—i.e., rationality increasingly applied to social, political, cultural, and economic worlds as well as to shaping and exploiting the material world—increasing problem of ritualistic, incomplete, or pseudo rationality
14. Increasing universality of the multifold trend
15. Increasing tempo of change in all the above

One of the most important assumptions that can be made about the future is that in most countries of the world it looks as if this multifold trend is going to continue, but with important differences in detail in various areas. In some countries it is getting to the point where it cannot go any further and another change in the kind of culture or quality of civilization is occurring. The continuance, or "forward movement," of the multifold trend does not necessarily suggest that this trend is beneficial in the way that nineteenth century writers assumed that progress was always desirable. This is just the way the world seems to be going in the long run, like it or not. If the multifold trend be the direction, then anything opposing or slowing the trend is necessarily not a forward movement, even though it may be a desirable or even a necessary thing to do at the time. The multifold trend is conceived of as a long-term base line which may include within it certain short-term fluctuations, some of which may temporarily reverse the trend and slow the general forward movement in the next fifteen years.

First and foremost in the multifold trend is the increasingly *sensate* culture. This term, derived from Pitirim Sorokin,* is best explained by contrasting it to Sorokin's other concept, *ideational.*

* *Social and Cultural Dynamics* (New York, 1937). Although we find Sorokin's terminology useful, we do not accept the substance of his theory of history.

To Sorokin, ideational cultures are those which are principally
motivated by other-worldly ideals. They tend to be charismatic,
commonistic, spiritual, and highly emotional. They rely upon
revelation and dogma for truth. In the Western tradition, the
early Middle Ages represents an extremely ideational culture. To
this concept Sorokin opposes the concept of the sensate culture
which is empirical, secular, humanistic, pragmatic, utilitarian,
contractual, and oriented to this world to the exclusion of the
next. Clearly, over the past thousand years of Western culture
there has been a steady, though irregular, movement from the
ideational to the sensate culture. For example, few modern artists
choose religious subjects, and relatively few modern writers approach religious themes. Even religion as it exists in modern
society tends to be pragmatic and worldly, rather than adhering
to its historic ideational goals. Most historians would agree that
the past one thousand years has seen a shift from religious cultures to more materialistic ones.

A sensate trend does not merely mean an increasing role for
science and technology, but a systematic erosion of the sacred, of
taboos and totems, and in some ways even of the very concepts of
authority and tradition. Obviously, there have been many ebbs
and flows in this erosion. The Reformation and Counter-Reformation, the Enlightenment and the Romantic reaction are the
best historical examples. Even making reasonable concessions to
religious humanists, secular humanists, and cultists who resent
and deny any formulation that attributes a lesser religiosity or
sacredness to their personal beliefs, it can be argued persuasively
that ever since the tenth or eleventh century there has been a
general decrease in the role of the religious and the sacred perspectives and attitudes and a general increase in the role of the
mundane, the secular, the practical, and the humanist perspectives and attitudes. We agree with many of the macro-historians
that this process may be the single most important aspect of the
long-term multifold trend.

Apparently we today are viewing pronounced tendencies toward a *late sensate* culture, particularly in the culture area of
Northwestern Europe (formerly Protestant Europe—Britain, the
Low Countries, Northwest Germany, and Scandinavia—and its
overseas settlements in Anglo-America and the Antipodes),
which has a very pronounced tendency toward what critics would

call cynical, nihilistic, superficial, transient, disillusioned, and alienated forms of cultural expression and social behaivor. A glance at any of the productions of the "underground press" will demonstrate this tendency. However, there also are strong movements in the world to counteract this movement. Millions of people are deeply affronted by the outward manifestations of late sensate behavior, such as the open display of pornography, and in some parts of the Northwestern cultural area, most particularly the United States, there is a strong possibility of a powerful "counterreformation" which might halt the further movement toward a late sensate society, at least for a time, and may affect its details for a longer period. The strength of such a counterreformation would depend upon many imponderable factors, including the vigor of the late sensate movement itself. Which movement will be stronger is still an open question, although it is one of the most important questions that can be asked about the next generation, having profound implications for the future of our society and its politics.

The second trend, the trend toward *bourgeois, bureaucratic, and meritocratic elites,* has been almost universal. In the last five or ten years there has, of course, come into being a rather spectacular revolt against middle-class bourgeois values—a revolt led by the youth of the upper middle class. In a way this revolt is a reactionary and even aristocratic, or "feudal," movement as well as one with (as many have noticed) certain aspects of the fascist ideology. This last comment is not intended as an insult or a derogatory charge, but merely an observation that many anti-bourgeois movements—whether on the left or on the right—have certain common romantic and traditional elements. How far these anti-bourgeois movements will go is another open question. However, the modern Western and non-Western world has seen an almost uninterrupted triumph of the bourgeoisie everywhere. (Even China, Burma, and other states which claim to be exceptions are, to a surprising degree, not. The most conspicuous real exceptions are in the Moslem world, and even there the changes have been enormous.)

There are very few traditionalist regimes remaining in the world and those few are almost all of extremely doubtful longevity, threatened either by revolution or by internal reform. Monarchy, the dominant form of government for four thousand years, is just about finished. The dozen or so ruling monarchs in the world may be deposed by revolution or coup at any time, and once ousted, they have little chance of regaining their thrones. This is true in Jordan, Morocco, Ethiopia, Afghanistan, Iran, and all of the various shiekdoms of the Arabian peninsula. Even while these countries remain monarchical, the traditional power, prestige, and position of the historical ruling classes—the aristocracy, landowners, and clergy—has eroded and has been largely transferred to a centralized government bureaucracy. Of particular importance in the embourgeoisement of the Westernistic countries is the existence of a Westernized military which in every country offers an alternative government to the status quo.

Not only has the bourgeoisie been expanding at the expense of the "feudal" classes, it is aggrandizing itself at the expense of the proletariat and the peasantry. In all Western countries, the more skilled elements of the working classes have been pretty thoroughly embourgeoised in the sense that they own property, hold traditional middle-class values, and increasingly consider themselves middle class (this is especially true of their wives). In most countries the traditionally debased illiterate peasantry has been brought into modern society and taught to be a functioning member of the modern bourgeois system. Except in the most backward corners of Quebec and the South, there are no peasants remaining in North America, only businessmen whose business is farming. Northern Europe has gone the same way; Southern Europe is going.

The proliferation of bureaucracies is one of the most striking characteristics of the contemporary world. Armies of clerks fill business and government offices from Mukden to Montevideo. Educational institutions proliferate to supply the demand (or perhaps to force the demand) for jobs. All social classes contribute their most bookish young to office work.

Meritocratic standards, that is, the assigning of prestige, position, power, and pecuniary rewards on the basis of ability, talent, achievement, and performance rather than birth, influence, style, or fortune, is spreading and contributing to the decline of traditional elites and societies. In more and more of the world persons are assigned their positions in society on the basis of some sort of personal attribute—whether it be by their true ability as determined by actual performance in the commercial marketplace or by some arbitrary standard such as passing a test—instead of by birth, although family status, even in the most rigorous socialist countries, still gives certain advantages. However, these advantages are held increasingly to be irrational and unjustified. According to good bourgeois principles, a man is supposed to make his own way in the world according to his own ability. All aspects of this trend should continue unchecked through 1985. But we must call attention to one less favorable effect which should become more pronounced and troublesome over the next generation. Increasingly, meritocratic standards of potential and performance are being measured by the passing of written tests or by the possession of formal educational requirements rather than by demonstrated ability. Both mandarinism and professional meritocracy are spreading, threatening to divide society and bar the multitudes from society's plums, not to mention the potential of filling our upper ranks with formally qualified, but less competent, leaders.

The third trend, *the centralization and concentration of economic and political power*, is another aspect that may show some reversal in the 1970s and 1980s. During the post-World War II era we saw a decentralization of political power in the breakup of the great European colonial empires. Since World War II, the number of sovereign states in the world has increased threefold and while there are a few possible states which could still be established and whose liberation or attempted liberation could create severe international crises, the number of such states is limited. The major remaining source of possible new independent political units is the multinational, or imperial, powers in the world—the Soviet Union, China, India, and Pakistan. White-controlled Africa could also provide a few more states to the world system, as could the breakup of many of the existing black African states whose boundaries are almost all irrational with respect to linguistic, religious, and ethnic, or tribal, divisions. However, these possibilities, especially the dissolution of the empires, are extremely unlikely during the next fifteen years. There are even some pressures to reassemble the now-divided states of Germany, Korea, China, and Vietnam.

On the whole, we do not think there will be many more states in 1985 than there are today. The great period of post-World War II state building is over. Still, the concentration of political power within the states is continuing. With a very few exceptions the typical pattern in most of the world is a transfer of power from the individual or the private corporation (in the medieval sense of a non-governmental collective body) to the government. In nations with a federal system there is a transfer of power from the lower to the higher elements of government, and a transfer from the legislative to the executive. These tendencies are most pronounced, of course, in the socialist countries, but they appear in the social democratic/liberal, capitalist, and even conservative states. Current quasi-decentralization of management may slow this movement, but there is no strong reason to expect reversal of the trend.

There probably will not be significant concentration and centralization of political power on the supernational level and the United Nations cannot be expected to appreciably increase its power over the nation-states. However, various regional groupings may have some effects. The most likely, and probable, candidate for supernational power is the European Economic Community, which seems to be developing very much along the lines intended by its founders; although serious divisions remain among its members, it seems to be going toward its goal of a united Europe. The adherence of the United Kingdom to the EEC will bring in most of the other European powers, creating a body with a complex constitution which, in the long run, has good prospects for playing the same role for Europe that the Continental Congress did for the English colonies in North America. Other possible regional groupings may have similar successes although they will certainly lag far behind the EEC in unity and importance no matter how rapidly they develop by 1985.

On the economic level there is increasing government control over economic activities in almost every nation of the world. Laissez-faire is just about dead and there is little prospect for its revival. Even in those industries and countries that have little government control, there is a very strong trend toward the private centralization of economic activities. In the advanced industrial countries we see more and more massive economic units created by conglomerations of firms. Now, it is likely that these units do not have, proportionately, more power than they did in the past; considering the total size of the economy, they still retain the same proportion of the total economic activity. Nevertheless, they are huge and powerful combinations of capital, managerial, and technical skill, and in most areas of activity there are larger, but fewer, competitors in the market. This can be seen clearly in Europe, North America, and Japan. Of course, the socialist nations have already achieved an almost complete economic unity along centralized and government-owned lines. Of particular interest regarding economic power is the obvious and growing importance of the international or multinational corporation in the world. This will be discussed in some length elsewhere so it will merely be noted here that these firms have a certain dynamic force which is likely to make them very powerful factors in drawing together the world economy, despite hostile national political reactions to their activities.

Despite the hostility to science and technology among certain elements of the social, political, and cultural elites in the world, we see nothing on the horizon which can halt the *accumulation of scientific and technical knowledge*. This trend should go on unchecked even though its velocity and impact may be slowed down as a result of attacks by its critics, and possibly, by recognition of scientists and technologists that these criticisms are to some extent justified. The accumulation of scientific and technological knowledge, once taken for granted as an unmitigated boon to man and society, is clearly being shown to have mixed blessings (see Chapter VIII). This reaction against progress may affect general acceptance of scientific advance, the funding for research and development, and perhaps even the morale of scientists and technologists. However, even though these modern Luddites might have some effect on the rate of accumulation, they are not expected to triumph in the next fifteen years, or even by the end of the century.

In terms of the direction of scientific and technical knowledge, it seems most likely that the most important advances will be in the various life sciences rather than the physical sciences. While the prestige of physics has not dimmed as much as some popular discussion suggests, it is no longer the unchallenged queen of sciences; the public interest and many of the brightest young science students are going into life sciences, particularly molecular biology, which seems to have all sorts of fascinating possibilities for great benefits to mankind as well as the most frightful horrors imaginable. The promise of such opportunities is bound to attract many of the brightest young scientists and technicians.

Many of the important technical achievements of the next fifteen years are already clear today. Almost from the moment of its invention the promise of the laser was widely recognized, and this promise will come to fruition both for military and peaceful uses long before 1985. In consumer technology one important new development is almost certain to be improved communications in entertainment facilities. Cable television, in particular, will provide a nearly unlimited smorgasbord of home entertainment for every taste. Its development will have an important impact upon the culture of the Western world. Because of labor costs and the spreading out of the population, it has become increasingly difficult to maintain the traditional forms of live entertainment. Theaters, concert halls, and nightclubs have been closing over the past generation. Cable TV will permit the revival of all sorts of entertainment which so far have had audiences too small or too scattered to support an electronic medium. Also of importance is the advent of various kinds of home television. American and Japanese manufacturers are perfecting cheap, simple, reliable, and easily-used home TV recording and replaying devices which should provide fascinating amusement for a good part of the masses of the most prosperous nations for some time to come.

The deliberate organization and *institutionalization of technological change* can be first detected in the support given by Renaissance princes to scientists and inventors such as Tycho and Leonardo. It was formalized in the seventeenth century with the founding of the Royal Society, which had many European and American (the American Philosophical Society) imitators. However, most innovation was still the result of activities by individual inventors and entrepreneurs until the late nineteenth century. Edison's establishment at Menlo Park marked the end of the predominance of the individual inventor, of which Edison was the exemplar. Starting in the early twentieth century the first modern research laboratories were founded. Great university research facilities were set up and have since mushroomed.

While it now seems likely that individual scientists may now drop out of institutional environments because of opposition to bureaucracy or to "immoral" research, such men will usually find it difficult to work successfully because of the need for comrade-ship, critiques, and research equipment and aids. Drop-out scientists will probably drop into small anti-establishment research groups, living marginally on contracts and foundation grants, but like the rest of the scientists, becoming more and more institutionalized in one form or another.

The long-term trend toward *increasing military capacity* is likely to continue despite attempts at arms limitation, but the speed with which more powerful and more devastating weapons are introduced is somewhat questionable (see Chapter VII). Happily, the arms race did not proceed as fast in the 1960s as it looked like it might in the 1950s. Few people would deny that this was a beneficial development in the world, and we may hope for (but not necessarily expect) an even slower development in the next twenty years. Everyone desires a major breakthrough in arms control, perhaps through the SALT talks, even though we recognize that this will be extremely difficult (but hopefully not impossible) to achieve.

Also very likely, despite attempts to prevent it, is the spread of sophisticated weapons to nations that do not now have them. There are certain tendencies in the world, particularly the "neo-isolationist" trend in the United States, which could cause many more nations to arm themselves. Although such weapons present certain difficulties, they are fairly easy for most industrial nations to obtain if they have the wish to do so. With the widespread sale of commercial jet aircraft, practically any country with a national airline can make minor adaptations and produce an effective long-range bomber. Many nations are now working on rockets, avowedly for purposes of scientific research, but these too can be put to other uses. Also, despite some attempts at restricting them, modern military hardware of various types is spreading around the world. Practically every state worthy of consideration has at least a few jet fighters capable of being converted into nuclear-armed fighter-bombers. This increasing military capability will certainly not spread evenly, and some countries will decline relative to others or even drop out of the arms race altogether, such as Costa Rica and Luxemburg already have. But the total weight and power of the hardware available in the world in 1985 is almost certain to be much more deadly than today.

Another part of the multifold trend is the expanding sphere

of influence of the Western society in the form of *worldwide industrialization and modernization.* We can trace the history of this trend back to the improvements in agricultural technology in the High Middle Ages, through the growth of urbanization and large-scale manufacturing in Italy and the Netherlands in the late Middle Ages, to the first dim beginnings of the factory system in early Modern England, to the Industrial Revolution. First England, then France, Germany, and Belgium, then the rest of Europe and the United States, industrialized. Then the non-Western world, with the example and help of Western techniques and capital or under pressure to emulate or compete with the West, followed suit. Japan, some parts of China, parts of India, the overseas China enclaves of Hong Kong and Singapore, can be described as approaching Western levels of industrialization and modernization, and almost all other societies (some exceptions are China, Burma, isolated mountain tribes, etc.) have at least a declaratory policy of rushing as fast as they can to achieve a modern industrial state.

While the simple and almost total acceptance of this objective will probably be increasingly challenged, the actual trend toward such industrialization should not only continue, but will probably accelerate through the entire 1975–85 decade. The decline in direct Western political rule over the rest of the world has been accompanied by an acceleration of these states towards Westernization. Colonial rulers had some romantic nineteenth-century notions of retaining and protecting the historical cultures of the areas under their tutelage, rather as the Americans at various times had with regard to the native Indians; however, the new native rulers of most of these states, despite lip service to their historic values and modern critiques of capitalist/industrial culture, have no such inhibitions against forced industrialization and modernization. Notions of the evils of modern industrial urban society, held by some upper-middle-class intellectuals in the West, go practically unheeded in "the third world." The elites of the underdeveloped states wish more than anything to achieve Western standards of prosperity and progress. Not only the governments, but the people in these societies show their preference for modern commercial culture by flocking into the growing cities. There will likely be some retrogression in this regard during the next few decades, principally through political upheavals in some countries. The one-sided civil war in East Pakistan has seriously injured developmental prospects in that part of the world, just as disturbances in the Congo in the early 1960s did. Some countries will suffer from incompetent or ideologically irrational governments, such as Castro's Cuba or Sukarno's Indonesia. Uruguay is going this route. Chile may also. But on the whole, it takes a very high level of violence, incompetence, or ideological fanaticism to seriously hinder this movement toward Westernization, modernization, and industrialization.

With the possible exception of some of the Chinese culture areas in Asia, parts of Mexico and Brazil, Latin America and the "left behind" enclaves in Europe, it is not expected that the industrializing countries will close the gap between their standard of living and that in the already-developed, Westernized countries. However, it should be noted that many of these countries (particularly the areas noted above) will show rapid growth rates that are extremely noticeable to the people of the country, and will convince them that they are making rapid progress, that they are much better off, and that their country is achieving something in the world despite the opinion of the bourgeois intellectuals of the West.

To the extent that these states become modernized in economic terms, they are almost equally likely to become Westernized in other ways. These *Westernistic* states will have Westernized bureaucracies, military, intellectuals, skilled workers, managers and/or businessmen, trade unions, farm lobbies, and universities. They will drink Coca-Cola, wear Western clothes, have transistor radios, ride bicycles, then motorcycles, and eventually drive privately owned automobiles. The only possible exceptions will be deliberately puritanical, extremely rigid, and egalitarian socialist states after the Chinese model, although these are expected to be few, if any. In 1985 the people of the world will be more culturally similar than they have been at any time in the history of mankind. Even the recently Stone Age natives of New Guinea will participate in the world economy, the world culture, and world society. To a remarkable degree, this "global metropolis" will be Americanized in that it will be a mass culture, mechanized, pragmatic, and cheerfully anarchistic; fundamentally philistine by highbrow cultural canons; and irreverent by traditional social standards. In 1961 the number one song on the

Italian Hit Parade was Elvis Presley singing "O Sole Mio" in English. In the sixties, with such manifestations as the Beatles, this "pop" culture, formerly a strictly American phenomenon, became even more internationalized. This sort of thing is going to continue. Perhaps in 1985 an Italian, Tanzanian, Bolivian, or Turk will listen to an Icelandic pop singer on a Thai-made transistor radio, wearing clothes first designed in a boutique in Seoul while riding on a Nigerian bicycle to see a Swedish movie.

Also very likely is a continued reaction against this "artificial, plastic, meaningless" American mass-consumption culture, particularly among upper-middle-class intellectuals in the United States. While much lip service may well be paid by many politicians, journalists, and others to this negative attitude toward this aspect of the multifold trend, in fact, we would expect little or no effect on the actual pace of change at least not before the decade of 1975–85.

There may, however, be an indirect reaction to the counterculture of the developed worlds that could affect this worldwide Westernization. In many third-world countries the leadership is very much troubled by the quality of the products currently coming out of America (and to a lesser extent out of England and the rest of the Northwestern European culture area). While many of these third-world leaders claim to be socialists or at least revolutionary, they are, in reality extremely "square." They believe that their countries need hard work, discipline, self-denial, and all the rest of the bourgeois virtues in order to achieve their national goals of development and prestige. They do not like the influence of the counterculture on their countries, particularly upon their youth. For example, developing countries trying hard to stamp out historically debilitating drug use do not take kindly to the open promotion of drugs by pop music. Several countries have expelled Peace Corpsmen, not because they were CIA agents but because they were seen as a corrupting force. To the extent that the international pop culture reflects the counterculture values of major media centers like New York, San Francisco, London, and Rome, the third-world countries may take a puritan position and cut themselves off from it. From their point of view, this would be a very intelligent policy. The last thing India, Iraq, Tanzania, or Bolivia needs is educated kids dropping out. Indeed, this is the position that

Communist China has taken toward Western culture. In China the reasons are essentially egalitarian socialist rather than developmental, but the moral factor is certainly present.

Increasing affluence in both the Western and Westernistic world is an almost inevitable result of the continuation of existing economic trends. The growth rates in gross national product per capita will probably vary from two to twelve percent per annum, which will increase the amount of funds available for both investment and consumption by almost all classes in almost all nations. In almost all more or less industrialized economies, whether communist, capitalist, or socialist, the distribution of income is relatively fixed in terms of the percentage of return to various economic levels (i.e., the so-called Gini curves are remarkably constant between countries with very different economies). These trends are expected to continue unchecked through 1985, although there are two very serious qualifications of this expectation. First, as noted before, it is possible that there will be physical violence, incompetency, and/or ideological irrationality which may delay or even reverse the affluence of some of the non-Western world. For example, Chile was a relatively affluent and growing economy until Salvador Allende came to power in 1970. If Allende and his colleagues carry forth their program for the social regeneration of Chile along the lines they plan, it is very doubtful if the Chileans can expect more affluence; indeed, the opposite is almost certain. (While it is too early to assess the long-term effect of Castro, it can be noted that Cuba's growth rate has been among the lowest in the hemisphere since he came to power in 1959.) Although the lowest classes may experience some immediate improvement in the quality of the government services available to them, this can easily turn out to have been at the cost of the future economic and personal improvement of all classes

The second qualification, which could have the most important impact upon the spread of affluence in the Western world, is the possible effect of the counterculture upon work discipline. Many people see serious problems in rectifying the values of the counterculture with the needs of a growing industrial technocratic society. Indeed, the counterculture enthusiasts recognize the same difficulties, but solve them by maintaining that affluence and economic growth in general is a "bad thing" and ought not to be encouraged. This is a consistent and respectable point of view. Less can be said for the position of those who recognize that the liberated values of the counterculture are the *result* of affluence and say that we can afford these "higher" values because of our affluence, assuming that the widespread adoption of these values will have no effect upon the economic machine and therefore on affluence. People often forget how fundamentally they rely for their survival and standard of living on the workings of the great economic machines of which they are a part. To a large degree, critics of the system are correct in saying that most people are "cogs" in that machine. But presently, those cogs are needed and if too many of them break, go soft, or drop out, the system is in real trouble. If society is to move toward a generally more liberated life style, the most pressing problem that it faces is how to rectify its economic needs with the more liberated values. Machines are not going to do all the work. One need not project a cultural revolution to see that there might be serious difficulties in this regard. Just a modest slacking in labor discipline in terms of output per man-hour or in the ability to count on people to do their jobs as directed could have important immediate effects upon both the cost and quality of the goods and services.

The *population growth* of the world seems to have been continuous for several million years, with some local and often devastating setbacks. However, since about 1500 this growth has been exponential. Projected growth rates indicate that by some point in the next century the whole world will be piled high with humanity. Of course, people concerned with population growth realize that this situation will not occur—what frightens them is what may happen to prevent this from occurring—famine, slaughter, ecological disaster, or mass insanity. However, this may not be a reasonable concern either, since such population forecasts have had a very bad track record. Demographers have been able to project the future size of groups already living; i.e., given a certain group of people the portion of that group still living at any specific time in the future can be predicted. However, they have been less successful in estimating the sizes of groups not yet born; that is, they have failed to adequately predict the birth rate. Historically, demographers have made huge errors in their projections of total population, principally because they assume the continuation of short-term trends into long-term.

For what it is worth, many intelligent planners are employing the U.S. Bureau of the Census' "D" projection, which has accurately forecast the past five years of population change in the United States and is consistent with the prime movers of birth rate in the U.S., which seem to promote a low birth rate compared to the 1950s (approximately 2.5 children per average married couple). However, by no stretch of the imagination does even this approach the zero population growth desired by those who are extremely (and excessively) worried about the problem. It is a simple matter to project U.S. population growth into the twenty-first century and find that there is plenty of available developable land area, natural resources, etc., for such a population (although pollution and access to specific, fixed places, such as, say, the Statue of Liberty, is another question).

The other industrial nations have even lower growth rates than the United States (Japan's is nearly zero). In the non-industrial countries, however, the traditionally high birth rate accompanied by major medical advances which sharply cut death rates, particularly the death rates of young children, has created problems of population growth. Most of these countries are going through the initial stages of modernization and industrialization and recent data suggest that as these countries develop industrially, they will follow the pattern of the previously industrialized countries.* Birth control propaganda and advanced techniques will probably have more effect as secularization causes religious taboos to be lifted. However, this is less important than the general recognition that having too many children is bad for the individual family. In an agrarian society, children were useful labor; this is clearly not the case in an industrial society where the "investment" in a child cannot be expected to bring any economic returns. Population growth is not accelerating, but slowing down and may even be topping out, although probably not before 1985.

The tenth trend, *urbanization*, will certainly continue unchecked during the period under examination. This is a worldwide phenomenon, felt in both the developed and underdeveloped, capitalist and socialist, Western and non-Western world.

* Donald Bogue, "The End of the Population Explosion," *Public Interest*, Spring, 1967.

The mushrooming cities of the third world are and will be the most striking manifestation of this phenomenon. Cities offer a more exciting life and more economic opportunities than the agrarian countryside, and people flock to them regardless of drawbacks such as crime, unemployment, and bad sanitary conditions. Yet the people still come. Many Western observers are appalled by the "bidonvilles" which have sprung up around the cities of Latin America, Asia, and Africa. By Western standards these are certainly terrible slums, yet by the historical rural standards of these areas, they are a great advance. The people who crowd in from the countryside are the most aggressive, upwardly-mobile, and optimistic people in their nations. These so-called slums represent hope, not despair, and in many cases the bidonvilles themselves are physically upgraded as the people in them advance economically and culturally. There are, however, a few places in the world where this is not so. In India, for example, city growth is less promising because the historic Hindu culture and various bad government policies have made economic growth very slow. Unlike Lima, Lagos, or even Saigon, Calcutta is a place where you go to die, not to advance. But these "human dumps" are rare.

In the industrialized world, urbanization takes a somewhat different form, which may herald the eventual development of the underdeveloped world. Urbanization is old news in the industrial West, but it still continues as people abandon the farms and hamlets, and even smaller towns and cities, for great cities. In some of the most highly urbanized parts of the world, like the Ruhr, the Netherlands, the Midlands of England, and the Northeastern United States, the cities have grown so large that they are beginning to blend into one another, into what the English call *conurbations* and we in the United States title *megalopoli*. This will continue in the Western world, despite a considerable and growing malaise with urban living. This malaise will not be expressed in a return to the farm, which is clearly economic and cultural foolishness, but in an attempt to have country living while in the megalopolis. This process, commonly called suburbanization, is accelerating the spread of the cities and their blending into one another. More and more affluent people are moving from the crowded cities and occupying large tracts of land on lots at very low densities. Sooner or later, of course, this process must stop, if only because all the land will be exhausted. Although North America, as well as Australia and South Africa, have plenty of land for urban sprawl of this kind for several generations, some traces of this constraining effect are already occurring in the Netherlands and, to a far lesser degree, in England.

This process of suburbanization is most characteristic of the Anglo-Saxon nations where a long history of suburbanization, largely encouraged by the historical equation of land ownership with individual honor and prestige, can be traced back to late medieval London. In southern Europe, and in the areas colonized by it, there was a more rigid division between the land-owning nobility and the urban bourgeoisie, which today is expressed by the much greater likelihood of prosperous people in France, Italy, Spain, and their colonies living in the centers of older cities, with the lower classes living in the less favored suburbs. However, there may be some tendency even in the Latin American countries toward adopting the Anglo-Saxon pattern, partially to imitate the dominant North American culture and partially to escape the same sort of urban problems that Americans seek to avoid by "the flight to the suburbs." Although there are many people, even in the United States, who would love to live in downtown areas, they are precluded from doing so for several good reasons, mentioned later. Since conditions in most of our cities will remain unsuitable for upper-middle-class and upper-class habitation in 1985 a continued movement to the suburbs by the middle classes, followed by the lower middle and working classes of all ethnic backgrounds, is expected to continue at least until 1985. This process will be stimulated and encouraged by the improvement of transportation facilities, particularly highways, in all countries; the increasing ownership of automobiles everywhere in the world; the higher standard of living which permits the ownership of more land; and improved communications which permit the dispersal of offices and industry as well as residency.

The *decreasing importance of primary industries* can be traced back to the beginning of the Industrial Revolution. Indeed, the industrialization of a country can be measured by the size of its primary industries (agriculture, husbandry, fishing, and mining). Most of the world is currently trying to industrialize and increase secondary industries and it will certainly continue to do so; however, some countries, already industrialized, have moved on beyond secondary (manufacturing) to service occupations and industries. In the most advanced industrialized countries, particularly in North America, there is a shift to a different kind of service industry. We distinguish between *tertiary* industries, which are services to primary and secondary industries, and quaternary industries, which are services done for their own sake, or services to such services, and are oriented toward ultimate consumption rather than toward production. Although these occupational shifts will probably continue and spread through the rest of the century, they will not cause earlier occupations and industries to disappear from the world, any more than the rise of the secondary industries eliminated primary ones.

Several persons, most notably John Kenneth Galbraith in his *The New Industrial State*, have expressed the theory that the increasing concentration of business, as well as the shrinking portion of the population engaged in the manufacturing industries, will have some sort of stranglehold on the whole economy. This can be argued against by analogy: imagine a forecast made in the late nineteenth century that the number of producers of agricultural products would become concentrated and shrink relative to the total economy; an analyst arguing according to the above principle would conclude that a small number of farmers would control the most critical sector—agriculture—and therefore utterly the nation. Historically, of course, the industries that are growing and spreading are most powerful and significant, not those that are static or declining. We may reasonably expect, therefore, that manufacturing will slowly go the way of agriculture in importance in the nation, and the really important economic forces in the most advanced countries will be those individuals and institutions engaged in quaternary occupations and industries. Important, but not decisive, shifts in this direction will be seen between now and 1985.

Increasing literacy and education in the world is another of the long-term trends that can be traced back to the Dark Ages. We need only to look around us to see that there is a continuing educational boom, and that more and more people spend more and more of their time attending formal courses of education. The quality of this education varies considerably and its very purpose is presently under dispute; but, despite the qualms held by both the intellectuals and the masses, it seems that the educational system fills certain basic needs in our society which will not be abandoned in our time. Men have and will continue to dispute the degree to which all this education actually meets the worldly and spiritual objectives which educators espouse, but most people who undergo it do learn to read, write, and count. Literacy is nearly one hundred percent in all industrial countries and nearly so among individuals raised in the industrial areas of developing, mixed economies. Formal education seems to be necessary to industrial development, and all ambitious nations invest a great deal in it, spreading literacy and producing a growing class of newly educated people who will be subject to enlightenment as well as commercial advertising and political propaganda.

A burgeoning educational system will also produce increasing numbers of intellectuals, that is, persons who to some extent define themselves and their role in the world by the possession of superior book learning. This development has occurred with a close symbiotic growth of knowledge industries, which deal, essentially, with the information needs of the greater society. However, the bulk of the people in the knowledge industries are not intellectuals as we would use the term. Indeed, the knowledge industries include all aspects of the printing and publishing trades, and business, the communication industry, libraries, accounting, etc. But they are also journalists, research scientists, and engineers; as well as social scientists both in academia and the bureaucracies, and people providing highly educated services such as policy researchers in "think tanks." Every industrial society produces large numbers of such persons, rewards them well and seems to find their services increasingly valuable. The more wealthy the society, the more such persons are produced. In the United States this is developed to its highest degree and as other countries approach current U.S. standards of industrial organization and economic conditions, they will probably follow suit. This is evidenced by the recent proliferation of universities in England, Japan, and on the Continent.

Intellectuals play an increasingly important role in the modern world and unless there is a serious "populist" or some other kind of backlash against them, their influence will continue to spread as it has in the last several generations. (Even a severe backlash against the intellectuals would probably, to a large degree, be led by intellectuals—e.g., Hitler, Goebbels, Kaltenbrunner, et al.) The intellectuals have a great effect on society. They indirectly mold public opinion. (Here it is important to note that these influences are the greatest on the intellectual and semi-intellectual classes. It is very difficult, almost impossible, to persuade non-intellectual people of any ideas that are against their own experiences in areas where their experiences apply. Such is not nearly as true for the intellectual and semi-intellectual). In any case, intellectuals influence important decision makers through the highbrow and national media, academic lectures, and personal contacts. Their power is directly felt by advice to people in power through staff jobs in governmental bureaucracies (and to a much lesser extent, staff jobs in industrial corporations), their occasional positions of authority in "line" positions, and less frequently, but increasingly, as elected public officials. It is striking how many former academicians are in the Congress of the United States, as well as the legislatures of other industrial countries. At the beginning of this century a professor was considered to be an educated fool; today he may be elected to the U.S. Senate.

This increased power of intellectuals is a mixed blessing. Certainly, an increasingly diverse and complex society requires people with a fundamental and theoretical knowledge of what the world is and what ought to be done with it. So it can be said that intellectuals, or at least highly intellectual people, are necessary to running the world. Unfortunately, the intellectual does not necessarily have other equally useful attributes such as courage, decisiveness, steadfast loyalty, and common sense. He may tend to believe more in the image of the world transmitted to him through books and other media than in the real world as it exists. This is one aspect of what we call *educated incapacity*, a problem which is going to become much more serious as the power of intellectuals in the world continues to gain and spread. For example, it is difficult to convince big-city intellectuals that people who own firearms and resist domestic disarmament legislation are not mentally diseased. They ignore the reality that half of all Americans own firearms, and half of the country cannot be mentally sick (if "mentally sick" means deviating substantially from the norm) and reply that the entire society must be sick.

Another of the multifold trends—the trend toward innovative and manipulative *social engineering*—points out a principal area in which the effects and weaknesses of intellectual thought may be most felt. This trend can be traced at least back to the Renaissance when many of the humanists, such as Machiavelli, attempted to apply reason to shaping the outside world. The trend seems to accelerate with the invention of statistics in the seventeenth century, the origins of modern anthropology and sociology in the eighteenth century, and the beginning of socialism in the nineteenth. The desirability of social engineering is an almost universal belief among the educated. Of course, many educated people, particularly political conservatives, claim to despise and fear this idea. However, a reading of their own products suggests that they too desire social engineering; but to achieve conservative goals rather than the liberal or socialist goals typically desired by public advocates of social engineering.

There is no reason why this trend among the elites should reverse before 1985, but there are good reasons why it will not accelerate significantly. Although the "Great Society" programs were remarkably successful, they failed to achieve the grandiose goals set forth by President Johnson and other Administration spokesmen. Also, many of the people who promoted these programs denigrated their real achievements in order to justify more funding and public support. The combination of overreaching and poormouthing led to the widespread impression that the Great Society programs were failures. The masses responded to the poormouth treatment by saying: "You've been spending twenty million dollars on this program and it's a failure, so why should we give you forty million dollars?" Clearly they were not convinced and it seems that, in the short run at least, the use of government power to promote social change in the United States has been partially discredited among the great mass of the people. Various attempts at social engineering may continue, and some are likely to be successful, but they will lack the enthusiasm with which, say, the original civil rights movement and the war on poverty were undertaken.

The last two items in the multifold trend are almost self-explanatory and should impact very strongly until 1985. *The increasing universality of the multifold trend* can be seen in its spread throughout the world and throughout all the classes of the societies of the world, although by 1985 this trend may begin to top out, if only because the universality will have become nearly universal. And overall *the increasing tempo of change* of the items of the multifold trend is clear enough, with the few short-run exceptions we discussed above.

II

La Belle Epoque– The Metaphorical Use of Historical Analogy

HISTORICAL analogy can be a dangerous exercise. Any historian will tell you that each historical phenomenon is discrete and unique, and attempting to draw perfect parallels between events in different periods is misleading and downright erroneous. Studies of historical situations obviously can be seriously misleading if applied to a specific situation of interest today, since various conditions of the example may not apply. Often the most that can be argued is that the historical analogy should be used metaphorically rather than analytically. However, these scholars can themselves be somewhat misled because of the organization of history into periods, nations, and fields of human endeavor. A medieval scholar, familiar with the institutions of feudalism in the Middle Ages in Europe, often has little or no knowledge of the strikingly similar institutions that appeared under similar conditions in Islam, India, and as far afield as Japan. In fact, historians use analogy all the time, for example, in assuming that Carolingian land law can cast some light on tenures in Saxon England. Still, there is some validity to this concept of all historical events being to some degree unique and prudent caution calls for great care in employing historical analogy. Certainly nothing can be proved by analogy; but it may illustrate, teach, make plausible, and clarify.

Actually, historical analogy has been misused as frequently as it has been used effectively. During the American Revolution, one faction of the revolutionaries, remembering the English Revolution of the previous century, was deathly afraid that George Washington might be like Cromwell and attempted to limit his power—and therefore his effectiveness—in military operations. If an analogy is used as a metaphor, no theory of historical inevitability or prediction can be assumed or argued. It merely facilitates and enhances communication. For example, in conjecturing about difficulties that the Soviets may have with any future foreign Communist or "pro-Communist" leaders, it is useful to be able to say, "He might play the role of a Tito—or a Mao—or a Sukarno—or a Castro—or an Ulbricht—etc." However, validity in old situations does not necessarily make something any more likely to be true in a new situation. Other important roles such leaders could play may not have occurred yet. Thus, in many cases the range of metaphorical discussion is unfortunately restricted to minor variations on what has already occurred. A major task of "presearch" is to identify new possibilities and to give them names (perhaps by using scenarios or artificially specified contexts).

For the modern man who, even though highly educated, may be relatively ignorant of history, the chief source of historical analogies is likely to be the events of the last four decades. This period includes the Depression, the rise of fanatic and chauvinistic movements in relatively developed nations such as Japan, Italy, and Germany and their subsequent, almost hysterically aggressive careers, the demonstration of weakness by the seemingly strong and powerful status quo nations, and the events of World War II and the Cold War. This brief span of modern history is rich in the kind of problems many believe can arise again. Some people, of course, argue that others are too preoccupied with these particular problems: having once experienced a Munich, they may be overly fearful of concessions to an opponent. Having experienced Pearl Harbor, they may be overly preoccupied with the danger of surprise attack. These judgments may be correct, but they may also be irrelevant. Such dangers as appeasement and surprise attack require a relatively high standard of prudence in a government and while popular or even professional discussion may overestimate these dangers, governments, as measured by actual preparations, have tended to underestimate them.

While the last four decades supply a fat cata og of historical examples of problems which could recur, it is not a complete spectrum of possibilities. It is startling how difficult it is for most people, even analysts and decision makers, to seriously discuss problems when they cannot find analogies in these last four decades. However, there are additional historical examples worth consulting for analogies to the future. Three of the most pertinent analogies for studying the immediate future are: the Hellenistic Graeco-Roman Classical Mediterranean civilization (for ways out of cultural difficulties), Augustan Rome (an exemplar of an "ideological renewal" government), and La Belle Epoque (c. 1900–1914). Of these, La Belle Epoque is probably the most fascinating and valuable.

Some characteristics of "La Belle Epoque," listed below, may seem familiar. The period from 1953 (end of the Korean war) to 1965 (before the disillusionment and bitterness surrounding the U.S. buildup in Vietnam began) was also a time of relative worldwide peace, prosperity, and economic growth. These years might be characterized as "La Deuxième Belle Epoque." In fact, this analogy is so persuasive it will be included later in our basic "Surprise Free" Projection.

La Belle Epoque
(1900–1914)

1. Relative peace
2. Relatively rapid economic growth
3. Vast expansion of world trade, investment, travel, communication*
4. Relatively free movement of world labor, goods, capital

* Even today we have not reached 1913 levels of world investment or world trade relative to the level of gross world product.

5. Among the upper classes growth of one world and world community concepts
6. Serious attempts in U.S. and Northwest Europe to impose upper middle class "bourgeois" morality upon lower classes —e.g., anti-prostitution, gambling, alcohol, drug laws, pure food and drug laws, "reform politics," women's rights, etc. (comparable to campaigns of '50s and '60s—e.g., women's rights, civil rights and freedom, worldwide concern for poor, "reform politics," etc.)
7. Eroding faith in traditional left and right ideologies, some turning to fin de siècle ideologies—anarchism, syndicalism, racism, nationalism, imperialism
8. Arms competition continued despite attempts at arms control
9. Disorder and minor wars in the "developing" nations which involved the great powers
10. Increasing hedonism among upper classes. Artists (and public) turn away from "Victorian" standards toward alien and violent styles and themes—Rousseau, Gauguin, Picasso, Stravinsky, Wilde, D'Annunzio
11. Some breakdown of public manners and controls and relatively great toleration of "discretionary behavior"—e.g., violent strikes, militant feminism, prohibitionists, etc.
12. Vague sense of "Indian Summer" and fin de siècle among upper classes

In fact there are many fascinating parallels between America in recent times and the twenty years preceding World War I in Europe. During that period, there were two seemingly contradictory movements at work—a striving for security, as expressed by demands for social welfare legislation, but at the same time a desire for insecurity, for action, for a breaking of the fetters of the dull, "bourgeois" society. England may provide the best analogies. During this time the English fought a "colonial" counter-insurgency war against the Boers. The English claimed to be defending the freedom of black Africans against Boer domination, but most liberal humanitarian people at home bitterly opposed the war, claiming it was an imperialist crime. Following the war there was an extreme anti-military, anti-expansionist, isolationist feeling in educated circles. Accompanying this were very serious attempts at arms limitation, as exemplified in the various Hague conferences which attempted to limit the use of weapons in warfare. However, England was engaged in a massive arms race with a formidable rival (Imperial Germany) which required massive investments in expensive new weapon systems (dreadnaughts). This raised a major question of priorities in England. In 1907 there was a furious debate over a new income tax in order to support heightened social welfare legislation (old age pensions) as well as to build more battleships. As a result of compromise, England felt it necessary to pull back in the Far East, and transfer influence there to the Japanese (the Anglo-Japanese Naval Treaties).

At home in England there was serious unrest. There was a militant feminist movement (suffragettes) accompanied by massive civil disobedience, terrorism, and the jailing of leaders. Moreover, there was ferocious labor unrest in the mines, utilities, and transportation industries, requiring the use of troops. Similarly, there was serious agitation among minority groups (the Irish) following which attempts at making concessions by the Liberal establishment were met by furious backlash (from the Ulster Orange) and the exploitation of the issue by the Conservatives. Anarchist terrorism of various kinds was an everyday occurrence. Throughout the period there was a noticeable breakdown in traditional British standards of public decorum. Speakers were howled down in the House of Commons. Interestingly enough, the group which one would expect to be the principal upholder of traditional standards—the educated elite—were the worst in this regard. Faced with the possible loss of their privileges, they became extremely nasty. Some were openly plotting with the potential Ulster insurrectionists, and when the Liberal government ordered troops deployed to suppress the Ulstermen, officers offered their resignations and the army was on the verge of mutiny. In the summer of 1914 it seemed as if the British Isles were about to explode, but the impending civil war was diverted by World War I. Some writers have claimed that the willingness of the British to guarantee Belgium's integrity and enter the war may have been unconsciously prompted by a desire to unite the nation against a foreign enemy. This was not the first time that such unity was gained at the cost of war.

By any historical standard, the countries of Europe were rich, were rapidly growing richer, and had much in common—religion, traditions, culture. There were no outside pressures to speak of. The colonies were essentially quiescent. Both the ruling class and the people seemed satisfied and self-confident. But, one basic theme of La Belle Epoque is a sense of fin de siècle; a world of relative peace and stability, expanding and developing at a great pace, but with an underlying awareness—or at least feeling—that an era is coming to an end. From the viewpoint of the troubled period after World War I, this time of "decline" and "malaise" looked beautiful; hence, the name La Belle Epoque given to it after the fact. Similarly, the second Belle Epoque was a period of unparalleled world peace, stability, and economic advance, a veritable golden age. Only after it was pushed out by the war in Vietnam and the advent of domestic violence in North America was it recognized how sweet it was for most of the nation and the world during the Eisenhower and Kennedy Administrations.

This analogy should not be pressed too far, however, if only because La Belle Epoque ended in World War I. At this point, the precedents of La Belle Epoque may be disregarded on the grounds of several vital differences between the two periods:

1. There was a slow, varied, and subtle, but nevertheless critical, change in the values, life styles, and beliefs which previously supported the international and domestic power structure (which might best be described as a turn-of-the-century version of the multifold trend outlined in Chapter I).
2. The stability of the first Belle Epoque was based first of all on a military/political/economic balance among the European powers and secondly on the possession by the Europeans vis-a-vis the rest of the world of an authority, power, self-confidence, and prestige which in turn allowed them to dominate and/or colonize the rest of the globe. There were probably good possibilities for evolution into a new stable international structure based on "balance of power" and enlarged Concert of Europe concepts. But the structure at the time was basically unstable as much for technical reasons as basic ones (World War I was caused as much by the characteristics of the mobilization systems as by any fundamental issues).
3. The rise of Imperial Germany obviously upset Europe, but we remember Germany was clearly the major power of Continental Europe as early as 1871. Its ambitions could have been absorbed into the system by peaceful evolution (i.e.,

by Germany's focusing on its Ostpolitik policy but also on not
generating a real rivalry with England—in particular, not
building a serious navy).
4. In La Belle Epoque both leaders and masses were not afraid
of a major war. When the First World War broke out enthusiastic crowds filled the streets and men rushed to the
colors. Europe was bored with La Belle Epoque. Everyone
thought the war would be glorious, exciting, and short. The
twentieth century has taught us a lot about war. Poison gas,
saturation bombing, napalm, nuclear weapons, and intercontinental missiles somehow lack the glamor of red panta-
loons, spiked helmets, and shakos.

Unlike the European catastrophe that put an end to the first
Belle Epoque, *we expect that the current Belle Epoque will
slowly erode or evolve into a new era.* This is not to rule out the
possibility of a cataclysmic end such as a World War III.* As a
matter of fact, the likelihood of major war may substantially
increase by the end of the 1970s—but hopefully not to the point
of being probable. The "end of an era" analogy means exactly
that. The basis of the current political/military/economic stability is eroding and thus there will be a period when new possibilities for real instability will arise. Or, other issues (see Chapter V)
might change everything. This surprise-free projection for continued peace and stability is based on the expectation that
erosion will be a gradual and evolutionary process (rather than
by revolution or even revolutionary evolution), perhaps to a new
basis for growth and stability.

This new Belle Epoque did not really end in 1964, and it will
continue to evolve relatively slowly, in some degree persisting
throughout the 1970s and the 1980s. Such a "good era" has, of
course, a tendency to erode, and there are many ways in which
the pace of erosion could quicken. There could be retrogression
to the pattern of behavior typical of the Cold War. "Internal
contradictions" (to use a useful Marxist phrase) could develop
within the West to the point where the system can no longer
continue without sharp change. Drastic and revolutionary

* Unless Vietnam is interpreted as a low-level substitute for a third
World War. Oswald Spengler predicted a world war every twenty-five years
in the twentieth century. 1914 + 25 = 1939; 1939 + 25 = 1964. This
illustrates how unwise it is to carry historical analogy too far.

change, or even "revolutionary evolution" might conceivably occur.

Probably, at least in the seventies, La Deuxième Belle Epoque will essentially continue, certainly so far as the underlying international political structure and character of Western society is concerned. Potential internal contradictions and revolutionary pressures will probably be held back by countervailing forces which already exist or will emerge rapidly and strongly enough to impose stability. Some of these countervailing forces are already beginning to oppose the so-called "counterculture" and many of its "reforms." If the counterculture is thought of as a kind of "reformation," then the countervailing forces make up a "counterreformation." However, there is likely to be a new synthesis emerging from this cultural tension and struggle which will strongly influence some of the values and forces of the counterculture in the future. Thus, the movement toward conservatism and reaffirmation of traditional values in the United States, in some parts of Europe, and elsewhere, includes a significant emphasis on environmental and ecological issues, on consumerism, and even on the welfare state (while opposing the alleged excesses of new Left, old Left), and many progressive programs. Much of the New Deal legislation of the American 1930s now appears as part of the conservative counterreformation program.

The Deuxième Belle Epoque will probably emphasize both internal and external stability; a fear of war, of revolution, and even of intense crisis; a growing adaptation to what is called the emerging post-industrial culture. In addition (and this in some degree contradicts other tendencies), there is likely to be, during the 1970s, a continued emphasis on economic growth, and rapid economic growth is likely to continue. Relatively free and open competition as well as successful exploitation of the less advantaged (much more so than occurred in the fifties and the sixties) is likely to accompany this economic growth. The people who finance and carry through these programs will profit greatly, and this may be seen by many as "exploitation" by the "establishment," but it is unlikely that the profits will be so disproportionate, or so exploitive as to arouse widespread concern or prevent a kind of "catching up" by the less wealthy—in particular, by the less wealthy in the five dynamic areas of the world.

When we say that the current Deuxième Belle Epoque is

slowly evolving, we are mainly emphasizing international relations and the fact that *external* political and economic pressures and trends in the world are not likely to prove terribly surprising or cataclysmic. However the growth of the five specially dynamic areas (see Chapter III)—initially economic, but eventually in political and perhaps military power as well, may cause economic, political, and perhaps military strains. Thus as the Russians gradually realize that Japan is likely to pass them economically in the eighties, dropping them to third rank among the economic powers of the world, there may be important internal repercussions. Despite all this there seems to be a growing consensus that, internationally, the Western world is entering a period of political and economic stability, at least as far as the frontiers and economies of most of the older nations are concerned. An expectation of relatively peaceful and evolutionary international relations is less easily justified for Afro-Asia, though it has some relevance even there.

A Surprise-Free
Projection–The World
of the Seventies
and Eighties

ONE of the most valuable tools in future studies is the *surprise-free projection*. This concept can be clarified by differentiating projections from forecasts and predictions. A *projection* is simply an extrapolation into the future. Sometimes the projection is done by an automatic extrapolation of past data; hence, the so-called *straight-line projection*; sometimes intuition, judgment, and speculation are also used. In either case there is no necessary assertion of validity.

In a *forecast* the analyst tries to establish which events are possible and then to assign at least rough probabilities to the various contentions, as for example, first finding out what horses are running in a race and then assigning odds to each of them.

A *prediction* is based on establishing high, perhaps overwhelming, probabilities in favor of a specific event, as for example the probability that a tossed coin will turn up heads at least once in five tosses.

A surprise-free projection is a projection which is not surprising to the author. It resembles the naive extrapolation of economics, though it is a somewhat more sophisticated concept and often more useful. In this so-called naive projection certain aspects of a situation are kept constant and others are permitted to continue or evolve in some prescribed manner—usually according to current trends. However, a surprise-free projection is often arrived at by using theories (or intuitions) that the author happens to believe or finds plausible. Therefore, if the analysis turns out to be true, he will not be surprised. This can also apply to multiple theories, even if they are contradictory—the author in this case is not sure which one is right but he will not be surprised if either one or the other comes out.

It is possible to have two or more contradictory surprise-free projections because many times two or more hypotheses or theories may be entertained simultaneously, and if any one or more of these actually occur, "we would not be surprised." However, although these projections are based on hypotheses, concepts, or theoretical ideas which may be entertained with reasonable seriousness they have not necessarily been proved or even documented and, therefore, may be incorrect.

In fact, the most surprising thing that can happen in a broad, long-range, surprise-free projection is that there will be no surprises. Therefore, any such projection should not be taken as anything resembling a forecast or a prediction. Indeed, since surprise will almost certainly occur, a surprise-free projection must be, at least to some extent, wrong. This projection should be

Surprise-Free Projection for the Seventies and Eighties

A. Revival, evolutionary development, and perhaps some erosion of *La Deuxième Belle Epoque.*
   1. Movement toward a half unified* but multipolar world with countervailing tendencies toward anarchy, preser-

* About fifty percent of the world's population lives in two relatively isolated cultures—twenty-five percent in Communist Asia (a relatively isolated Sinic culture) and twenty-five percent in a relatively isolated Indian culture (India, Ceylon, Burma, and perhaps Pakistan).

vation of ethnic culture and a "convergent" world order, *net* movement is probably a general but fragile tendency toward synthesis and unity for the half which participates

B. But *politically an increasingly multipolar world* will see in the seventies the end of the post-World War II era (including an effective political settlement of that war)

    2. *Relative decline of the two superpowers* in power, prestige, and influence (both within their own blocs and toward the rest of the world)

    3. *Rise of Japan* as superstate (and superpower?)

    4. *Full recovery of both Germanies*

    5. An enlarged EEC, with perhaps a *new role for France* as the leading nation of the community

    6. Possible creation of an *Eastern European EEC*

    7. Many new possibilities by 1980: e.g., "intermediate" powers—new alliances, new arms races, challenges for world leadership, political unification in part of Europe, a partial or complete breakup of the enlarged EEC, or even of some nation-states

C. Above sets context for *further development of a unified but multipolar and (partially) competitive (half) global economy*

    8. A general understanding of the process and techniques for sustained economic development

    9. A *worldwide "green revolution"*; also a worldwide capability for modern industry and technology

    10. Growing importance of multinational corporations as *innovators of economic activity* and *engines of rapid growth*

    11. High (3-15%) GNP growth almost everywhere—especially the five dynamic areas (Japan, other Sinic culture areas in Pacific Asia, Eastern Europe, Southern Europe, and important parts of Mexico and Brazil)

    12. Sustained *growth in trade, communications, travel*

    13. *Increasing unity of technology, private industry, commercial and financial institutions*, but relatively little by international legal and political institutions

D. One result is a relatively anarchic but also relatively orderly and unified world with *new issues of international control*

    14. Continuing growth in *discretionary behavior*, corresponding worldwide (foreign and domestic) *law and order issues*. Some growth of violent, deviant, or criminal behavior

15. Probable increase in terror, violence, subversion, unilateral changes of international rules, etc.

16. Probable increased influence of anarchism, syndicalism, neo-nationalism, counterculture

17. *Persistence (despite some alleviation and normalization) of chronic confrontations* (e.g., four divided countries, Arab-Israeli, India-Pakistan, and Sino-Soviet-U.S. triangle), perhaps a Sino-Japanese confrontation

18. *New conflict and turmoil in Africa, Middle East, South Asia:* perhaps Latin America and Pacific Asia

19. Nativist, messianic, and/or "irrationally" emotional and violent movements; some decrease in rationalist and (materialistic) interest-oriented politics

E. Some acceleration, some continuation but also some selective topping off of *multifold trend* (and perhaps some temporary reversals)

20. Further intensification of many issues associated with *1985 Technological Crisis*; growing need for worldwide (but probably ad hoc) zoning ordinances and other environmental and social controls

21. Other problems in coping with sheer numbers, size, and bigness

22. With important exceptions, erosion of *twelve traditional societal levers*, a *search for meaning and purpose*, some *cultural confusion, polarization, conflict*

23. Increasingly *"revisionist" Communism, capitalism* and Christianity in Europe and the Western hemisphere; perhaps a "crisis of liberalism"

24. *Populist, conservative, backlash,* "counterreformation" movements and/or ideological renewal movements

25. Increasing problem (worldwide) of *educated incapacity* and/or illusioned, irrelevant, or ideological argumentation—greater explicit emphasis on feeling and emotion —on "value oriented" research, argumentation, and operation

F. *Emergence of various styles of post-industrial culture* in the currently developed nations (with about 20 percent of world's population) and in enclaves elsewhere characterized by:

26. *New political milieus;* rise of "humanist left"-"responsible center" confrontation in at least high culture of developed nations (but in particular in the U.S. and Northwest tier of Europe)

27. Emergence of *"mosaic cultures"* (at least in U.S.) incorporating esoteric, deviant, communal, and/or experimental life styles; some increase in anarchistic behavior and movements
28. Possible successful synthesis between old and new in France, Japan, Scandinavia, Northwest tier, or elsewhere

considered mainly as a context to be used in analysis and discussion; one with which disagreement may be as useful as agreement. (A purpose of the context is to identify possible disagreements or deviations and put them in perspective.) However, at least the central tendencies of the basic surprise-free projection described above have more of the validity of a forecast or prediction than of an ordinary projection—at least for the next five or ten years.

LA BELLE EPOQUE

As indicated in the previous discussion of La Belle Epoque (Chapter II), the most reasonable "surprise-free" projection for the seventies and eighties is, essentially, a continuation of worldwide economic development and progress. We expect the GWP (gross world product) to exceed six trillion (1970) dollars by 1985, up from 3½ trillions in 1970. Overall this economic growth will far outstrip population growth, permitting a 1985 per capita GWP of 1,200 dollars, up by two-thirds over 1970.

These economic gains will be in the already developed world and also in the five dynamic areas of the developing world (see page 63). Because of low growth rates in parts of the developed world (e.g., Britain) and the underdeveloped world (e.g., most parts of Africa and Latin America), the gap in wealth between the already developed countries and the rest of the world will not change appreciably. Still, most of the developing world will be richer (or less poor) than it has ever been, and most of its people will benefit to some degree from that additional income, although elite groups who compare their economies with the developed countries will be aware of a growing gap and be less sensitive to the real progress. Nevertheless, the developing countries will still be scratching: the conscious beneficiaries of the projected Belle Epoque will be the half of the world that is industrialized.

Despite the survival of the nation-state system, the relatively advanced industrial half of the world will feel very much a part of a world community. The residents of this half of the world will have remarkably similar urban bourgeois life styles, will enjoy the same or similar consumer goods and recreation, and will see, hear, and read much the same material in their media (although there will be different languages, English, Spanish, and French may be even more widespread than today). Better communication and transportation will link the world together. Managers will ordinarily travel abroad for business and secretaries for pleasure. Even a rise in protectionism would probably only temporarily slow the growth of world trade. People will use foreign goods (and perhaps even services) as a matter of course. In short, a large part of the population of the industrial (and post-industrializing) societies will see themselves participating in world society, much as did the haute bourgeoise of Europe and North America in La Belle Epoque preceding the First World War.

To describe this world we use the term *global metropolis*, which we prefer to McLuhan's term *global village*. A village is characterized by the involvement of people with one another, by complex ties and emotional interrelationships within the village. A village is not a private place. It has strong communal strengths of mutual aid and support, a strong commitment to communal social, political, and moral action. Villagers have a limited group of relatives and friends who are also their neighbors.

In contrast, global metropolis describes a world where individuals live in a metropolis and work, say, in a stock exchange. They have very different relationships from people who live and work in a village. Politics, social action, and charity tend to be organized and professionalized. Community action is often ad hoc, enlisting people who are otherwise strangers in transient and particular causes.

Contemporary city-dwellers also have a small group of relatives and friends, but they are probably not their neighbors. Most of their neighbors and the rest of the hundreds of people they encounter each day are strangers or impersonal "business acquaintances."

The distinction between these two terms is important. The global metropolis image is central to an understanding of the reasoning that underlies a number of expectations. For example, the possibility that worldwide law and order problems may become a major issue by the late 1970s or early 1980s is characteristic of a city or global metropolis problem. Banditry in the countryside has often been common, but the bandits have usually struck from beyond the village. Traditionally village societies have been almost immune to internal crime and disorder, whereas crime and disorder are characteristic of urban civilizations.

Similarly, the global metropolis image is important in understanding the concept of an emerging mosaic culture (see page 85), in contrast to a uniform, homogeneous culture. Characteristically, the city has been a place where many cultures and peoples mix, maintaining (within established constraints) their own customs, dress, and language; living in close proximity, but generally in their own quarters; bargaining and conducting business in the marketplace, but maintaining a separate, private existence.

MULTIPOLAR WORLD

To persons who have become accustomed over the past generation to a world organized around two power poles, the prospect of a multipolar world may seem uncomfortable. Actually, it is a bipolar world which is unusual. If we count China and Italy, there were eight great powers in the world in 1939. Five of these (China, France, Italy, Germany, and Japan) were later devastated, defeated, and their territories occupied. A sixth (Great Britain) was exhausted by the strain of six years of war. Small wonder that the two powers which survived intact and victorious dominated the world. Today, the defeated powers of World War II are returning. China and France made their first major independent moves in the world in the late 1950s. Japan and Germany have much of the potential strength and importance needed to take an independent or military policy. However, in the cases of France and Germany, it is useful to compare their potential for independent foreign policy with the pretensions of Britain to being a world power in the late 1940s and early 1950s—they are not very convincing, simply because these countries (as well as

Britain and Italy) do not and will not have the necessary population, natural resources, technical or economic potential, or, most important, national will to play a great power role in the world.

If Germany, France, and Britain wish to play a major role, they may find it easier within a united Europe which, of course, would itself be one of the principal powers of the world (at least on paper). The political difficulties involved in getting these still diverse European nations to support the policies necessary to their playing a great power role within the next fifteen years, seem almost impossible to overcome. Still, emerging Western Europe, under French leadership, or possibly a triumverate of West Germany, France, and Britain, must be counted as a potential player in a multipolar world game. If we add Western Europe to the two existing superpowers, the United States and the Soviet Union; the would-be superpower, China; and the emerging superpower, Japan; we have a pentapolar world. From the point of view of present day U.S. responsibilities, this world looks a lot better in some ways. To the extent that the United States sees its role as world policeman and supporter of the free world as a burden (which is precisely the way more and more Americans are viewing the current situation), that burden will lessen. Of the five projected superpowers, three are liberal/democratic/capitalist free world countries that have at present no serious conflicts with one another, no life or death economic interests which clash, and no fundamental ideological divisions or historical rivalries. This cannot be said of Russia and China, which have excellent reasons for being at each other's throats. But an international power equation with five variables is necessarily more complex than one with only two; more difficult to compute, and more prone to miscalculation. However, many analysts believe it will be essentially more stable.

THE RISE OF JAPAN

In the fifties, the output of the Japanese economy more than doubled. This large (but not unprecedented) growth rate was admired but it did not make much of an impression on the world since, in an absolute sense, the Japanese economy only grew from small to medium size. The economic impact on the rest of the world was minor. During the sixties the Japanese economy more than tripled. This was spectacular, especially since it followed on top of the rapid growth rate of the fifties. Furthermore, the economic impact on the rest of the world was considerable because the economy grew from medium to large, passing France, England, and West Germany to become the third largest economy in the world. Of course, Japan was not yet really comparable with the two superpowers. In 1970 the Japanese economy was only about 20 percent of the American and 40 percent of the Soviet. However, the Japanese economy will almost certainly double and perhaps even triple during the seventies. Any such growth would represent a mushrooming from large to gigantic. Indeed, such a growth would make Japan an economic superpower—even though the Soviet Union and the United States had not yet been passed. In any case, Japan may soon outstrip them. In particular, Japan has probably already passed the Soviet Union in GNP per capita. Furthermore, because the Japanese economy will be focused more on the external world than on the largely self-sufficient economies of the United States and the Soviet Union, Japan may play a much more pervasive role in world politics, world economics, and even world culture (see Chapter X).

FULL RECOVERY OF BOTH GERMANIES

Although both of the German states have recovered economically from World War II and have achieved most of the prerequisites of statehood, they will lack full legitimacy. Both states still recognize themselves only as parts of the German nation. Although they may be resigned to the current situation as a matter of necessity, they still have not abandoned the idea of a whole German state and necessarily see their positions as somewhat transitory. We cannot expect these feelings to completely fade by 1985, but by that time the German states will be thirty-five years old and anything that venerable must necessarily generate some loyalty or at least habit, regardless of strong surviving national feelings. Probably officials and citizens of both the DBR and DDR will be less apologetic for their existing governments (although certainly individuals may, particularly in the East, disagree with specific policies, they will not necessarily be in opposition to the existence of the state). The venerability of both states will lead many outside nations to move from de facto to de jure recognition. It will be increasingly difficult for the West to maintain that the thirty-five-year-old, powerful, economically advancing East Germany is a mere puppet of the Soviet Union. Both Germanies will insist that the world officially forget the Third Reich and recognize them as legitimate states on a par with other states in the world. They may even attempt more independent foreign policies—although, of course, they will probably be restrained by the great powers and each other.

ENLARGED EEC

With the British joining the Common Market, most of the remaining nations of Northern Europe will probably follow suit. Portugal may also follow, and even Spain, although serious political problems are in the way. Besides having the obvious effect of increasing the potential economic power of the EEC, these additions will raise several other issues. First, the national character of the Market will change. So far it has been dominated by Roman Catholic Europe, but the new Northern European members are from Protestant (or ex-Protestant) Europe. In politics, one of the most powerful groups promoting the present market has been the Continental Christian Democrat-style conservatives, whereas Social Democrats are much stronger in the North.

Second, Great Britain is going to be a very large lump for the Common Market to digest. The British public has had mixed feelings about abandoning their historic insular and extra-European outlook. After joining the Market they are likely to take the position "this far, but no farther" and resist further attempts at European integration. Britain may even indulge in some other forms of at least symbolic nationalist behavior in an attempt to prove to the world (but mostly to itself) that it still is "This royal throne of Kings, this sceptred isle."

Such a "Gaullist" reaction by Britain may be all the more necessary because France is likely to continue as the "first among equals" in the Common Market. The disparity in growth rates between the two nations, if continued, will result in France having a GNP half again as large as Britain by 1985. Furthermore, residents of France, Germany, and the Low Countries will enjoy per capita GNP considerably larger than that of Britain. Of course, British supporters of entering the Common Market hope that the stress of adaptation will help the British economy. This is possible, but the economic growth rate of Britain is remarkably stable. Britain has grown two to three percent per annum for two hundred years.

France and Germany should have growth rates around five per cent, leaving the United Kingdom behind—at least until the disparity between Britain and the major Continental powers becomes so large as to create countervailing pressures and mechanisms. The factors in Japan's growth (see Chapter X) suggest reasons for the relative slowness of British GNP growth: almost every one of the factors that are positive for Japan are negative for the United Kingdom. One of Britain's key problems was stated by the Tory election slogan of the 1950s—"You never had it so good!" Despite the country's many fiscal problems, that statement is still true. One cannot find any class of people in England who are in a real sense worse off than they were ten or twenty years ago—at least in terms of wealth. But the roots of what appears to be Britain's relative apathy have to be sought elsewhere. Throughout the nineteenth century Britain's economy grew by approximately two percent a year, and this was considered the miracle of the age. By the end of the nineteenth century and the beginning of the twentieth however, other countries had started to grow even more rapidly. Today, Britain's problem is not that it is growing slowly as compared to its historic past, but that other countries are growing at two or three times its rate (Japan at about five times the rate). Unless the British change (and it does not seem that they intend to), they will simply be outdistanced.

In fact, Britain's relationship to Europe may develop into something much like Canada's relationship to the United States. Canada's GNP per capita tends to be sixty to seventy percent that of the United States, the Canadian economy being dragged up and down by the United States' performance. In this case, it will make a great deal of difference to the British whether they have, say, seventy to eighty percent of Europe's per capita GNP, or just fifty to sixty percent. In the first case, it seems unlikely that they will have a severe problem. But if they drop into the latter range, a tremendous national self-contempt, frustration, or even self-hatred might develop. (Though, even then, this might not prove enough to motivate great changes.) The difference between the two ranges is probably exactly the difference between the likely outcome of good and bad British government policies, and thus both are well within the realm of possibility. On the other hand, it does not seem feasible—or at least likely—that any British policy could shake the country out of this fifty to eighty percent range of Europe's prosperity. Consider this statement by British author-scientist Sir Charles Snow in his *The Two Cultures and the Scientific Revolution*:

> More often than I like, I am saddened by a historical myth. . . . I can't help thinking of the Venetian Republic in their last half-century. Like us, they had once been fabulously lucky. They had become rich, as we did, by accident. They had acquired immense political skill, just as we have. A good many of them were tough-minded, realistic, patriotic men. They knew, just as clearly as we know, that the current of history had begun to flow against them. Many of them gave their minds to working out ways to keep going. It would have meant breaking the pattern into which they had crystallised. They were fond of the pattern, just as we are fond of ours. They never found the will to break it.

We might add that Venice decayed very comfortably for three hundred years and only now has come to a point of crisis in which "business as usual" is recognized as completely unacceptable.

AN EASTERN EUROPEAN COMMON MARKET?

The spread and obvious potential of the EEC will likely prompt Eastern Europe to attempt development of the present Comecon into a more unified economic structure, able to compete or even cooperate with the West. The obvious problem is that no single country in Western Europe has the economic, political, economic, and military power that the Soviet Union has in the East. The East European Communist powers strongly resist being economic vassals, "hewers of wood and drawers of water," for the Soviet Union, and the Western European model of economic unity as a first step toward political union will not be attractive in Eastern Europe—a Comecon turned into a political union would essentially mean expanding the Soviet Union to include Poland, Czechoslovakia, etc., as new constituent republics similar to Byelorussia. On the other hand, the establishment of an East European economic union without Russia would be hardly less tolerable to the Soviet Union than the accession of any of these nations to the EEC.

Historically, East and West Europe have had strong cultural and economic ties and most of the East European regimes will have powerful temptations to deal with the West. If East Europe is viewed as one of the five dynamic culture areas (see page 63) it makes sense for both East and West to have "early industrial" type plants in the East to take advantage of the low wages and lack of trade union power there. Again, the ideological and political interests of the Soviet Union are the principal obstacles to such developments. However, despite the obstacles, something less than full economic and political union of the East is possible and may be made necessary by the obvious success of the EEC. Many variations and possibilities are available to Eastern Europe even within its constraints.

NEW POSSIBILITIES

Of course, in our picture of the next generation we cannot ignore many new political events which are possible, though they have a relatively low degree of probability. In particular, some of the intermediate powers may flex their muscles more than is expected. New alliances, conflicts, crises, and arms races are always possibilities. Many of these possibilities are discussed in Chapter V. One of these possibilities, although an improbable and perhaps bizarre one, comes from the political effects of the Common Market.

Today we take for granted the legitimacy of the existing nation-states of Western Europe. With a few trivial boundary adjustments caused by the World Wars, they have had essentially the same configuration for a century, and some of them can be traced back several centuries. These nation-states are taken so much for granted that we sometimes forget that their existence within their existing boundaries, with their current populations and languages, is based upon a long series of historical accidents and coincidences. That we have nation-states named Belgium, Austria, France, and Spain instead of Flanders, Wales, Brittany, Catalonia, Naples, Bavaria, etc., is the result of a long series of dynastic marriages, the outcomes of long-ago wars, and other historical events which are long forgotten. Each of the existing nation-states has developed a national history which claims that their development was inevitable and destined by Providence, such as the French myth of its "natural frontiers" of the Pyrenees and the Rhine. However, with the possible exceptions of the smallest and most homogeneous nations, government attempts to impose unity on the varied peoples who have come under their sway have not been completely successful. A Breton is still a Breton in addition to being French. A Scot is still a Scot in addition to being British. A Catalan is still a Catalan in addition to being Spanish.

Each of the European nation-states has been established for a good deal of time and obviously has offered the residents of the incompletely assimilated provinces certain political and economic advantages of being part of a large state. But these historical advantages are rapidly eroding. The present world stability as well as the existence of NATO and other European security arrangements has made the defensive functions of large European nation-states nearly obsolete. France is no more secure than Belgium and neither of them is more secure than Luxemburg (in fact, Luxemburg has disbanded its army). The impending economic unification of Europe in the EEC eliminates the principal economic reason for a large European nation-state. Again, France is not necessarily any more economically healthy than Belgium, and neither of them any more so than Luxemburg.

Why then should a Breton (or a Sicilian, or a Scot, or a Fleming) continue to tolerate being part of a larger state which takes his taxes, sneers at his provincial manners and dialect, may discriminate against him, and at the very least may diffuse and dilute his individual representation and his ethnic personality? Perhaps it is time for a revival for the submerged nations of Europe. Now, critics of this idea will claim that these provinces are not really nations at all. A Frenchman from Paris, a Britisher from London, a German from Berlin, an Italian from Rome, or a Spaniard from Madrid could say that these people do not have the characteristics of a nation. They might say, for example, that they do not speak a different language, merely a dialect. However, the historically dominant central areas, which have been the cores of the nation-states, have imposed their version of the language upon the outer provinces and have merely relegated the local version to the status of a dialect, or so the provincials might claim. Was it Sombart who said a language is a dialect with an army? Or, they might say that even if it were true that local national feeling survived and that vital nation-states could be created in these areas, the idea of separate nations has long since been discarded as impractical by these people. Hardly. There are very active movements for regional autonomy or absolute separation in Wales, Flanders, Brittany, Sicily, and others. Surely there would be such movements in Spain if the government allowed it. Also, there are many Germans whose primary loyalty is still to their *länder* and who feel that the creation of a German *reich* was and still is a mistake.

For the most part the areas we are talking about were originally seized and forcibly held by the states which created the present nations of Europe. Most of these states are now liberal and relatively pacific. Most of them had colonial empires which they could have fought much harder to keep if they had really been serious about maintaining national territory. If some of the provinces of the nation-states of Europe should desire their individual nationhood to the degree that serious repression would be necessary to keep them within the existing states, we may seriously doubt if the present governments of West Europe (obviously excluding Spain) would apply severe police measures, much less tough counter-insurgency operations against citizens of their metropolitan states. Yet there could be serious disturbances in Western Europe caused by the strivings of various provincials for equal rights, self-government, regional autonomy, or even outright independence. If any one of these provinces should attempt and achieve independence, the process might spread throughout Europe. Just one new nation-state could create a persuasive example, placing the existing European nation-state system under serious strain. Particular candidates for such strain are Spain, Italy, the United Kingdom of Great Britain and Northern Ireland,

Belgium, Yugoslavia, and perhaps Czechoslovakia and West Germany. When Franco dies, a lot of nationalists are going to be heard from again. The Basques already have an underground organization and the Catalans will probably be as vigorous as in the 1930s. All this is particularly true if it could be carried out in a framework of a relatively secure EEC. Under these circumstances independence would bring about few if any negative economic disabilities. Nor should we be surprised at the above possibilities. The major function of the nation-state—defense—has greatly eroded. The examples of Finland, Norway, and Denmark show how viable and successful a small state can be.

As for Italy, we cannot forget Metternich's description of it as a "mere geographic expression." Today, the Italian state is functioning badly. The individual Italian's primary loyalties are to his family, his community, and his province. Italy is still a vague concept (although the migration of millions of workers has made it much more unified than a generation ago) and the Italian state is widely regarded as a fraud and a racket by all too many Italians.

The United Kingdom, historically one of the most stable states in the world, is also subject to strains. Note how the very term "United Kingdom" seems odd. It does not exist in the mind of its individuals. Even the term "Great Britain" is limited to foreigners, the government, and upper-class journalists. Individual subjects of Her Majesty are English, Scots, Welsh, or Irish; only the royal family and BBC commentators are "British." If, as projected, British growth rates should lag behind those of the Continent, the gap between the British standard of living and that of other Europeans could very seriously undermine the interests of the Scots and Welsh in maintaining a connection with the predominantly English government. A religious issue could also be involved. The ancient and empty churches of England stand mute witness to the defection of their parishioners to Mammon, football pools, and "the telly." England, particularly big-city England, is in the vanguard of the late sensate culture of the Northwest European culture area. Scotland and Wales, however, despite some erosion from their historical position, remain much more strongly Protestant. If England looks incompetent, corrupt, contemptible, and even silly, Scots and Welsh nationalist movements could find fertile soil.

It is instructive to watch the current struggle in Northern Ireland. Protestant Ulster (two-thirds of that province) is firm in its desire to remain independent of the Roman Catholic Irish Republic. To what degree they are also loyal to the British Crown and the United Kingdom except as an alternative to and protector from Catholic Ireland is open to question. Currently the Catholic minority in Northern Ireland seems united in its determination to resist the Ulster and British governments and to seek unification with the rest of Ireland. Presently the United Kingdom is engaged in trying to repress, or at least accommodate, the Catholic population. Let us assume that the British government is unsuccessful (and given the dismal record of England in Ireland, it is more likely that Whitehall will fail than succeed). We may doubt if the British government and people will then have the stomach for a long drawn-out campaign against urban guerrillas. Ulster has already been called the British Vietnam, with tens of millions of viewers watching the horrors of civil war on their "telly." Already some British writers and politicians are calling for a withdrawal from Ireland.

Although British abandonment of Ulster would solve Britain's problem, it would only begin those of Ulster. The Protestant Irish, led by the Orange Society and other fanatic nationalists, would almost certainly attempt to establish an independent Ulster state (possibly somewhat smaller than the existing six-county area) and try to hold their own against the Republic and the Irish Republican Army. If they succeeded, and they might, then this new nation-state might be the trigger for an independent Scotland or Wales and then an independent Brittany, Flanders, Sicily, Bavaria, etc. Note that there is a very long string of "mights" leading to this possibility; nevertheless, the possibility must be recognized. The prime reasons for the European nation-states are being liquidated; they might be historically obsolete, and if so, can be replaced.

Although this reorganization or fractionalization of Europe would lead to all sorts of dislocations and problems of citizenship, it probably would not make much difference to the total world scene. Fractionalization would only be possible because Europe is essentially united; the EEC might consist of twenty members instead of ten, as would European security arrangements, but Europe would still be Europe. In fact, there might easily be a forced growth of community-wide political institutions. Indeed, a Europe of fragmented nation-states might form a more effective European political community than the current system.

A BETTER UNDERSTANDING OF ECONOMIC DEVELOPMENT

In many areas—especially less-developed areas just beginning a rapid growth—there is a developing dynamism, simply because of the momentum of the economic development already achieved. For this purpose there is an enormous difference in the politics of growth among rates of 2.5, 5, or 10 percent per annum. In the eighteenth century the British discovered how to grow economically by a rate between two to three percent per year. (Let us call it 2.3 percent since this simplifies calculations.) Any country growing at this rate will achieve growth by a factor of ten in a hundred years. If applied to per capita income, this would ordinarily solve the problem of poverty as it was understood at the start of the process and from almost any historical perspective such growth would be a spectacular achievement. However, in any particular period of five or ten years a 2.3 percent annual growth rate simply implies a twelve or twenty-five percent improvement respectively, and this is not so noticeable in the five- or ten-year time frame. If, however, income grows by 7.2 percent a year, then it doubles every ten years. This is highly visible. The five dynamic areas are already growing by around seven percent a year or more. Excitement over visible, rapid growth can generate a commitment among large numbers of people, a dedication to preserving the mechanism producing this growth.

The attitude that the system is more or less succeeding is, of course, not universal. The problem of sharp differences of income within a country is extremely important in Latin America, and is going to be still more important in the future. This resembles the classic North-South problem in Italy (or the United States), but in Latin America it is likely to be seriously worse, particularly in the more successful countries where the dynamic portions tend to leave the less dynamic areas far behind. If the "success" of a country is measured by egalitarian criteria, or by looking mainly at the lagging regions or sections, then some countries which are very successful in important but limited areas, or even by the criteria of overall indices, may seem to be failing.

The importance of such gaps can be exaggerated in moral and political terms. Consider first the political issue. Few people compare their lives with the richest people they hear of or see in movies; rather, they make their comparisons with themselves five years ago, their neighbor, their relatives, friends, and so on. Many Hudson Institute audiences have been asked if they feel depressed because they do not live as well as a Rockefeller or Rothschild lives—practically nobody ever does. Few people can imagine living a dignified and self-respected life at about twenty per-cent of their current income, and yet many readers of this book will have had fathers or grandfathers who lived quite well at such a twenty percent. The current emphasis on gap thinking forces large areas of the world into a kind of semantic poverty and often leads to inefficient programs.

Let us imagine for example, that there are two programs to improve Northeast Brazil. One of them promises to double or triple the per capita income of half the population over a certain period, the other half receiving "only" some fifty percent increase. Many people would consider this a rather impressive pro-gram. The other program wants to move about half the popula-tion of the Northeast to the dynamic areas of Brazil, where they will enjoy a doubling, tripling, or even quadrupling of their income in ten or twenty years; the other half of the population will be left where it is and still achieve a fifty percent increase (or even more since such an increase would be easier since fewer people left in Northeast Brazil means not only more resources per person but also that the dynamic South can contribute more per capita). The second program is not only more successful in de-creasing poverty but is also much more practical, but to most casual observers (and even many experts) Northeast Brazil would not seem much of an improvement at all. In fact, with its deserted villages and overgrown farmland, it may even seem worse. This judgment fails to take account of the fact that the "invisible" migration of half the population of Northeast Brazil would be more successful than anything that could be done locally.

Fortunately, there is a strong tendency in the later stages of industrialization for all classes and areas of a society to share in improved income, and this tendency becomes general by the time the society becomes one of mass consumption—though there may still be great inequalities. If countries are not misled in the short-run by "gap ideology" thinking, and if the appreciation of just how much richer everyone will be even in the short-term future spreads throughout the country, it could serve as a stabilizing and unifying force in previously low morale and strife-torn areas.

THE GREEN REVOLUTION

The awarding of the Nobel Prize in 1970 to Dr. Norman Borlaug called the world's attention to the "Green Revolution," which is changing the face of the underdeveloped world and promises to delay widespread famine or perhaps even postpone it indefinitely. The new Philippine "miracle" rices, new Mexican wheats and sorghums, and the successful transfer of these to India and elsewhere, have created the possibility of doubling or tripling production per acre. As a result, a food surplus rather than a food shortage seems likely in the mid-seventies. Thus, the length and intensity of a world agricultural depression, due to overproduction, is more likely to be a problem than the often predicted famine due to increased population (though there may still be many local food deficits—particularly in protein foods).

On the other hand, the ability to produce food much more rapidly and efficiently may provide an enormous impetus to development—and thus be an important force through the 1970s and into the 1980s. In general, if a country is sixty or seventy percent agricultural, an increase in agricultural productivity of ten to twenty percent makes an important difference, permitting the release of manpower for industrial development and perhaps permitting agricultural exports to industrial states for capital goods.

MULTINATIONAL CORPORATIONS

The multinational corporation will probably be playing the central role in the development of an interdependent world economy. Production will be internationalized despite pronounced tendencies toward regional and national political multipolarity and competition. The emergence and growth of the MNCs can be compared to the formation of the great corporate organizations in the United States at the turn of the century. By the time of the first Belle Epoque, this formation had been completed and the transition to a continental economy was underway. Corporate organizations were both a cause and a result of the economic expansion during this period. The combinations were justified by the emergence of a continental economy as a result of the tremendous development of the railroads in the previous decades. They tended to be large, vertically structured, departmental, professional organizations with national marketing practices and they continue today as the central instrument for expansion in the U.S. economy.

In much the same way, the great multinational corporations, which have grown up in the past two decades, could be the major instrument in the creation of a truly international or global economy in the next generation. They may or may not account for the majority of international business transacted in the next two decades, but they should set the tone for the expansion in international business and act as a carrier of "capitalist" values to the "transitional," developing Third World. They are presently especially competent at performing the following functions:

1. Raising, investing, and reallocating capital
2. Creating and managing organizations
3. Innovating, adopting, perfecting, and transferring technology
4. Distribution, maintenance, marketing, and sales (including financing all of these)
5. Furnishing local elites with suitable—perhaps ideal—career choices
6. Educating and upgrading both blue collar and white collar labor (and elites)
7. In many areas, and in the not-too-distant future, serving as a major source of local savings and taxes and in furnishing skilled cadres (i.e., graduates) of all kinds to the local economy (including the future local competition of the MNC)
8. Facilitating the creation of vertical organizations or vertical arrangements which allow for the smooth, reliable, and effective progression of goods from one stage of production to another. In many cases, such organization is a negation of the classical free market. It is a very efficient and useful method of stable production
9. Finally, and almost by themselves, providing both a market

and a mechanism for satellite services and industries that can
stimulate indigenous local development much more effectively than most aid programs

Because they are so capable of performing these economic functions, the multinational corporations could become highly efficient at supplying any particular area or economy with missing
factors of production. Furthermore, the technostructure elites—
and perhaps almost everyone else associated with these dynamic
organizations will probably have high morale and commitment to
growth. This is particularly true for companies operating in the
five dynamic areas of the world in comparison to the "decadent,"
"low morale" atmosphere of much domestic business activity in
the United States and Western Europe.

The complexity of operating in a number of countries whose
laws, policies, and customs vary and may even conflict, suggests
that large corporations with international experience have a distinct and probably enduring advantage over new entrants into
international business. These multinational corporations can
profit not only from their own activities but from the raw materials and excellent labor sources of countries in Pacific Asia,
Latin America, and the underdeveloped areas of Europe. And
once these countries start developing, they will become an excellent market.

Individual countries will find it increasingly difficult to act
unilaterally to resist these corporations or international investment in this multipolar economic world. Almost every country,
with the possible exception of the United States (and the United
States may be a little too blasé in its lack of concern) worries
about the special problems presented by large multinational corporations operating within its borders. Many concerns arise—
ranging from fear of internal political manipulation to a perceived inability by the government of the nation-state to control
the multinational corporation. Actually, even though the multinational corporation looks like a threat to many states, and even
in some cases looks more powerful than the state, it is in fact a
weak political instrument when compared to the nation-state. A
multinational corporation does not have the nation-state's cluster
of loyalties. It has no sovereign authority and no armed forces.
No one will kill or die for General Motors. The greatest and often

only power or leverage the multinational corporation has is that it can choose to enter a country or not, or to expand or cut back already operating facilities. This leverage is usually small. In almost any serious direct confrontation between a nation-state and a multinational corporation today, the multinational corporation is almost certain to lose.

In the world of 1985, despite their great importance, most multinational corporations will try to adapt to the native political environment. Their major reaction to politics in the host country and to international politics in general is likely to be to take account of and adjust to political developments without trying very hard to influence politics directly. There may be a few "banana republics" where one or a group of the corporations have so much economic muscle relative to the host government that they will be tempted to dominate local politics. But such cases should be rare and are likely to be contraproductive for the corporation concerned.

Of course, even a policy of non-intervention could unintentionally influence politics. If the local and national political scene is radical, irrational, or erratic, the multinational concern may choose to invest little or nothing in the errant country. This may cause the country to adjust its politics to prevent such a "boycott." Further, any country which discriminates strongly against multinational corporations is likely to find its economy falling behind. In 1963 the French began a campaign of discrimination against multinational concerns, particularly American corporations. As a result, the Americans set up operations in Belgium, Germany, etc. The French soon began to fall behind and by 1970 the French Government had largely changed its policy. Thus the multinational concerns had a major effect on French policy, but not in a deliberate or premeditated way. Each separate corporation simply took account of the situation and adjusted to it.

Of course, the results of the individual actions were collectively very large and the French simply had to take account of this collective result. Conceivably, the multinational corporations may learn to cooperate to enhance the effectiveness of their collective actions in much the same way that European bankers in the nineteenth century refused to deal with any government that had repudiated its debts until a settlement had been made with the debtors. Whether or not the multinational corporations learn to cooperate in this way, they are still lucky to be one of the most important institutions of the late twentieth century. In fact, it seems quite plausible that historians of the distant future, writing of this period, will focus on the multinational corporation as the engine of progress and as a uniquely dynamic institution that imparted a good deal of its dynamism to the society as a whole. Whether or not this happens will depend to some degree on the self-consciousness of the personnel of the multinational corporation and on how well they communicate the consciousness of their mission to others. Such a consciousness will generally increase their effectiveness, but it need not be based upon purely self-serving considerations. What we suggest here is that just as national trade acted as an engine of progress and industrialization in the nineteenth century (although for a number of reasons it is not doing so today), the multinational corporation may play exactly this role in the future.

The developing countries especially are at once attracted and repelled by the presence of multinational corporations. The appeal of added taxes and employment, and the development of unexplored resources conflict with the challenges that major foreign activities seem to present to sovereignty and self-determination. Some countries will view themselves as forced to choose between neocolonialism (prosperity with foreign domination and corruption) and national socialism (independence with poverty and tyranny). Few such clear-cut choices will actually have to be made, although local politicians will accuse each other of "selling the country" or "starving the people." In fact, almost all countries will arrive at some workable compromise between their nationalist ideology and their national economic interest. Even those developing countries which call themselves socialist will adjust and adapt to the presence of the multinational corporation. Most of the developing world has decided, and will likely continue to decide, to open the doors to foreign investment.

Ambivalent—or contradictory—attitudes toward foreign investment can exist in a developed country as well. Many Canadians, for example, have resented U.S. multinational corporations' ownership of so much of the Canadian productive plant and of many key areas of Canadian industry and commerce. Still, the Canadians have refused to take any really serious action which would slow down the rate of U.S. investment in their country. The Canadians have tolerated U.S. investment because it seems likely that any slowdown in U.S. growth would be reflected in a slowdown of the growth of the Canadian economy. The Canadians, like many other countries, do have a tendency to encourage investment by non-U.S. multinational corporations, particularly Japanese and British, but this has had very little effect in lessening U.S. involvement.

There are other factors in addition to government actions that might slow multinational business expansion. For example, excessive labor agitation or political instability or anything else which threatens major cost increases and inefficient or disrupted operations may retard major investment commitments even when official government policy favors investment.

Even so, it seems very likely that, in the next fifteen years, the multinational corporation will emerge as one of the major driving forces of world economy, and of world culture and society. We can get perspective on this process by considering the record of the 1960s, and we agree with many Marxists that this record is likely to repeat itself in the 1970s and perhaps even in the 1980s. We can think of gross world product as growing about 5 percent a year and gross world trade as growing about 50 percent or more faster than gross world product. This by itself would mean an increasing internationalization of the world economy. The multinational corporation seems to grow about twice as fast as gross world product and one-third as fast as gross world trade. Already, the American owned multinational corporations sell abroad five dollars for every dollar that the United States exports.

THE FIVE DYNAMIC AREAS

About one-third of the increase in gross world product in the next decade should come from the five dynamic areas—Japan, Eastern Europe, parts of Latin America, parts of non-Communist and Pacific Asia, and Southern Europe. Each of these areas has about 100 million people directly involved in the specially dynamic economic zones.

These areas seem to be closing the gap (at least geometrically, and in some cases even arithmetically) between themselves and the more developed countries of the world. All possess or are creating local economies that are growing between six and fifteen percent a year, much faster than the rest of the world.

Japan, whose growth rate in the last five years of the 1960s averaged about twelve percent (in real terms) is the best known example but increasingly the four other areas are becoming recognized as having been and likely to continue being especially dynamic economically. Much of Eastern Europe grows at seven percent a year or better, about fifty percent faster than the highly developed areas of North and Western Europe. It also has the largest source of relatively inexpensive manpower trained in the European tradition, and that manpower is becoming increasingly available to the United States, Western European, and Japanese business. There are some indications that the same may soon be increasingly true of the Soviet Union (while we note this possibility and its importance if it succeeds, we are also skeptical of any great degree of success). This reserve of professional, skilled, manual labor, without free unions or the right to strike, is not subject to as many labor disturbances as in Western Europe or America, and receives much lower wages. There is a new political emphasis now on "bridge building" and economic interchange between Eastern Europe and the West. As a result, one important phenomenon of the seventies is likely to be a spectacular increase in East-West trade, and more important, in East-West production and marketing agreements. We have seen the rapid growth of these kinds of relationships in the last two years, and this growth seems to be accelerating, although the political issues and risks involved should not be underestimated.

The economic performance of the dynamic areas of Latin America (principally South and Southeastern Brazil and "Europeanized" Mexico) is even more impressive. The concern of foreign observers and even cultured natives with the terrible poverty of some decaying rural areas seems to have blinded them to the impressive economic growth in some major urban centers. For example, in Brazil the poverty-stricken agrarian Northeast is now serving as a labor source for the booming São Paulo-Rio area, much as the American South provided labor for the industrial growth of California. Much the same thing is happening in Mexico. Mexico's growth has also been helped by intelligent government policies and the presence of a continuing source of foreign exchange from *yanqui* tourists and retirees, while some Brazilians are forced to boast that "the country grows while the government sleeps," that Brazilian urban dynamism can overcome even counter-productive public policy. But in both these places and in other areas of Latin America, there is a growing awareness of "compound interest."

The less developed part of non-Communist and Pacific Asia (mainly South Korea, Taiwan, Hong Kong, Singapore, Thailand, and perhaps even South Vietnam, Indonesia, and Malaysia) is an especially interesting dynamic area. Already a significant portion of Japanese and American industry is moving, or considering moving, many operations there, spurring on an already dynamic development. For example, Japanese manufacturers have found that they can produce textiles and consumer electronics in this area at about one-half of the cost of production in Japan. One important question mark in this area is Indonesia. With its 120 million people, natural resources, and improved administration, it is potentially very prosperous indeed—at least certain areas if not the country as a whole. At present, about one and one-half billion dollars has been pledged for investment in Indonesia by various private sources, and foreign aid is running about six hundred million dollars a year; yet the development process seems to be just starting.

Southern Europe (Spain, Portugal, Southern France, Southern Italy, Yugoslavia, and Greece) is also important because it is supplying millions of foreign workers to the rest of Europe and has dynamic indigenous industrial and agricultural development and in the future there is likely to be an increasing tendency to bring the work to the worker, instead of vice versa as today.

SUSTAINED GROWTH IN TRADE, COMMUNICATIONS, TRAVEL

We have already discussed the fact that international trade and communications will increase substantially in the next decade or two, as more and more of the world becomes a global metropolis. One of the most important growth industries of this global metropolis in the 1970s will be the care and feeding of transient and resident foreigners, which should grow about three times as fast as the global economy as a whole and play an increasingly important role in the economies of many countries. These foreigners can be divided into four categories: tourists; students; business, academic, and governmental executives and technicians who travel frequently or spend long periods abroad as part of their jobs; and retired people. The growth of tourist and business travel should break down psychological and physical barriers to foreigners; and people used to studying, vacationing, or conducting business in foreign countries will be less hesitant to retire there. In particular, an increased emphasis on learning foreign languages is a cause and result of the above.

The retired person provides some especially interesting and often overlooked possibilities. With the likely increase in both the expectations and cost of services and commodities, many elderly couples in the United States or in much of Western Europe who retire (say on an income of $10,000 to $15,000 a year) may not be able to live up to their expectations. But they would be able to live extremely well in much of Southern Europe, many parts of Latin America, and some parts of Pacific Asia. As travel costs decrease (permitting trips home to visit children and grandchildren and vice versa), as communications improve (bringing international TV programs), as world markets increase (making available familiar products), this phenomenon should increase. Retired couples will be able to stretch their incomes further, afford servants, more luxurious housing, relatively inexpensive medical care, etc., without sacrificing a feeling of connection with their home country. And as international retirement increases, the "expatriate" communities will provide increasingly important markets, leading to tailored services that will, in turn, encourage this phenomenon. American retirees are already living in Mexico and other areas of Latin America and Southern Europe.

A particular pattern which has sprung up in Mexico seems worth commenting on. Many retired American couples have bought homes just far enough away from resort areas that the prices are not high, but close enough so that they can still be rented during the season for enough to pay for a full year's expenses. During the time the houses are rented the owners can spend time with their children in the States or travel around the world. Further, because they have servants, it is easy for them to take their grandchildren when they have vacations, so all in all it is a very nice pattern of life.

There may be native reactions against tourism and "tourist pollution" of the home country, but it is unlikely that' many governments (or the people themselves) would consent to shut off such an easy source of money, although some will. Many more may grumble loudly—but on their way to the bank. Still others may try to restrict the foreign intrusion to those tourists with the most desirable economic, cultural, and social characteristics.

LITTLE POLITICAL UNITY

The surprise-free projection describes the world as half-united, multipolar, with a tendency toward synthesis and unity. By 1985, international politics will have increasingly felt certain effects of the trend towards the post-industrial economy and culture, but the political consequences are not likely to have been either radically destabilizing or radically innovative. In its essentials, the international system is likely to resemble the system of today, which is to say that it will still be a system of *nations*. The world may be smaller, but this will not alter the nations' view of themselves as sovereign political entities, the autonomous judges of their own interests and policies.

WORLDWIDE LAW AND ORDER ISSUES

A general decrease in political and ideological consensus and freely-conceded authority is notable in the West today. This is a very important issue from the practical point of view, and ideologically it reflects the decline in force of the twelve traditional societal levers (see page 78). Today, not only are the economic imperatives and incentives of life sharply reduced in the industrial West (a condition which could, of course, drastically change, greatly affecting the projection), but the old forces of national security, national interest, and the marital virtues have been weakened (see Chapter V).

Authority is only indirectly connected to power, wisdom, or knowledge, or ability—though any of these can play an important role in creating and maintaining authority. The naked use of power is coercion, not authority; the naked use of wisdom or knowledge is persuasion or subversion, not authority; and the naked use of ability is usually in providing lessons or examples. Pure authority is simply the right to say, suggest, or order something, and to be listened to seriously simply because the speaker has authority. The essence of authority is concession. One who exercises authority has that authority because he is conceded to have it. Some cultures have heavily emphasized authority (Roman). Some cultures never really understood it (Greek), and kept searching for it because, so to speak, they needed it to make the system work. The following example is useful in explaining authority to young people. Imagine two basketball teams, each composed of half of five pairs of identical twins. But one team has the institution of authority and the other does not. The one with authority simply has the custom that if one of the members wears a red arm band, the others will obey his instructions; not because he is stronger, or smarter, or older, or a better player, but just because he wears the arm band. The other team has no way of selecting a leader; clearly the first team will have a much greater chance of beating the second team.

Without authority, freely conceded, society and governments are faced with the alternatives of anarchy and coercion. This may be a key issue of the 1970s for most Western nations. At present not only is deviant and violent behavior on the increase among groups which are—or believe themselves to be—alienated from the larger society but also among important elements in the larger society itself. This raises the question of what Daniel Bell has called *discretionary behavior. Discretionary income* is the economist's term for money that you can spend on whatever you like. Just as you only have discretionary income available when your basic needs are satisfied and you feel financially secure, discretionary behavior is possible only when you feel socially secure, when you feel you can get away with it.

Certain groups and individuals with a private or group cause will defy the conventions of society, believing that extreme or disruptive behavior is the most effective course for gaining their goals and that they will not be seriously penalized for using such tactics. Examples are disruptive "job actions" by unions, civil service and police strikes, disruptive "sit-ins" and demonstrations, punitive harassment of individuals or groups by such organizations as the Jewish Defense League or black militant groups.

Today, society's toleration of this kind of behavior is high, but it clearly is—in the nature of political society—a toleration with finite limits. The counteraction may be sharp repression; and repression in turn may either succeed or provoke a much wider defiance of authority, further discrediting it. The character and quality of the political milieu of the 1970s will be heavily influenced by whether the political and social elites of Western society (new ones, or the established elites) attempt to regain real authority through a renewed competence in their roles, through ideological or coercive measures, or through changes in the educational and/or ideological milieu.

TERRORISM AND VIOLENCE

A new form of insecurity threatens the seemingly secure states of Europe and North America, as well as the Third World. This kind of law and order issue is now a central issue of U.S. domestic policies and is likely to take an international form. By 1980 there may be a serious and widespread problem of unauthorized or semi-authorized violence. Analogous problems occurred in La Belle Epoque: those raised by anarchists and nihilists attempting what they called "propaganda by deed"; problems exemplified by the assassination of the Archduke Franz Ferdinand. Respect for authority and traditional standards may decrease, particularly among the more frustrated members of the less developed nations and many of the more idealistic (or disturbed) of the developed. There is likely to be an increasing number of individuals willing to "bear witness," "confront," or otherwise communicate their "message" through violent demonstrations, assassinations, or activities such as the Palestine guerrillas' against Israeli civil aircraft.

The world's economic and social system is so complex that it is very sensitive to disruption. The new technology raises fantastic opportunities for acts of sabotage and terrorism by individuals or small groups. The faceless anonymity of great megalopoli makes crime and other forms of antisocial behavior more difficult to prevent and punish. The "educated incapacity" of lawyers, judges, and other persons in authority, particularly in the United States, makes it extremely difficult to deal rationally with crime and criminals. In the early 1970s a few dozen dedicated men are destroying the political stability and economic possibilities of Ulster and Uruguay. The I.R.A. and the Tupamaros will be an inspiration to angry and ambitious young men everywhere—perhaps they will be the Guevaras of the later 1970s.

One might imagine that while the developed nations—Europe, North America, and even the Soviet Union—may have a common interest in controlling such violence, some of the underdeveloped nations might be in sympathy with the perpetrators of this violence and therefore unwilling to allow the United Nations or other worldwide groups to control it. This could lead to differentially invidious, or otherwise onerous, controls on the international movement of people, as well as to international tensions and the development of unfortunate political or social attitudes and practices within some states.

NEW IDEOLOGIES

One of the obvious conclusions of the experiences of the 1960s is that the prevailing ideologies in the world do not adequately serve the aspirations of many people, particularly young people in the West. Historical liberalism, conservatism, and Marxism seem archaic and "irrelevant" to these young people* and they are searching for new ideologies. One of the real weaknesses of the New Left elements in the 1960s was their lack of some firm ideological commitment. They had a vague idea of what they wanted and a very clear idea of what they did not want, but no coherent view of the world as it is or ought to be.

There are several obvious candidates for a new ideology (or rather, a revived ideology since the late twentieth century does not seem very good at inventing new ideas). Some of these are: *neo-anarchism*, or the revival of the violent anti-statist ideals of the mid-nineteenth century; *syndicalism*, or the revival of the La Belle Epoque revolutionary socialist "gang" ideology that organized groups waging war upon the entire society (and perhaps each other) give a meaning and purpose to life (the "community control" agitation in the United States may be a harbinger of this sentiment); *neo-nationalism*, or revived nationalism might con-

---

* William Pfaff, *Condemned to Freedom* (New York, 1971).

ceivably replace the cosmopolitanism of some disaffected elements in Western Europe, perhaps in response to the emergence of the submerged nations; and *neo-fascism*, or crypto-fascism as the memory of the evils and failure of fascism fades from the mind of Europe (the recent Italian elections suggest this possibility).

PERSISTENCE OF THE CHRONIC CONFRONTATION

We see nothing on the horizon which is likely to change the character of the chronic political confrontations which threaten the stability of the world today. Perhaps some of these confrontations may be alleviated or normalized but it must be recognized that each confrontation is based upon fundamental political differences. These chronic confrontations, listed below, are discussed in some length in Chapter V.

The Chronic Confrontations

Triangular	1.	United States vs. Soviet Union
	2.	Soviet Union vs. China
	3.	China vs. United States
Divided Nation-states	4.	Germany
	5.	China
	6.	Korea
	7.	Vietnam
	8.	Arab-Israeli (divided Palestine)
	9.	India-Pakistan (divided India) and perhaps
	10.	Japan vs. China (?)

Note that a possible Sino-Japanese confrontation has been added to the list. Because Japan has been quiescent for a generation, and because mainland China has been embroiled with the United States and the Soviet Union during this period, we tend to forget that China and Japan were almost continuously at each other's throats for the fifty years preceding 1945. The rapid Japanese capitalist growth is likely to be received most unfavorably by Communist China. Japan may threaten China's currently accepted primary position in East Asia and the Chinese are not likely to respond cheerfully to such a development.

The Chinese have traditionally thought of themselves as the

"Middle Kingdom," the center of civilization. Today the Japanese have an economy more than one and one-half times larger than China's and growing at about twice China's rate. It is reasonable to think that the Chinese might not, therefore, choose to compete economically. They could argue that the important criteria for measuring a culture, a society, a nation, should not be crude indices of the gross national product, but the quality of human life, the quality of the culture and of the society. From a Chinese point of view, it is possible to argue that all that a good Chinese government owes its people is adequate food, adequate clothing, adequate shelter, adequate medical care, and adequate education. (Adequate by traditional Chinese standards, not by Western.) All of these guarantees seem to be available to the Chinese people or on the way to being made available. From this point of view, then, the pressures within China may not be for accelerated growth rates, but pressures of quite another sort. The Chinese may want to suppress what they see as the artificial values and decadent demands of Western industrial society. From the leadership's point of view they may want—or need—to emphasize that China is a lean, hard, purposeful, dedicated, austere, ascetic, *serious* nation, and that the capitalist nations (and revisionist Soviet-style Communist states) are decadent, corrupt, and materialistic. It may become important to the Chinese to single out the phenomenally prosperous Japanese as the "corruptors" of Asia—in effect as the agents of the "neo-imperialist" West. This conflict of values is far more subtle than the simple political and economic arguments which may develop in Asia. And China may serve as a powerful inciter and organizer of various indigenous forces of reaction against modernization or Westernization, and at the same time claim to represent a unique form of modernity. If this is true, the Japanese may again assume an important place in the Chinese hierarchy of devils, which would, to put it mildly, poison Sino-Japanese relations—as well as affect the Japanese people's view of themselves.

Currently, though, most Japanese seem anxious for continued good relations with Communist China and want to get along with the Chinese at least as well (if not better) as they have in the recent past. There are, of course, many complexities in this relationship. One is especially worth noting. In some ways the mainland Chinese are one of the proudest peoples in the world, as anxious for prestige as the Japanese. It may seem particularly important to the Chinese to assert a superiority in values and culture over those Chinese enclaves in Southeast and East Asia which enjoy a better economic performance than Communist China. Thus the Hong Kong Chinese today have a per capita income of around five hundred dollars and this seems likely to continue to increase rapidly. The Chinese in Singapore are doing very well. Such countries as South Korea, Taiwan, Malaysia, Thailand (with about three million ethnic Chinese), are also likely to do very well in the future. If the Japanese have large capital resources available, which they choose to invest in these countries, they may play an increasingly important role in their economic growth and prosperity. The Japanese could then be made subject to condemnation as "lackeys of the West," exploiters of and traitors to Asia.

TURMOIL AND VIOLENCE IN THE THIRD WORLD

It is safe to predict that there will be much turmoil in the underdeveloped areas of Afro-Asia and perhaps even Latin America. One of the principal forces encouraging turmoil is the penetration of well-established Western ideas into these areas. The concept of nationalism has a particularly devasting effect in Afro-Asia where the existing states, whose boundaries were largely drawn in European chanceries in the nineteenth century, have very little relationship to the true cultural, racial, religious, and linguistic patterns of these areas. As elitist Westernized intellectuals attempt to impose Western forms of nationality and state organization upon the peoples of their areas, trouble is bound to occur. Nation-states are made of blood. People who have not yet made their nation-states will fight. In Latin America this pattern will perhaps be less severe. Although a similar situation exists in the contrast between the thoroughly Hispanic (and in Brazil, Portuguese) dominant classes and their Indian and/or African underclasses, there are no irredentist problems.

This turmoil will forcibly impact the billions of people involved, but as far as the First and Second Worlds are concerned the significant thing to note about what will happen in the Third World in the 1970s and 1980s is that it will not be any more important than it is today. The Third World has little economic strength, less military power, and even its much publicized population is considerably exaggerated in importance. Now, this does not mean that the Third World will be of no consequence whatever in the world; to be sure, it will be particularly important, if one lives or does business there, or is engaged in some sort of governmental activity dealing with those areas of the world, but by the very nature of things the Third World will not be as important as the First and Second worlds—that is, North America, Europe, Japan, the Soviet Union, and China.

In some ways it is useful to view the Third World as filling the role in the world today that the Balkans performed in Europe during the period, say, 1878 through 1945. The Third World, like the Balkans, is essentially backward, agrarian, and industrializing, but industrializing at a very slow and uneven rate which is in itself causing great dislocations. It consists of more or less states hacked out of decaying empires, having artificial boundaries and including many hostile and conflicting nationalities. Many Third World countries have highly productive and hated mercantile minorities, but instead of the Jews of the Balkans they have Indians or Chinese. Like the Balkan states they have adopted governmental institutions and theories from Western Europe, and find them of little relevance to local conditions. Also like the pre-Communist Balkans, the ruling classes of the Third World look toward Western models for language, education, and material culture. They speak French and English, wear Western style clothes, eat in a Western manner, read Western books and newspapers, and measure their cultural level by Western standards. Third World states must have a company of paratroopers, a modern Hilton Hotel, and a jet airport, just as in the late nineteenth century a good self-respecting Balkan state had to have a squadron of hussars, a rococo opera house, and a railroad. Also like the Balkans the Third World states, despite their freedom, are in economic thralldom to the industrialized states, relying upon Western capital for development (either through direct investment or some sort of international body), supplying agricultural goods and raw materials to the West, and importing capital goods.

However, unlike the Balkans, which had real military significance because of their geographic position and dogged infantry, the Third World can contribute little to a world struggle. The new states are significant as a human problem and as a political arena for the rivalries of great powers, and possibly as a place for wars to be provoked or prevented.

VIOLENT MOVEMENTS

The next item in our projection points out a principal threat to the achievement of the rosy picture of economic growth presented above. Nativist, messianic, or other irrationally emotional mass and elitist movements in both the Western and developing states could lead to economic stagnation (as in Cuba and the Congo in the 1960s) and other difficulties. This would represent a decrease in "rational" politics—that is, politics based on calculated economic, national, and class interests.

An extremely fertile area for irrational political movements in the next fifteen years is the Caribbean. The Caribbean islands have achieved their independence with what the Marxists call *neo-colonialist* regimes, that is, regimes essentially the same as the preceding colonial regimes but with natives in the positions of power. This situation is extremely unattractive to certain elements in the intelligentsia as well as a strong segment of the urban poor in these nations. Most of these island nations are almost without natural resources, capital, and technological know-how of any kind. Because their only resources are their climate and beaches, their only possible business is tourism. But, demagogues maintain that this turns them into nations of busboys. In the contemporary world, very few people take pride in personal service. In practically every one of the Caribbean nations there is strong potential for an irrational, ferocious, anti-white, anti-foreign, anti-capitalist revolutionary regime. These regimes could, possibly, come to power legally, but more likely it will be through insurrection and riots. The effects of such governments would be terrible in material terms, but could conceivably infuse pride into the masses. Perhaps it is significant that Franz Fanon was a West Indian. Under certain circumstances, there is a good chance that Britain could be drawn in (as in the Anguilla incident) and/or the United States (as it nearly was in Trinidad). The appearance of a militant black government in the Caribbean could also have effects on the United States, giving black militants and separatists a nearer and more relevant base and model than Africa or Cuba.

1985 TECHNOLOGICAL CRISIS

This phenomenon seems so important and may have such far-reaching ramifications that we have devoted Chapter VIII to the subject. Very briefly, the concept of the 1985 technological crisis was originally derived from an article by John von Neumann in the mid-50s, in which he argued that "the environment in which technological progress must occur has become undersized and underorganized." This is happening not accidentally or as a mistake, but is inherent in technology's relation to geography on the one hand, to political organization on the other. Von Neumann discusses the likelihood that a number of technological trends may come to a crisis stage sometime around 1980, or soon afterwards. A multitude of very real physical threats and moral problems caused by advanced and advancing technology has led to an increasing disillusionment with technological and economic progress (e.g., the popularity of environmentalism), especially among those historically most enamored of "progress" —the upper-middle class. Both the problems of advancing technology and the revolt against technological progress may play a significant role in the next decade or two.

PROBLEMS OF SHEER NUMBERS, SIZE, AND BIGNESS

Many problems caused by sheer numbers, size, and bigness are so obvious they require little comment. As groups grow in size, they come more and more to dwarf and render insignificant each individual within them. For example, when the Constitution was ratified, a Congressman represented fifty thousand people; now he represents a half million. Like an individual voter, an individual consumer now has very little weight. Even our "great men" feel themselves impotent—generals and corporation presidents laugh bitterly when they hear critics complaining about their vast power.

Even those developments which are increasing an individual's ability to do what he wants have costs. For example, contemporary transportation and communication systems allow people to do all kinds of things they could never do before, but at the cost of gargantuan (and potentially fallible) artifacts. If a DC-3 crash was a grave tragedy, what is it when a 747 goes down with a full load? The *Torrey Canyon* befouled miles of Channel coast with its hundred thousand tons of oil; but what happens when a million-ton tanker hits a reef?

Obviously major increases in size offer great and desirable opportunities for new and greater human achievements, and make previous achievements available to more men. But with these opportunities come growing problems. What can be even more serious is when a cumulative series of fairly small, often irreversible, quantitative changes leads to a qualitatively different situation or environment, one less desirable than what existed before these changes began. A dystrophian sequence of controlled increases in size can create a situation essentially beyond control.

SEARCH FOR MEANING AND PURPOSE

Historically, the twelve societal levers (listed below) have moved Western man or, to use the contemporary cliché, provided "meaning and purpose to life." One of the most widely publicized and discussed phenomena of the 1960s was the startling change among upper and upper-middle class young people in the United States; in much of Western Europe; in such Latin American countries as Mexico, Venezuela, Chile, and Colombia; and (before August, 1968) in parts of Eastern Europe such as Czechoslovakia, and to some degree even in Japan. In these upper and upper-middle classes—there was a substantial waning of these levers.

The 12 Traditional Societal Levers

*(i.e., traditional sources of "reality testing," social integration,
and/or meaning and purpose)*

1. Religion, tradition, and authority
2. Biology and physics (e.g., pressures and stresses of the physical environment, the more tragic aspects of the human condition, etc.)
3. Earning a living
4. Defense of frontiers (territoriality)
5. Defense of vital strategic and economic interests
6. Defense of vital political, moral, and morale interests
7. The "martial" virtues such as duty, patriotism, honor, heroism, glory, courage, etc.
8. The manly emphasis—in adolescence: team sports, heroic figures, aggressive and competitive activities, rebellion against "female roles"; in adulthood: playing an adult male role; similarly a womanly emphasis
9. The puritan ethic (deferred gratification, work orientation, achievement orientation, advancement orientation, sublimation of sexual desires, etc.)
10. A high degree (perhaps almost total) of loyalty, commitment, and/or identification with nation, state, city, clan, village, extended family, secret society and/or other large grouping
11. Other sublimation and/or repression of sexual, aggressive, aesthetic, and/or other instincts
12. Other irrational and/or restricting taboos, rituals, totems, myths, customs, and charismas

The eroding or disappearing of these levers from many current life styles—particularly among upper and upper-middle-class members of societies which feel that they get their "security for free"—may make an enormous difference in events by 1985. Indeed, it seems a reasonable generalization that much of the New Left and many "dropouts," in almost all countries, come from upper-middle-class homes where these levers have been almost fully eroded. It should, of course, be mentioned that newer pressures and life styles seem to be appearing in these same societies and classes in answer to the current search for "meaning and purpose." Some of these are indicated below:

Interim Meaning and Purpose

A. *Probably healthy*	B. *Probably unhealthy*
1. High-consumption materialism	1. Semi-permanent adolescence
2. Neo-cynicism	2. "Bread and circuses"
3. Neo-epicureanism	3. Cultism
4. Neo-stoicism	4. Fanatic reformism
5. Neo-gentleman	5. Protest, revolution, and violence
6. Self-actualization	
7. Charismatic projects	6. "Drugs and fornication"
8. New religiosity	7. Other kinds of "dropouts"
	8. Emotional "backlashes"

C. *New politics* (not necessarily healthy or unhealthy)

We are "square" enough to hope that most of our "elite" youth will choose the left side of the table above, but we are not necessarily optimistic. The question of how people are to justify their lives on this earth is one of the most crucial issues of the last third of the twentieth century. No one yet has the Word.

REVISIONIST COMMUNISM, CAPITALISM, AND CHRISTIANITY

Closely related to the impact of confusion, polarization, and conflict are the possibilities for increasingly revisionist communism, capitalism, and Christianity (and even combinations of the three) in Europe, the European colonial areas, and possibly Latin America. Any changes from the existing systems may be first received as aberrations or revisions of the "true" faith. However, all things are subject to change, and, in fact, most advocates of revisionist forms of these ideological systems will claim that their innovations are actually the "true" and "pure" versions. Certainly, it is clear that the historic Leninist-Stalinist form of communism has very little attraction to either the proletariat or the intelligentsia of the Western or Westernistic nations. The same can be said of historical forms of capitalism. As for traditional Christianity, it too is in great disarray. All of these belief systems are subject to major modification, both from within and without.

These changes, along with the other factors, will tend to decrease the consensus and authority of all established ideologies, institutions, and organizations. The general challenge to authority will be uneven, come from different directions, be based on different grounds and grievances, and lead to an increased diversity in ideologies, value systems, and life styles. This will almost necessarily lead to increased polarization between persons holding different views and strong possibilities of social conflict or, in extreme cases, even violence between the various elements of the Western and Westernistic societies.

CONSERVATIVE AND BACKLASH MOVEMENTS

It is apparent that law and order issues and other aspects of the surprise-free projection open major opportunities for popular and/or conservative backlash and revolt. The rapid changes in society will leave huge segments culturally and socially behind. The development of new ideas among the intelligentsia may promote pronounced or even extreme reactions among the fundamentally traditionalist masses. If most of the intellectuals and the upper class support the "elite" humanist left and responsible center positions, then any movement from the masses must either have traditional right wing or populist leadership and organization. The possible outcome of such movements, especially in the United States, may lead to grave difficulties in the next generation (see Chapter IV).

EDUCATED INCAPACITY

By educated incapacity* we mean an *acquired or learned inability to understand or see a problem,* much less a solution. Increasingly, the more expert, or at least the more educated, a person is the more likely he is to be affected by this. Education necessarily involves selection, indoctrination, a special intellectual environment, the development of a framework of accepted "givens" or "facts," and learning to think about a subject in a certain required way. However, when a problem or the solution to a problem lies outside the accepted framework, an expert is often less likely to understand the situation or see the solution than an amateur. For example, we naturally prefer to consult a trained doctor rather than an untrained man about our health.

* We modify Veblen's term "trained incapacity" to our purpose; he was concerned with engineers; we are mostly concerned with social engineers.

But when a really new type of cure at variance with accepted concepts is developed, the doctor is often the last to accept it. The history of medicine is full of instances exemplifying the reluctance of the medical profession to accept new methods. Military history also abounds with blatant cases of this. This is essentially true for all professions. "Educated incapacity" describes this type of limitation.

Educated incapacity is accentuated in the modern world because huge contemporary organizations proliferate new forms of expertise and specialists for them. This is a basic characteristic of bureaucracies and of technological society. Even business seems to be in danger of becoming a specialty. And we would guess that the more prestigious and the more academically difficult the business school, the more likely the graduate will be a technician rather than a decision-maker in contact with the pressures and insights of the real world.

Large organizations, long formal training, and expertise are most highly developed in the United States, and so is educated incapacity (although it should soon become important in much of the developed world). The educated incapacity that seems important in the United States today is derived less from a specific kind of education than from the general educational and intellectual milieu. On an increasing number of issues, upper class and upper-middle-class elites are having difficulty with relatively simple degrees of reality testing, especially with issues related to the attitudes or behavior of the lower-middle-classes or with issues of national security, prestige, welfare, race, and crime.

The following table indicates tentative, but salient, features of this phenomenon.

Why Educated Incapacity?

1. Classic tendency to exercise favorite or accustomed muscles (skills or formulations)
2. Normal parochial professionalism and emphasis
3. Misleading or constraining bureaucratic or organizational ground rules or commitments
4. Misplaced glamor or incentives
5. Ideological (political or apolitical) biases
6. Insufficient imagination, courage, expertise, etc., for useful innovation or creativity

7. An increasing use of irrelevant experience and intuition: a growth of simplistic, theoretic, illusioned, and/or wishful thinking and utopian objectives; and a general lack of reality testing and hard-headed or "tough-minded" analysis (perhaps most important of all)

The whole subject of educated incapacity is very controversial. The little educated incapacity that is recognized is usually "the other fellow's," and he is accused of being evil or stupid rather than suffering from a case of educated incapacity. The authors of the Pentagon Papers have been called vicious, stupid, or ignorant individuals; actually they were highly skilled and highly educated, devoted, dedicated, and decent men who were doing some brilliant things that had little to do with Vietnam, rather like a brain surgeon operating on a rubber duck. Educated incapacity can thus lead to domestic polarization and to misadventures. We don't know how pronounced educated incapacity can or will become, but every indication suggests that it is going to become even more of a problem in the near future.

Many writers, including the sociologist Daniel Bell, have maintained that the dominant class in the future is going to be the highly-trained "brain workers." However, if people perceive that the suggestions and policies of all too many trained people are non-productive, or even counter-productive, intellectuals will be discredited as the appropriate people to manage the economy or society. There may indeed be extreme hostility against these people and their ideas and methods. Remarks such as Governor George Wallace's about "pointy-headed professors" may be more widely and openly accepted in the seventies and eighties than they are now.

HUMANIST LEFT—RESPONSIBLE CENTER CONFRONTATION

The next item in our surprise-free projection is the confrontation between two points of view, the *humanist left* and the *responsible center*. These two positions are being delineated today, though not under these names.

Responsible center refers to the basically rationalist, reformist, melioristic, essentially liberal establishment. It ranges from pure technocrats concerned only with keeping the existing system going, to those who are extremely skeptical of the humanist left's ability to use power wisely or efficiently, to those who truly value the system as it stands. Many people in the responsible center are relatively close to the old liberal consensus of the 1950s and early 1960s, but their thoughts have been modified by the arguments of conservatism. They have many of the historically conservative concerns for public order, decency, and organization and mobilization to compete with the opposing forces in the world. They do not believe that the ideals of the humanist left are practical or desirable and while anti-authoritarian and generally anti-traditional, they distrust utopianism and extreme permissiveness. While the responsible center does share some of the goals, values, and characteristics of the humanist left, it tends to define itself as an alternative to the humanist left for the control of society and its values.

Humanist left, on the other hand, defines the rising opposition to the entrenched position of the responsible center. The humanist left consists of persons who highly value transcendence and impulse, freedom, idealism, participation, and self-actualization. Such people are principally interested in human relationships, and are very much concerned about problems of alienation, conflict, and things which artificially divide people. They are intensely anti-hierarchical and anti-bureaucratic, favoring participatory democracy and a reduction or elimination of external and "irrational" restraints of all kinds. Sometimes this tends toward anarchy, which to many humanist leftists represents a desirable state of individual and collective freedom and well-being which will occur when natural man (who is basically good) is liberated from the artificial and corrupting restraints of present society. (Humanist leftists tend to believe in environmental determinism.) Today the humanist left includes most of the countercultural and radical student movements in the industrial world, as well as many "fellow travelers" in such establishment institutions as the universities, foundations, the press, and the judiciary. It even has sympathizers among significant elements of the old wealthy classes. The humanist left has also influenced many former old-line liberals, and to some extent humanist left values have penetrated rather widely, but shallowly, into the traditional middle classes, particularly in the eastern seaboard cities and the Pacific coast area where many people holding ordinary middle-class positions are sympathetic to liberal concepts of personal experience through drugs and sex, to the problems of the oppressed and poor, and even to political radicals.

Some of the differences between the humanist left and the responsible center are summarized below:

Humanist Left	*Responsible Center*
1. Revolutionary end of industrial society	1. Threshold of new technological, affluent, and humanist society
2. Destruction or radical revision of system, confrontation tactics valid to shock the masses or dramatize issues	2. Reforming system from within, preventing confrontation, so as not to polarize politics and vested interests
3. Emphasis on moral issues, including a tendency to concede the moral judgments of the young	3. Concessions not the prevailing pattern; firm and moral decisions needed from leaders
4. Radical transformation of social and political institutions is needed; electoral process has become inadequate; government must be remade to respond to the popular will, not the power of interest groups	4. Parliamentary government remains valid and vested interests are an inevitable (and valid) political phenomenon; only change to confident, competent, and dynamic leadership and charismatic programs can prevent malaise and erosion of popular morale

The differences between the humanist left and the responsible center also indicate some of the similarities between the two groups. There seems implicit (if not explicit) agreement on the limits and goals of their debate. Both groups can be thought of as modern groups. They are mostly middle and upper class in origin and are interested in innovation and progress (but in different areas and directions—one being revolutionary, the other evolutionary). Both groups tend to be relatively intellectual and, moreover, both are likely to be relatively uninfluenced by the twelve societal levers although the humanist left rejects these traditional levers much more violently and completely than the responsible center. Both groups are interested in social justice, both are against the use of nuclear weapons, cosmopolitan, anti-militaristic, anti-aristocratic, anti-hierarchical, and anti-authoritarian. They are a product of the current crisis of values and search for meaning and purpose, while they respond with differ-'ng—but not diametrically opposed—reactions and proposals.

In a way, the coming confrontation will represent a falling-out among the liberals who have triumphed in the Western world in the last generation. It seems that historic conservatism, both its ancient agrarian, religious, and hierarchical "Tory" form, as well as its nineteenth century bourgeois, industrial, laissez-faire, "Whig" form, has been defeated in all the Western countries which have achieved the economic level of mass production. The situation is similar to that of Italy during the thirteenth century: the great struggle in Italy was between the Guelfs and the Ghibellines. After the Ghibellines were smashed, the Guelfs divided into two factions and began to fight it out among themselves; what was left of the Ghibellines supporting the more moderate White Guelfs. Some of the old conservatives can be expected to support, to some extent, the responsible center. Even though the responsible center is liberal in traditional terms, it is defending the status quo and is not hostile to order, capitalism, the old morality, etc.

By 1980, most governments in the West will probably be run by members of the responsible center, though others will have some say. The most serious challenges may come from the humanist left, but there may be others. Customary political groups including economic and romantic conservatives, old-line democratic socialists, and orthodox Communists should survive and may be important.

EMERGENCE OF A MOSAIC CULTURE

The term *mosaic culture* can be applied to a society with a number of different life styles. A mosaic culture may have divisive tendencies for society as a whole and lead to tensions and conflict, but it could also promote social harmony through mutual withdrawal, exclusion, and tolerance of groups with differing life styles and values. Groups could maintain differing life styles (based on political affinities, cultural values, ethnicities, etc.) that are internally cohesive and exclusive, but externally non-aggressive and tolerant.

At present, hippie communes and the areas around university

campuses are obvious manifestations of the beginnings of a mosaic culture. Such counterculture groups may continue to drop out in the future, but if society as a whole continues to move toward a more "sensate" culture, movement toward a mosaic culture will not be regular; elements will lag or even move in the opposite direction (there may be substantial elements in society which are disaffected not from the left but from the right). People in the United States and other Western nations (including many young people) who strongly hold traditional values, such as fundamentalist Protestants, traditionalist Roman Catholics, orthodox Jews, Mormons, conservatives, old-line Social Democrats and orthodox Marxists may wish to drop out of society and form their own bastions against its "corrupt" torchbearers. A century ago, the Amish decided they did not like the "worldly" direction of American society so they spiritually, and to a large extent physically, withdrew from it. There are many possibilities for movements of this type.

Such movements need not be limited to persons who wish to uphold traditionalist values. Various ethnic groups may withdraw to preserve their historical identity. This tendency can be detected in Black Muslims and black cultural nationalists, in the Jewish Defense League, and even in the Italian-American Civil Rights League. Other groups may simply have a shared interest and form old-age or retirement homes, apartment houses exclusively for "young swingers," and nudist colonies.

Furthermore, in modern times political scientists have become accustomed to viewing unitary societies as desirable, recognizing that fundamental differences in such things as religion, language, and degree of Westernization have led to major conflict. There is nothing historically unusual about a mosaic culture and in most of these societies (Roman Empire, Ottoman Empire, Austrian-Hungarian Empire) there has been some strife and conflict, usually with one group dominant as the ruling class. When some mosaic cultures break up (Congo, Cyprus, and Pakistan) it is extremely ugly. But many do not break up (Singapore and Lebanon) or break up without great intramural clashes (the Roman Empire). And, of course, in the United States many different immigrant groups have always lived more or less peacefully side-by-side.

POSSIBLE SYNTHESIS BETWEEN OLD AND NEW

People are amazingly adaptable, and despite obvious difficulties, should find a way to synthesize the diverse elements of the global metropolis of the 1980s. Such a synthesis is most likely to evolve in countries with advanced post-industrial societies—the Northwest culture area (ex-Protestant Europe and its overseas settlements), France, and Japan (see Chapter IX). What form this synthesis will take cannot be said, but we can hearken back to what may have been a similar synthesis of old and new, of Hellenistic Greece and Rome. Major political, social, economic, and even moral changes were shaking the world, with frightful class and national conflicts. The savagery of twentieth century revolutions and wars pales before the experience of classical man. Yet out of this conflict men eventually found ways to live well in the world. They developed "Hellenistic" civilization, adapting "Hellenic" culture to new and changing conditions, needs, and opportunities and incorporating elements from other cultures where needed or desired. Perhaps Hellenistic civilization built no Parthenon, and produced no Euripides or Thucydides, but it did produce the Roman baths, Aristotle, and Virgil, and a full, satisfying, productive, and eventually peaceful life. Historians sometimes describe the Hellenistic period as a falling off from the Hellenic, a period of decay. Perhaps so, but it was a period of decay that lasted some seven hundred years, in which people lived relatively well and did some remarkable things. If a Westernistic syncretic culture and society can grow out of the Western experience the way the Hellenistic did from the Hellenic, we should be more than satisfied.

Our conjectural mosaic society of the next couple of decades will be based more on political/cultural differences than in the past (although ethnic consciousness has by no means died out); but we even have a precedent for that in the coexistence of the vastly different life styles and attitudes of farmers and city-folk throughout the industrialized world. Our present mosaic society may simply develop more different (and perhaps overlapping) patches than before.

IV

Counterculture or
Counterreformation–
Countervailing Forces

ONE of the most insidious tendencies in future studies is to assume the direct continuation of an existent and clearly visible trend without seriously considering what the "prime movers" pushing that trend along are, whether they will continue to operate, and whether or not the trend will come up against various limits or countervailing forces in terms of saturation, counteracting trends, or dialectical effects. As an exemplar of this, we may look at a social phenomenon which was extremely striking during the 1960s. During these years, certain cultural manifestations among the upper classes, particularly the upper-class youth in the Northwest European culture area (and areas, such as the United States, that are largely derived from the Northwest European culture area) were, to say the least, startling and shocking to persons who highly valued or were accustomed to more traditional forms of culture and personal behavior. These manifestations have been given several names—the youth rebellion, liberation, and the new values. They could be called the *counterculture* of the humanist left. To clarify what we mean by counterculture we have found the following paradigm a useful heuristic device.*

Fundamental world perspectives (*Weltanshauungen*) or ideologies are classified under one or more of these columns. Probably most people reading this book are in column 3. A generation ago, those reading it would probably have been in column 3 and column 4. Two generations ago, they would have been exclusively in column 4. Today, column 2 probably looks more reasonable than column 4; in fact, the younger you are, the better column 2 looks.

This chart is another way of considering value shifts. For example, the bottom, or pathological half, of column 2 is almost the same as the critical description of late sensate culture. Generally there is a movement in Western society, particularly among the educated, from the right to left side of the chart. (The layout of "left" and "right" has no direct correspondence to political alignment, but there are relationships.) This movement is slow, normally taking at least a generation to drop one column and pick up another. In a few individual cases the change is faster, but usually has some of the character of a new life, conversion, or severe internal dislocation.

* Although we apologize when we use these unfamiliar terms, they seem to be the only ones which properly describe much of our work. A "paradigm" is an explicitly structured set of assumptions, definitions, typologies, conjectures, analyses, and questions giving both a framework and a pattern of relationships: it is halfway between an analogy and a model, more rigorous than an analogy, not a model, relevant to the subject, but not a theory. It is a set of interrelated questions, typologies, conjectures, speculations, tentative theories, intuitions, insights, lists, and so on, which covers a subject about as far as you can go. It offers you a framework, at least, for thinking about the subject. "Heuristic" means serving to discover or to stimulate investigation; a method of demonstration which tends to lead a person to investigate further by himself but with no connotation of the scholarly or rigorous. We also use "propaedeutic," which means conveying preliminary instruction in an art or science (but with no connotation of the elementary or oversimplified). This book is propaedeutic. See Chapter X of *The Year 2000* for further discussion of heuristic and propaedeutic paradigms.

U.S. Social and Political Ideologies Tend to Emphasize:*

(1) Transcendence	(2) Impulse	(3) Reason	(4) Conscience	(5) God's Will	Common Possibilities
		(Leading to, at best, a Reasonable or Acceptable Emphasis On)			
Spirituality	Freedom	Rationality	Dedication	Revealed Truth	Individual Meaning & Purpose
Mysticism	Creativity	Synthesis	Loyalty	Worship	Social Cohesion
Reverence	Perception	Calculation	Responsibility	Salvation	Humanism
Idealism	Spontaneity	Planning	Order	Awe	Inner Tranquility
Altruism	Self-actualization	Prudence	Organization	Dignity	
Pan-humanism	Participation	Comprehensiveness	Tradition	Eschatology	
Perspective	Sensory Awareness	Flexibility	Justice	Righteousness	
Detachment	Joy and Love	Moderation	Obedience	Submission	
Openness	Ecstasy	Meliorism	Self-sacrifice	Fatalism	
		(But with a Corresponding Potential for a Pathological Degree of)			
Dropping Out	Anarchy	Dehumanization	Fanaticism	Fanaticism	Elitism
Passivity	Lawlessness	Scientism	Despotism	Dogmatism	Self-righteousness
Unworldliness	Chaos	Technocracy	Authoritarianism	Bigotry	Intolerance
Cultism	Violence	Rationality	Sado-masochism	Intolerance	Cultism
Withdrawal	Nihilism	Meritocracy	Vindictiveness	Superstition	Hypocrisy
Mysticism	Selfishness	Theorizing	Punitiveness	Hypocrisy	Pharisaism
Faddism	Promiscuity	Abstraction	Guilt	Pharisaism	Bigotry
Superstition	Other-Indulgence	Calculation	Rigidity	Passivity	Rationalization
Naiveté	Self-Indulgence	Indecision	Callousness	Fatalism	Callousness

* Anthony J. Wiener is largely responsible for this chart.

Of course, columns 1 and 2 are the counterculture. A person who has abandoned column 4 altogether is, at most, only marginally loyal to column 3, and gives his full ideological loyalty to columns 1 and/or 2, we identify as being in the "humanist left." The change of the meaning of the word "humanism" is fascinating. The nineteenth century historians who coined the term used it to identify Renaissance intellectuals who promoted column 3 at the expense of column 5. In the early and mid-twentieth century people who called themselves humanists emphasized column 2 over column 4. Today, younger humanists reject column 3 for column 1.

Most observers of the counterculture agree that most of its effects have been limited to a relatively small group of people (particularly the upper-middle-class, highly educated youth) but nevertheless, that it has penetrated or at least had some effect upon the wider society. If this were merely a fad or fashion among the children of the elite, it would be of some interest, but not of very great significance in world or national history; however, there are many observers of contemporary phenomena who believe that this counterculture is the wave of the future. Many people have made what is technically called a "naive extrapolation" of these trends toward new values in America and have assumed that these would continue to move and would eventually dominate our whole society. Much discussion of future values is based upon the assumption that our culture will inevitably continue to move to the left on our chart. (One recent publication called columns 4 and 5 "dying values.") It is widely claimed, and even more widely assumed, that the values and standards now held by young people in Cambridge, Berkeley, and Aspen will disseminate throughout the entire society and, indeed, eventually become the dominant cultural form in Anglo-America, the rest of the Northwest European cultural area, and perhaps eventually the entire world. This projection assumes a "trickle down" theory of cultural change; that is, innovations come from the highest classes and penetrate slowly to the more stolid, inert masses. There is plenty of historical evidence to justify such a projection. However, other historical evidence suggests that this pattern is not always true. Sometimes a new phenomenon is first manifested in the lower classes and penetrates to the upper—for example, "rock" music had its origin in American Negro "rhythm and blues."

Also, many twentieth century "waves of the future" have not spread far up on Western shores. Those over forty may remember the Henry Wallace Progressive movement of 1948, when many highly publicized youths were leftists and pacifists and were strongly opposed to the beginning of the Cold War, American rearmament, and particularly nuclear weapons. Thousands of our most academically gifted students, particularly in the big cities, enthusiastically supported Henry Wallace and his movement. Two years later, nothing was heard of them. We heard more of Joseph McCarthy, his followers, his admirers, and his victims. Similarly, the "silent" generation of the 1950s was believed by some observers, including some very perceptive observers, to represent a primary condition in our society. People who somewhat misinterpreted Daniel Bell's essay on an "End to Ideology" said that henceforth our culture would be more rational, pragmatic, and less subject to ideological fits of enthusiasm. Looking at the youth of the 1950s told you very little about the youth of the 1960s.

To what extent does the youth culture of the 1960s reflect on the total culture of the 1970s and 1980s? Although the evidence is mixed and fuzzy, it is more likely that the counterculture of the 1960s has peaked than that it will continue unchanged. There are many reasons for this. First of all, the counterculture must top out, if only because it doesn't have too much farther to go. Take the issue of the public display of previously private sexual acts. We already have fornication, fellatio, and cunnilingus in public media. What can be added to this? Bestiality, rape, and incest are all that are left. On the question of drugs, millions of young people are already experimenting with drugs, and even though there is great potential for the further spread of drug use to youth, the "entrepreneurial" period is over. There is insufficient market left to continue at the rapid expansion rate of the 1960s. In terms of politics, already the leading edges of the counterculture are, for all practical purposes, what once were called "Trotskyites," that is, communists who do not take orders from Moscow. A few have even gone beyond this position to almost pure nihilism. This extreme alienation could spread to terrorism, including assassination and sabotage of various important facilities, but this seems unlikely. In any case, the period of initial and rapid growth also seems to be over. Can clothing become much more bizarre than it is today, or can music become much more basic and unintelligible, or can the underground press become much more snotty and scurrilous?

Second, whatever deep cultural trends may underlie the counterculture, it is clear that there are significant frivolous and faddish elements in it. Young people are notorious slaves to fashion and conformism to the standards of their peers. Also, they are very changeable. The counterculture may very soon be very old hat indeed. It is easy to imagine a situation in which the younger kids coming to school will be relatively "square" and sneering at the "old-fashioned" radicalism of their elders.

Also, no one would deny that the counterculture has been exploited for all sorts of commercial purposes. The purveyors of the news media necessarily need to write about what is new. The counterculture, the hippies, youthful revolt, drugs, promiscuous sex, etc., all were very interesting and in some degree very shocking. They made good stories and presumably sold newspapers and magazines. In the early 1970s, these are old stories. The media will need new ones.

Furthermore, there was a direct exploitation of the counterculture for marketing purposes during the decade of the 1960s. As a result of the "baby boom" following World War II, young people were a rapidly growing group both in absolute numbers and in their relative percentage of the total population. Because of other social changes they have had unparalleled affluence for such a group and plenty of leisure time in which to enjoy this affluence. The youth market was noticed and exploited deliberately and coolly by the consumer industries which catered to their taste. Marketing campaigns must necessarily change their tone and emphasis to retain attention and attract new notice.

Another element in cultural change also bodes ill for the counterculture. It has been so widely publicized and at least its outward manifestations have been so widely accepted by the larger world that the counterculture can no longer be described as "avant-garde." The psychology of an avant-garde artifact is clear—once it has been widely accepted by the wider society, the avant-gardists move on to other things. That Charles Reich's *The Greening of America* was number one on the American bestseller list (that is, it was the most popular book of suburban housewives) indicates that these ideas have become commonplace, accepted, respectable, middle-aged (Reich is over forty), and therefore banal and commonplace. It is high time for the avant-garde to drop the counterculture.

Although it is too soon to identify trends clearly, there are other signs that the humanist left counterculture may be on the wane: the decline of demonstrations on college campuses, the fragmentation and factionalism of the New Left, the apparent deflation of revolutionary organizations such as the Weathermen and the Black Panthers, the advent of terrorism and hysteria among radicals, the failure of rock festivals, the switching of pop singers from revolutionary to religious themes, and the turning of avant-garde youth to drugs and quietism.

Most obvious is the decline in student radicalism and activism in the United States and elsewhere. A partial cause of this is that both university authorities and society at large are getting fed up with violence and disorder on campuses and engaging in some modest but noticeable and effective repression. To some extent, the majority of the students have similarly become disenchanted with the abuses of the more vociferous and alienated radical elements. Certain events which have come as a result of student activities or persons acting in accordance with the principles of the youth culture may have had a cooling effect: the murder at the Altamont rock festival (casting cold water on the "Woodstock nation"), the Manson-Tate murders (discrediting charismatic leadership and "doing your own thing"), the death resulting from the University of Wisconsin bombing and the explosion at the Greenwich Village bomb factory. Perhaps more important, was the realization among students that they were not, in truth, "the people," and that the people as a whole generally reflect the views of the "pig" police. The Wall Street "hard hat" riots of early 1970 were the most striking example of this. But perhaps most significant of all was the widespread display of the flag and other patriotic emblems. Students came to realize that they were a small minority in the total population, and that they were in many ways a despised minority. This is not a very good attitude for a "forerunner"—to be the avant-garde one must believe that the rest are following.

So far we have discussed reasons why the counterculture might top out of its own accord, but still other influences might affect the counterculture from the outside. There is apparently a very strong reaction against the counterculture in the U.S., and perhaps to some degree in other nations as well. This phenomenon can be labeled the "counterreformation." The traditional values of Western society, such as hard work, public morality, respect for legitimate constituted authority, deferred gratification, and so many of the other aspects of the "Protestant ethic" or "middle-class values," have long been taken for granted by the overwhelming majority of people in all industrial nations, so much so that they have been scarcely challenged, and more important have not had to be defended against attack. These values and the people who have held them have been an amorphous mass. The challenge to these values by the counterculture has had some effect of mobilizing people who consciously held them, has obliged many millions of people to redefine these values, at least in their own minds, and to decide whether or not they are worth maintaining in their historical form. Plenty of people, certainly a vast majority of the people of the United States and probably other industrial countries as well, very strongly hold to the traditional value system, and despise the counterculture and its adherents.* These people are by no means limited to uneducated workingmen; in fact, the historical middle-class values are most strongly held exactly where you would most expect to find them—among the bourgeoisie. With few exceptions most managers, officials, engineers, technicians, businessmen, and other principal historical bourgeois groups have remained fundamentally untouched by the counterculture. Particularly attached to the traditional values are the recently embourgeoised lower-middle classes—the people with backgrounds and occupations which were historically working class, but who in the past generation have moved up to middle-class incomes, standard of living, and value structures. The recently embourgeoised lower-middle-class American (or Englishman) greatly values his newly gained and hard-earned position and does not appreciate having it scorned or spat upon by "kids," especially upper-class kids. Survey data taken in the United States over the 1960s showed a hardening of positions on fundamental cultural and moral values in the United States—on such things as marijuana, sexual prom-

* Our discussion of middle-American opinion is based, in part, on public opinion studies of Frank Armbruster to be published in his forthcoming book, *The Forgotten Americans.*

iscuity, pornography, and religion. The great majority of the people are more concerned with at least the public display of traditional moral standards than they were a decade ago. Insofar as these traditionalists (columns 3 and 4) react against the humanist left (columns 1 and 2) we have the phenomenon commonly called *polarization*. The cultural, social, and political expression of that reaction we call a counterreformation.

Now it is possible that there could be a very serious "backlash" against the counterculture. To some extent this is taking place all over the United States today. It is impossible to say how far or what form this backlash will take; however, we think that there will be very strong dialectical effects involved: the stronger the push against the traditional values by the counterculture, the more vigorous the reaction is likely to be. If the counterculture should truly threaten the sanctity of the family, or if, for example, the eighteen-year-old vote should lead to a takeover of the university towns by college students with the public promotion or sanction of radicalism and/or public orgies, the reaction is likely to be extremely severe, conceivably even resembling the reaction against the Weimar culture of the 1920s. On the other hand, if the counterculture is peaking or topping out, at least temporarily, then most of those elements could be relatively easily absorbed into the mainstream. We could have a situation in which, in Hegelian terms, the traditional society is the thesis, the counterculture, the antithesis, and the result of the conflict and/or combination of the two would be a new synthesis. A society under a new synthesis could be pretty much like the traditional society, but significantly modified in the sense that people would be more willing to engage in or condone premarital sex, salacious literature would be more widely accepted and the general standards of what constitutes pornography would be lower, the roles of men and women would not be as clearly delineated, there would be much less racism, sexual deviation would be more tolerated, men would wear flashier and brighter clothing, drugs would be more widely accepted for pleasure (indeed there might be a de facto legalization of marijuana), hard work would be less highly regarded, the traditional martial values would be held in lower regard, and so forth.

Many conservative Cassandras call the counterculture decadent, and think that a society that compromises with its values cannot function. However, a synthesis of traditional society modified by counterculture values could work quite well. In fact, most of the historically successful societies were characterized by both hard work and orgies, virility and vice. The Greeks, Romans, and Byzantines took these for granted. Renaissance financiers could patronize the arts, but did not forget to extract their pound of flesh from their debtors. It took religious fanaticism and two-to-one odds to overwhelm the "foppish" Cavaliers of Charles I. The French nobility that Louis XIV kept as lap-dogs at Versailles demonstrated their devotion and courage in the fields of Flanders and the wilderness of Canada. "Corrupt" Georgian England defeated revolutionary France. Even today, the European ruling classes surround themselves with luxury and are prone to vice by puritan standards, but they function effectively in furthering the interests of themselves, their institutions, their class, and their nations.

But what about the spectre (or idyll) of a victory by the counterculture? Several years ago, the Hudson Institute drew up a list of alternative futures for the United States. On the first draft list "fellow travelers and sympathizers of the humanist left take-over" was included, but it did not take us very long to realize that this was an impossible alternative. The humanist left just does not have enough strength to take over legally and its adherents are too poorly equipped to conduct a successful insurrection. The incompetent and hysterical terrorism of the Weathermen and the Berrigan group reflect a low level of political potential. Effective revolutionaries need intelligence, organization, and discipline to conduct effective propaganda, plan successful insurrections, and seize and hold power. What Trotsky unkindly called the "vegetarian left" and Orwell even more unkindly called the "pansy left" noticeably lacks these virtues. Even if a humanist left-leaning government came to power, perhaps in the guise of a moderate liberal administration, its program could not be carried out without inciting the mass of the nation against it, including the military, the police, the National Guard, and twenty million gun owners.

Some of the extreme elements of the new left recognize this. Their avowed strategy is to promote disorder to incite backlash leading to fascism. This is to expose American "repression" to all, thus uniting the "masses" for the "revolution." By waving their red flags, they hope to provoke the Establishment bull into charging to its death. But they are matadors without swords. A fascist America would wipe them out, together with their sympathizers and apologists, and since this would necessarily have been provoked by terrorism and other assaults on public order and decency, the masses would cheer. In fact, an American fascism, properly prepared by leftist frontlash, could be immensely popular, even democratic, if it required extreme patriotism and traditional public morality, wiped out the drug traffic ruthlessly, ended forced integration and reverse discrimination, regulated public employees' trade unions, and took a tough *Machtpolitik*, or even isolationist, line in international affairs.

There are many historical precedents for a counterreformation. In the late Middle Ages, the people, especially intellectuals, rulers, and educated persons, were largely abandoning the traditional religious emphasis of life in Europe. People, particularly educated people, were much less interested in religion and in the condition of their souls, but seemed to be principally devoted to the improvement of their lives on earth and the enjoyment of the blessings of the material world. This mood came to a screeching halt when Martin Luther nailed his Ninety-five Theses on the church at Wittenberg in 1517. For the next 150 years the intellectuals, princes, and commoners of Europe were concerned and convulsed with the questions of religion. Interestingly, historians have maintained that one of the factors involved in the Reformation was the widespread disgust by the fundamentally religious people of Europe for the highly educated, materialistic, and secular ecclesiastical officials of the day. Popes and prelates were more interested in politics, art, and scholarship than in pastoral care. They thought more of the good opinion of the educated classes than they did of their religious duties; were attempting to be "relevant to the issues of the day."

A similar but perhaps less studied turn took place at the end of the first third of the last century. Early nineteenth century England, called "Regency England," was a notoriously materialistic, hedonistic, secular, skeptical, and corrupt society. This was the age of Beau Brummel, scurrilous journalism, and cynical politicians. The English prime minister, Lord Melbourne, was a cheerful skeptic. A duchess of this time described her nieces approvingly as "comfortable girls who enjoy a dirty joke." But within a few years there was an almost complete reversal of the moral tone of British society. The British ruling classes soon became staid, serious-minded, religious, and at least outwardly chaste. "Victorian" morality appeared from within a fairly sensate society. There was a time when the older members of the House of Lords had to be careful with their language lest they shock their younger peers. We really do not know what made this happen. We can identify certain harbingers of it in the form of a Romantic counterculture which grew within the bosom of Regency society. Perhaps one explanation is that the corrupt upper classes of England were deeply frightened by the revolutionary upheavals which shook their country—most notable the Chartist movement—and recognized that they had better shape up or they would go the way of their French cousins a generation before.

An even more recent example is that of Stalinist Russia. The triumph of Bolshevism in Russia was accompanied at first by many "liberated" manifestations in personal and social morality, as well as in art and other forms of general culture. These flourished in Russia during the 1920s, but Stalin put an end to them. Today the public and private morality of Soviet Russia resembles that of Victorian England.

Going even further back into history, there was a very serious and important reform movement in Athens after the defeat in the Peloponnesian War. At that time, there were certain subversive teachers abroad who were undercutting traditional religion and morality among the elite youth of the day. One of these subversives, Socrates, was put to death by a democratic "ideological renewal" government.

A counterreformation may have many aspects but a heightened resistance to further reformation is a common element in all of them. The resistance may or may not be successful in its own terms but at the very least it will affect the shape of the reformation. The reformation may be defeated, its growth may merely be slowed, or it may turn violent and even nasty in order to break through the resistance. It is also possible for a compromise of choice, exhaustion, or a new synthesis may come out of the conflict. Let us consider some possible effects of a counterreformation in America.

BACK TO RELIGION

It may be useful to conjecture upon the effects a counter-reformation might have upon the organized Church. The most obvious effect would be a change in the character of the clergy. Although many of the currently liberal, "concerned" clergy are deeply sincere in their beliefs, many other clergy, perhaps more, seem to be espousing liberal social causes because it is presently fashionable to do so. Too many ecclesiastical and theological fashions in the last decade—"the death of God," "situation ethics," "reparations"—have come and gone so rapidly that many of their supporters must be highly faddish. Should the tone of the times become more conservative and more traditional, many of the clergy would follow. If the dominant tone should change, and if the leadership reflect or encourage this change, many of the lower clergy, who embrace new ideas in order to ingratiate themselves with their ecclesiastical superiors, would change.

Several current phenomena would tend to promote such a shift. Many of the laity are appalled and shocked at the turn their churches have taken. These people are not normally very well organized, and have been, in the past, easily manipulated by the more aggressive minorities who support new ideas. The religious conservatives have expressed their displeasure by not attending church or not contributing to it. Donations to many of the most "advanced" churches have dropped sharply. People have suggested that funds currently being used for "social action" be given to the poor. They have not felt that the Black Panthers, draft dodgers, and militants are proper objects of Christian charity, nor have they felt that Christianity is furthered by support for the Viet Cong, Al Fatah, the Grape-pickers' Union, the Southern Christian Leadership Conference, or the Memphis garbage collectors. Those who have stopped giving have been roundly attacked by the liberal clergy as "racist," which they have not appreciated. Currently, many of the churches most active in the social area are having to lay off staff because of declining contributions. There is a noticeable softening of the radicalism and militancy of the clergy, and a glimmering of the idea that perhaps their primary duty is to tend to the spiritual needs of their congregations. This idea is likely to grow in strength during the 1970s, and may even become fashionable among the most forward-thinking young seminarians.

On the other hand, if the high clergy should continue to actively promote what are, in effect, secular humanist values, they are bound to lose many parishioners. The United States and Canada may well become like Finland, where many of the people are deeply religious but do not attend church because it has totally adopted modern, progressive, liberal, secular humanist values. In Finland a religious person does not go to the "atheist" state church. We have the possibility in the United States of underground churches, based upon the Bible, extremely Protestant and individualistic, coexisting perhaps with far left underground churches. One scenario would have the Roman Catholic church remaining predominantly conservative, with liberals (predominantly upper-middle class) forming small underground churches with dissident priests. There could also be traditionalist Catholic groups surreptitiously holding Latin masses. The mainstream Protestant churches, such as the Episcopalian or Presbyterian, could become increasingly "liberal" and "concerned," with underground conservative cells maintaining the traditional forms. Similar effects are possible among the Jews.

PROTESTANT PAROCHIAL SCHOOLS

A counterreformation need not affect the entire society; it is possible that only certain minorities will feel its full impact. Perhaps our culture will continue its general shift toward sensate values, but some groups will strongly react against this trend and may become traditionalist chips of a mosaic culture.

Protestant parochial schools are a possibility. So long as the U.S. public schools were essentially Protestant schools (which is why the Roman Catholics felt the need to operate a parallel school system), church-related Protestant sectarian education was unnecessary. But today, an orthodox Protestant Christian (not to mention a Fundamentalist) can make a good case that, from his point of view, the public schools are proselytizing secular humanism and its explicitly anti-Christian values. Thanks to the U.S. Supreme Court, children at public schools are not even permitted to pray; and they are taught "value-free" sex education, while from the historical Christian perspective sex ought *not* to be a value-free expression of love and joy, free from shame and guilt. The whole issue of permissiveness cuts deeply against the Protestant ethic. If these counterculture tendencies in the schools continue, as some of the best young educators want them to, the public schools will become "corrupt" and "immoral" institutions that no "decent" Christian would want his children to attend. Under such circumstances the establishment of Protestant sectarian schools would be reasonable.

Further, many parishioners who are currently responding to "social action" by withholding their contributions may seek out and give to traditional congregations that engage in more traditional activities, such as Christian education.

POPULISM

Populism refers to fairly spontaneous lower-class or mass movements, particularly those which are not led by upper-class or left-wing intellectuals. In American and European history, populist movements have often appeared suddenly and unexpectedly. They were poorly organized, were usually directed against "the establishment," almost always lacked ideological justification, and usually failed. Left-wing intellectual radicals have usually failed to mobilize these movements for their ends; right-wing reactionaries have had some short-run successes. But populism is both radical and reactionary—radical in that it seeks radical changes in society, "reactionary" in that it often reacts against perceived undesirable changes which are undermining the economic position, social status, and/or traditional values of the "people." It often evolves into chauvinism or attacks minorities or "scapegoats" who are blamed for the evils in the land. Populist targets in American history have included "monarchist" Federalists, "aristocratic" Whigs, "papist" Irish, "anarchistic" foreign immigrants, "monopolistic" capitalists, "bolshevik" Jews, "communistic" upper-class liberals, and, of course, Negroes.

Today the "middle Americans" are increasingly conscious of their alienation from the liberal consensus which is reflected by the expression of humanist left values by the national media, Federal judiciary, and universities. "Middle Americans" tend to have moved upward recently, but to still consider themselves (with some justification) financially hard-pressed; indeed, these people's economic status presently seems to be stagnant and may in some cases be slightly regressing. These people are relatively racist but prefer not to use racist arguments. (In fact, if they become willing to use racist arguments openly this could lead to serious difficulties in our political scene.) They enjoy traditional non-intellectual pursuits such as hunting, fishing, and outdoor and spectator sports, as well as non-sophisticated TV and movies. In their personal life they prefer manly behavior and democratic ways, having great contempt for upper-class values and styles which they consider effete and/or depraved. The populist fiercely supports traditional American and orthodox Christian values and strongly resists attacks on them. To the extent that the elite in our society today deviate from or attack "the American way of life," there is the potentiality of a traditionalist populist movement hostile to and directed against the "effete snobs" and the "liberal establishment."

There are three possible scenarios for the rise of populism in the United States. The left-wing scenario is essentially a return to the New Deal. Liberals hope to ally with the working people, minority groups, and the poor against the Establishment, which *they* identify as the great corporations, banks, and those elements of government involved in defense, intelligence, and an aggressive foreign policy. Their program would take the form of vastly expanded government powers over the economic life of the United States, presumably to cut corporate profits, and the diversion of revenues from the military-industrial complex to human services (such as medicine, housing, and other social welfare programs). The government would scrupulously refrain from intervening in moral issues.

A right-wing populism would seek to unite the productive elements of the population (the lower-middle and working class) against the unproductive elements—the welfare poor (particularly in minority groups) and the liberals. The enemy is the "liberal establishment," and minority groups who are seen as "pawns" of the liberals. The liberals are attacked principally upon moral grounds; they are held to be corrupt, degenerate, irreligious, and generally un-American. Conservatives who sought to manipulate populist feelings in their own behalf would try to ignore or fudge over economic issues.

The third possible scenario that might conceivably come to

the fore under certain conditions is a mass movement against both the liberal and corporate establishments. Presumably this would be a true populist movement in that it would not serve the interests of either important elite group. However, no mass movement can succeed without leaders, and there seem to be no real populist leaders on the scene today, as well as no populist organizations, publications, or explicated ideology. The only obvious populist leader in America today is George Wallace, who may be the most important man in America, not for what or who he is or what he represents, but because his position in the American political framework prevents any other populist leader from coming to the fore. Because of Wallace's obvious drawbacks as a potential national leader, he cannot himself expect to achieve power, but his presence in the field blocks anyone else from coming to the forefront. An American populist movement would need as its bases the South and the industrial workers of the North. But Wallace's clear and obvious racism makes it quite impossible that he should achieve anything resembling national success. For a true populist movement to have effect nationally, Wallace would have to be removed from the scene. Since he is an exceedingly ambitious man, it is hardly likely that he will withdraw in the near future. If he were out of the picture and a competent, more widely accepted, populist leader were to appear, American politics in the 1970s might change radically.

IDEOLOGICAL RENEWAL GOVERNMENTS

One political aspect of a counterreformation would be the establishment of an *ideological renewal government,* that is, a regime dedicated to the preservation of the traditional values of the society. Such a regime could take any number of forms, ranging from a "do-nothing" government which would pay lip service to traditional values through a whole spectrum of regimes which would take positive steps within historic frameworks to extremely repressive regimes which would be essentially conservative, use Bolshevik techniques, and probably be best identified as "fascist."

An ideological renewal government in the United States would probably be unlike that in other Western countries. Based on historic American values it would be at least avowedly democratic or populist. It would promise to end the movement toward late sensate values in the United States and would act particularly against pornography, obscenity, drugs, crime, political demonstrations, terrorism, the formation of paramilitary political groups (except that of the ideological renewal movement). It would probably claim to be sympathetic to the worker and small businessman (though in practice it might continue trends towards bureaucratization, government control, and collusion with large enterprises). In Europe, almost by definition, an ideological renewal government would be nationalist and probably somewhat elitist, while in Japan the Soka Gakkai offers a possible vehicle for national ideological renewal.

Certain general rules can be laid down about ideological renewal governments: they seek to revive or restore some historical or traditional values, they are hostile to and despised by progressive elements at the time (and later, which is one reason why few of them look very good to historians), and they lack a clear program, making do with vague concepts of what they want and specific complaints about what they don't like. Ideological renewal governments frequently come to power after a government has been discredited by defeat in war. Some examples of ideological renewal regimes might be Gaullist France, Dollfuss' Austria, Gambetta in France, the "democratic" regime which took power after the Athenian defeat in the Peloponnesian War, Augustan Rome, Marshal Mannerheim's regime in Finland, and most recently the Greek military regime. Most of these regimes could be called right-wing, largely because they were explicitly opposed to "the left" of their particular country. However, it would be a serious mistake to see them merely as reactionary or fascist. They all expressed deep democratic feeling, certainly not liberal democratic sensitivity as expressed through civil rights, due process, and parliamentary majorities, but democratic in the sense that they sought to promote the values and sensibilities of the masses. And in most cases they made significant concessions to the masses at the expense of some element of the ruling cosmopolitan elite.

Should anyone doubt the attractiveness of an anti-liberal ideological renewal government, he might consider the existing regime in Greece. Throughout the world "the Colonels" who rule Greece are excoriated in the media as fascists and tyrants on the basis of a bad record on fundamental political rights, and rightly so. However, although there have been no elections in Greece, Greek Gallup polls (which seem to be honest) indicate that under the reign of the Colonels, the Greeks are one of the most happy and optimistic people in the world. The Colonels seem to have widespread support among the Greek masses, who are traditionalist, religious, and have a strong sense of being both economically and morally exploited by their "liberal" elites as represented by the ruling parties which were thrown out of power by the Colonels' *coup d'etat* of 1967. The politicians and the upper classes of the old, liberal regime were thought of as rich and somewhat corrupt. The "little people," particularly in the villages and small towns referred to the people in the capital as the "eaters." On the other hand, the Colonels are all small-town boys of lower-middle class, or even lower, origins. For example, one of the Colonels is from Crete, the Greek equivalent of Arkansas, where his brother is a manual laborer on the roads. Insofar as the Colonels represent anybody, they represent the little people of Greece and are apparently making some reforms which are economically benefiting them. A critic of the Greek regime would perhaps be little impressed by the Colonels' attempts at moral regeneration through promoting the "Hellenic-Christian tradition" (the Greek equivalent of the "American way of life") and "discipline," against what they perceive to be corrupting liberal, cosmopolitan standards and values (sensate culture). The possibility that this moral program of the Colonels has significant and substantial support, particularly outside the capital, cannot be denied. To some degree at least, the current regime in Greece is a populist regime representing the values and aspirations of the "little people" in Greece.

If there should be an ideological renewal government in the United States, it would barely resemble the present Greek regime, the Gaullist regime, or any of the fascist or near-fascist regimes of the period between the wars. For example, the United States has no tradition of direct military intervention in politics. A *coup d'etat* in the United States is an impossibility. But that does not preclude individual soldiers entering politics, nor would it prevent officers sympathetic to a political movement from permitting political propaganda to be circulated through the army. However, we have in America a phenomenon for which, as far as we know, there is no historical precedent—the politicaliza-tion of the police. Already, two major U.S. cities have police mayors elected by "middle Americans" against almost monolithic opposition from the business and intellectual elites.

NEO-RACISM

Another possibility in the 1970s and 1980s is the revival of another characteristic of the late nineteenth century—racism. Racism has not been fashionable in the Western world since the Nazis demonstrated the possible disastrous results of such an ideology. However, like so many other things, Hitler, World War II, and the Final Solution seem a long time ago and may have been nearly forgotten by large numbers of people. A racist revival in the United States would most likely be directed against Americans of African ancestry. Racism has been unfashionable in the United States for the past couple of decades; we tend to forget that previously racism had been a near-constant in our history. Since the first slave landed at Jamestown in 1619, almost all Americans have believed to one degree or another that blacks were fundamentally inferior to whites. American racism may be about to make a comeback.

Neo-racism could easily be explained by the perceived (mis-perceived?) failure of our racial policies of the 1960s. Govern-ment involvement in the race question was based on the ideology that Negroes were equal to whites but had suffered from oppres-sion in the form of segregation and discrimination which had kept them from achieving their potential. Governmental policy was designed to eliminate segregation and discrimination; then Negroes would be equal. These governmental programs have been implemented and hardly a vestige of legal segregation or discrimination exists in the United States today. Most Negroes responded to this liberation with the anticipated results—like men who had previously been forced to run in chains, when the fetters were shattered they sprinted ahead. The social and eco-nomic status of the *majority* of black Americans has been catch-ing up to that of white America at an extremely rapid pace throughout the sixties.

However, there remained a subgroup within the Negro

group which did not respond well to the government's treatment. People in this sub-group were typically of extremely low social and economic status, poorly educated, very frequently from fatherless families, and had been living on welfare. To aid these people, advocates of Negro progress demanded not just an end to segregation and discrimination but *reverse* discrimination, that is, discrimination in favor of some Negroes in order to truly equalize opportunity. To gain support for such a policy, its advocates denigrated the very real progress made by most Negroes. The liberal media generally minimized the gains made by most Negroes, exaggerated the size and poor condition of the remaining severely depressed subgroup, and devised new concepts such as "de facto segregation" and "institutionalized racism." Unfortunately, they did not convince the public that the new programs were desirable, but rather persuaded most of white America that the earlier programs were failures—that most Negroes, despite the removal of artificial restrictions, remained in a depressed position. Instead of being persuaded that whites ought to be discriminated against or that fundamental institutions had to be radically changed, many Americans adopted the position that because Negroes had allegedly failed to respond to equal treatment, they must be unequal to whites. In any event, while the majority of white Americans were willing to take steps to remove existing racial restrictions against Negroes, they have been singularly unwilling to impose restrictions on whites.

Of particular interest has been the revival of what some consider racist (or "racistic" or "crypto-racist") ideas in academia. The physicist Shockley's demands for serious examination of the racial differences between human beings, and particularly the educationalist Arthur Jensen's article which suggested—pretty much in passing—that the "median" Negro I.Q. may be fifteen points below the "median" white may (much against the wishes of these men) tend to make racism slightly less unrespectable (though still not respectable) than it has been for the past generation. The widely asserted "failure" of civil rights programs, as well as the public performance of assorted agitators and hoodlums whom the national media characterizes as responsible and legitimate Negro leaders, cannot but have tended to impress some white Americans that Negroes are not capable of competing with whites on equal terms. Therefore. . . .

We recognize this is unpleasant speculation. However, it should be noted that there has been no major additional civil rights legislation for the past four years. The dramatic phase of the Negro revolution seems to be over. Has the counterrevolution begun? This may largely depend on the media and public policy makers. The great strength shown by George Wallace in the presidential election of 1968 and the great strength he is almost certain to show in 1972 is causing most responsible people to pause. The widespread and growing fear of crime, perceived as black crime (which much of it is), is having considerable effect. But it is also true that millions of Americans are now dealing with Negroes in responsible positions—policemen, bank tellers, army officers and non-coms, salesmen, clerks, skilled workers, bureaucrats, and white-collar workers of all kinds. There is also a strong, almost conservative movement among the majority of Negroes who are "making it" in our society. These people are purchasing homes, making sure their kids get a good education, moving to the suburbs—in sum, coming to have a real stake in our society, a stake which they do not like to see threatened either by black punks or white goons. They may even ally with their white neighbors against both (this is already happening to a certain extent).

In the next decade, the gains that are made by black Americans will probably be made by them as individuals competing in the larger society according to the ground rules established in 1968–1972. There is little chance of massive programs of reverse discrimination or widespread direct transfers of funds from the rich to the poor, nor will there be the "backlash" that would probably result from such a program being pushed through by the national government.

Most Negroes in America will likely continue to make substantial and significant economic and social gains, but there will likely be a minority (perhaps twenty-five percent) who will not or cannot participate fully in our society as presently constituted, and who will remain a major recognized social problem throughout the decade. Their existence will keep the economic and social indicators of the "statistical Negro" below that of the statistical white, and if these people continue to be heavily publicized and the majority of Negroes ignored, the white image of all Negroes will be lowered.

ANTI-SEMITISM

A black racial problem is almost unique to the United States among the industrial nations.* However, the United States has another minority which *does* exist in Western Europe—the Jews Again, it has been unfashionable to be anti-Semitic for the past generation. But like anti-Negro feeling, anti-Semitism is the norm rather than the exception of Western society. Anti-Semitism was almost a standard social and political position in any country where there were enough Jews to matter. Many Jews did not take it too seriously until German National Socialism showed what it could lead to. But Hitler was some time ago and some of the fundamental causes of anti-Semitism are becoming prominent again, together with some new ones stemming from the establishment of the Israeli state.

Perhaps the most obvious source of potential anti-Semitism, or at least the end of philo-Semitism, is the widespread association in the United States of secular humanist views and Jews. The Jew is somehow associated with the promulgation of anti-traditionalist, anti-Christian ideas in the United States. As a generalization, of course, this is incorrect; there are large numbers of conservative and traditionalist Jews in the United States. However, poll data reveal that Jews are much more likely than Christians to support government intervention in the economy, the legalization of marijuana, legalization of pornography, legalization of abortion, and student radicalism, and to be "anti-patriotic" and "anti-religious." This last item is perhaps a key—for a re-emergent anti-Semitism would not be directed against Jews but against *ex*-Jews, people of Jewish background who have long since left the synagogue and have thoroughly adopted secular humanist values. Many of these people are to some degree assimilationists and would like to see Jews disappear as a distinct group and be absorbed into society, but not a traditionalist and Christian society. Despite the popular association of Jews with

* The action of the British Government in the sixties to restrict "coloured" immigration will almost certainly prevent the emergence of a racial problem in Britain similar to that of the United States, and will help to speed the assimilation of the West Indians and Pakistanis into British society.

business activity, most American Jews come from a social democratic, anti-capitalist background in Eastern Europe, and have to
a large degree passed their values on to their children, even
though they themselves may have become successful in business.
Therefore, it is consistent with their values to work for the dissolution of traditional Christian society and the creation of a truly
secular, truly "human" society. Most of the extreme advocates of
such a policy do not even consider themselves Jewish. Unfortunately, the rest of society is all too clear about who they are. The
association of Jews with liberal secular humanist ideas has reached
the point that in many areas of the United States the words
"liberal" and "New Yorker" are euphemisms for "Jew."

Another factor that might spur anti-Semitism of this type is
the association of the Jews, or rather ex-Jews, with the liberal
national media. And again, unfortunately, when one lists publications which are taking an extreme left liberal position on
moral, social, and political issues, one finds that most of these
publications are owned and staffed by a disproportionate number
of Jewish names. Fortunately, the effects of National Socialism
are not entirely forgotten and that group in our society which
might be expected to exploit anti-Semitism, that is, the anti-secu-
lar right, is very cautious about being tainted with anti-Semitism. American conservatives, with very few exceptions, have
utterly rejected anti-Semitism, because they don't believe in it
and because it would discredit their movement.

The state of Israel raises all sorts of complications for Jews in
the Western world. Most obviously, it brings up the whole issue
of divided loyalties. Everyone expects that Jews will be sympathetic to Israel.* During the Six Day War of 1967, many of the
people who were picketing for support of Israel were the same
people who had been picketing against support of South Vietnam. This did not go unnoticed. Furthermore, persons on the
left (some of them Jewish), particularly those who are romantic
about Third World "anti-colonialism," oppose "Zionism" to illustrate their solidarity with the resurgent masses of the Third
World. The struggle between Israeli and Arab is seen as the same
one which is going on in South Africa, Angola, Algeria, and Indo-
China. Support for Israel is the support of imperialist aggression

---

* In the Suez expedition, the English Expeditionary Force left their
Jewish troops behind.

against the Third World. So long as the Communist powers support the Arabs against Israel, anti-Zionist slogans are going to be heard in leftist circles, even among persons of Jewish ancestry.

No serious anti-Semitic outbreaks are expected in the next decade or two in the Western world, including the United States. In a strong counterreformation, however, there may be a slight, subtle, but nevertheless significant tendency among educated Gentiles to note that there are differences between Jews and Gentiles and perhaps to make anti-Semitic remarks and jokes. This may subtly affect their relations with their Jewish co-workers, friends, and neighbors which in turn may increase Jewish consciousness. Possibly, this will result in a slightly increased rate of emigration of American Jews to Israel, giving that country much-needed Western educated people. More likely, it will heighten sensitivity among Jews toward the more traditional forms of Jewish cultural and religious expression. Already there seems to be some trend in this direction. Many Jewish families, even those which have been thoroughly secularized for several generations, are feeling the need to inculcate Jewish culture and tradition in their children. Conservative and Orthodox Jewish congregations seem to be gaining adherents; many children of Reform or non-believing Jews are turning to traditional modes of belief and expression, rejecting Reform Judaism, rock services, and assimilation. In a strange sort of way, mild anti-Semitism in the counterreformation may encourage a sort of counterreformation among the Jews themselves.

Despite the ugly possibilities speculated about above, it seems that some sort of "new synthesis" is the most likely outcome for the 1970s and for the early 1980s. Of course, there could be an extension of the counterculture, with a concurrently savage reaction. But even a conservative (or, as we prefer to call it in these circumstances, ideological renewal) government is unlikely to return to the cultural and moral standards of the 1950s. We are not likely to return to a situation in which marijuana is considered to be as evil as heroin, where alcohol is suspicious, gambling is fundamentally bad, no one dares to speak ill of the Presidency, women are expected to be virgins at marriage, and the police are automatically obeyed. The counterculture has had some permanent effects on American society.

Now, we do not mean to say that our projected new synthesis

will be some sort of permanent solution for cultural problems. Indeed, we expect that the long-term trend to a more sensate society will continue. However, we expect the discontinuities will not appear probably until the 1980s or perhaps even later. It is reasonably likely that the long-term prospects for humanity still remain unchanged, despite whatever short-term reactions might take place in the next ten to fifteen years. But we think that Western society feels a need for a rest, time for consolidation, for absorption of the cultural innovations of the 1960s into the mainstream before pushing off in new directions.

V

Sources of Stability and Instability in the International System— Where we are and where we are going

ONE of the most difficult problems in futurology is charting how we get from here to there. Any look at the future must begin with the present, or at least begin with that immediate past which, for all practical purposes, is identical with the present. However, all too frequently, we have an extremely poor notion of what is going on at the present time. We may have various ideological biases, a lack of understanding, or pure ignorance, but most obvious of all, we may be unable to see the big picture, the overall view of the present day system.

Although there are, and probably always will be, differing ideas of the relative importance of continuity and change in human affairs, it is almost always useful to look at the world as it is—to "fix" it, so to speak—before examining what forces of change are at work. This chapter draws upon national security studies conducted at the Hudson Institute, to examine the fundamentally important issues of what the international system is like, what factors made it that way, how those factors could change, and what new factors might appear.

The world in the sixties was relatively stable rather than prone to international violence. To an extent which would have seemed incredible in the 40s and 50s, most analysts in the 60s argued that it would have been extremely difficult to bring about an intense U.S.-Soviet nuclear confrontation. A Nasser or a Castro might say that only his self-restraint prevented the world from nuclear conflagration, but the choice really was not his. The choice belonged to the United States and the Soviet Union, and they were anxious to avoid escalation-prone confrontation. But the stability of the 1960s was based on more than this U.S.-Soviet choice, though clearly the U.S.-Soviet choice was important. To some degree, stability and relative safety from World War may continue in the early and mid-1970s, but there are now many events threatening the world scene.

The principal sources of stability and instability in the current international system are outlined in the following charts. On the right-hand page are factors which seem to promote stability, world order, and peace; on the left are some remaining and some new sources of instability. Up until 1968 the right-hand stable elements were most influential, so long as reasonable concern for the destabilizing elements was taken into account. But since 1968, the balance has begun to shift. The Soviet invasion of Czechoslovakia, the effects of the Vietnam War on the home front, the increasing perception of neo-isolationism, the changing strategic balance between the United States and the Soviet Union and even such minor (from world perspective) events as the resurgence of communal strife in Ulster and Bengal have somewhat shaken the relative safety of the world. Indeed, such events as the full recovery of both Germanies and Japan, while having many stabilizing aspects, do raise new and disturbing issues. This is not to imply that the world is now "unsafe" but that it is less safe in 1972 than in 1968 and that it threatens to be even less safe in 1976.

Now, perhaps when this discussion began some readers thought: "Vietnam, Cuba, the Middle East, the Congo, Berlin, hydrogen bombs, ballistic missiles and the world seemed *safe* in

Sources of Instability

The Basic Political Environment

1. General distrust and/or disillusionment in government—appearance of anarchist and nihilistic movements
2. Relatively strong, but probably weakening, sanctions against nuclear diffusion
3. U.S.-Soviet detente—two-way deterrence—almost no power vacuums
4. Sino-Soviet split—NATO and Warsaw pacts in disarray
5. Complex mixture of bipolarity, polycentrism, multipolarity, and obsolete sovereignty
6. Increasing nationalism and regionalism generally, but European nation-state system in flux
7. Extreme and nationalistic behavior in France, Rumania, China, Cuba and many places in the Third World. But not yet West Germany, Japan, Canada, Poland, Brazil, etc.
8. Limited retrogression of U.N.—growth of ad hoc groups
9. Many old hostile emotions (nationalist, racial, greedy, vengeful, ambitious, etc.) partly eroded but mostly coerced, restrained, diverted or sublimated
10. Many new hostile emotions

Some General Political Trends

1. The current small world is getting smaller and leading to:
   A. Worldwide welfare state
   B. Urban indifference
   C. A disappearance of *Lebensraum*—maneuver space—safety factors
2. Frustrated expectations:
   A. Re-raise social order vs. social justice issues
   B. Exacerbate domestic divisions
   C. May tend to increase existing envy, racism, nationalism, class conflict, and messianic movements
   D. Are turning U.S. toward neo-isolationism
3. West may have tendency toward a lack of assurance (or ancien regime morale) in dealing with progressive and/or humanist left revolutions or even criticisms
4. New political issues and groupings and religions—or quasi-religious —movements
5. Gradual erosion of political, moral, and morale legacy of World War II, colonialism, and even the Cold War

Some Classical Reasons Why Major Violence May Still Occur

1. Miscalculations or unintentional escalation
2. Shocked, hysterical, or irrational behavior
3. Deliberately (most likely as a result of defensive reactions, but even this is not certain)
4. A revival of ideological zeal in communist parties
5. A taste for violent ideologies (crypto-fascist and crypto-communist)—particularly in the Third World and among the young
6. Development, in Afro-Asia, of a desire for revenge against the ex-imperialists
7. An Afro-Asian drive against Rhodesia, South Africa, and/or Portugal, or even against the West generally, etc.
8. Claims and pressures of China, West Germany, Japan, etc.
9. Other revisionist territorial and political claims in central Europe

Sources of Stability

The Basic System

1. Nation-state as basic unit characterized by territoriality, sovereignty, center of loyalty and protection, some self-determination
2. About 150 states—of whom more than half are serious nation-states
3. Each state more or less the judge of its own cause
4. Some limited international authority—some limited Great Power authority
5. Some bipolarity, some multipolarity
6. Dilemmas of competition and cooperation
7. Both balancing and disruptive processes
8. Much self-restraint and self-deterrence
9. The war system—increasingly considered abnormal, increasingly unusable, and yet always there
10. However, force and military calculations do seem increasingly less relevant

Why Do Force and Military Calculations Seem Increasingly Less Relevant?

1. World is one human community—there are no outlaws, barbarians, or *Untermenschen*—everybody has human rights—indeed many pluralistic security communities (a political and moral content that makes legal war and even the use of force unthinkable in most situations)
2. Internal development is both the efficient and the fashionable technique for achieving most national objectives—including achieving a base for power and influence as well as wealth itself
3. Modern technology and other developments have either obviated, lessened, or made transitory the historic strategic value of many geographical areas
4. As a result of the above, nations no longer, by and large, seek for ways to use force to gain plunder, slaves, foreign territory, commercial advantages, income, power, military manpower, or even to collect debts, avenge insults, enforce international law, etc.
5. Ideological and religious pressures to use force are—at least relative to many past eras—also weak
6. In addition:
   A. The U.S., U.N., and others act not only as policemen and protectors but to limit the ultimate success of an initially successful aggression
   B. All-out war (and therefore, to some degree, any war) is unthinkable or impossible
   C. Little serious irredentism in Europe, except possibly for Germany, North and South America, and Japan
   D. General (but waning) fear of extremism
   E. Current relatively high standards of behavior
   F. As a result peace seems to be based as much on satisfaction and acceptance as on deterrence and weakness
   G. As well as some illusionist and/or wishful thinking about the likelihood of certain areas of the world being kept—under almost any policy—free of national wars

Sources of Stability (continued)

Some Specific Reasons Why the World Seems Relatively Safe

In General:
1. Recovery of Europe and Japan
2. Weakness of Germany (and Japan?)
3. Holding of Africa, Middle East, Chinese rim and Latin America
4. Weakness of underdeveloped nations
5. U.S.-S.U. detente and growing belief in stability
6. Increased crisis incredulity
7. Continued U.S. strategic superiority over S.U. (?)
8. Soviet Thermidor—loss of enthusiasm and/or nerve

In Strategic Area:
9. U.S. (and S.U.) strategic forces relatively invulnerable (?)
10. Organizational and technical safeguards—arms control
11. Controlled response and crisis management policies
12. Nuclear incredulity (nuclear war is unthinkable)

In Limited War Area:
13. Few power vacuums
14. Greater (U.S. and S.U.) capability and understanding

In Technology:
15. Expense and complexity of strategic weapons systems
16. New strains of rice and wheat

the 1960s?"—not "safe," but *relatively* safe compared with the 1950s. The curve on the chart below represents the estimates of independent professional defense analysts of the probability of an international disaster. The vertical scale is purely subjective—up is dangerous. In effect, the chart estimates the probability of one of the following: (1) outbreak of major European or World War—a war in which some millions, perhaps even hundreds of millions, might be killed; (2) a major act of appeasement; or (3) a collapse of NATO. It shows a sharp downward trend in the late fifties and early sixties.

Despite the habit of crisis thinking inherited from the turbulent mid-century years, probable scenarios for large-scale war—or even scenarios plausible enough to cause serious and specific concern—were hard to write in the 1960s. This was quite a change from the fifties.* In the 1950s there was a widespread belief that

* During the 1950s analysts such as those at the RAND Corporation had perhaps a dozen scenarios for accidental or deliberate war, almost all of which were taken seriously by the decision-makers. In many cases officials or members of their staffs lost sleep until the underlying conditions that made these scenarios plausible were corrected or modified. In 1962 Hudson Institute undertook the writing of another dozen scenarios for accidental or

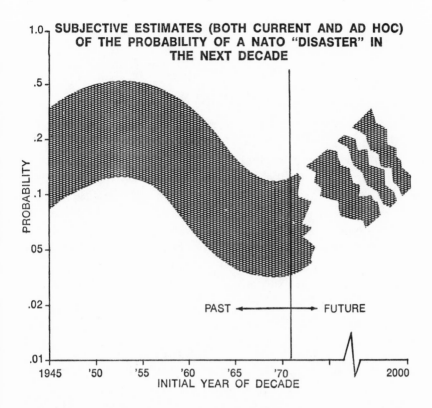

SUBJECTIVE ESTIMATES (BOTH CURRENT AND AD HOC) OF THE PROBABILITY OF A NATO "DISASTER" IN THE NEXT DECADE

the world was exceedingly dangerous. Many today, even in retrospect, agree that the probability of deliberate or accidental nuclear war was high. In the 1960s most analysts tended to believe the opposite was true. A general conviction spread that the world, far from teetering on the brink of nuclear war, actually was a relatively safe place. In part this was because "war is unthinkable." This is the mood that Raymond Aron called "nuclear incredulity," a complacent belief either that "nuclear war is unthinkable" or—less extremely and illogically—that no likely

---

deliberate war. None of these, however, were plausible enough to cause decision-makers to lose sleep or otherwise react decisively, although all of the scenarios were taken as reasonable. We do not claim that the world is necessarily safe because Hudson Institute cannot write frightening scenarios. This could easily be due to the fact that we were insufficiently prescient, observant, ingenious, creative, etc. Somehow we cannot help but feel that the world is safer if it is hard to write such scenarios. Today, it is easier to write disaster scenarios.

issue or escalation-prone threats could justify the use of nuclear weapons.

STABILITY

The first chart on page 117 reminds us that today's international system is one of nation-states and that this system is relatively complex. Despite much criticism and concern the nation-state system is hardly likely to change enormously in the next two or three decades, at least in lieu of a war or really intense crisis or some other event that profoundly shocks human society. Despite many statements about its obsolescence, nationalism is still the major source of social energy—the nation has, in varying degrees, the morale, spirit, and ability to generate unity and sacrifice. However, possibilities of some slow evolution from nationalism cannot be denied, e.g., arms control.

Still, the nation-state as characterized by territoriality, sovereignty, self-determination, common history (real or contrived), and usually a common race and language, is the fundamental unit of the world system. There are approximately 130 such units, up from fifty at the time of the founding of the United Nations. More than half of these are "serious" nation-states in the sense that they are, at least theoretically, capable of engaging in an independent economic and foreign policy, and of undertaking that real test of national sovereignty—war. Since decolonialization is almost completed, there are few opportunities for its leading to any substantial increase in the number of nation-states, especially serious nation-states as defined above. For the most part, the remaining colonial territories are tiny islands hardly capable of independent political life. Still, the sense of security in the world is such that even these may attempt to go out on their own—as the semi-farcical case of the Anguilla independence movement demonstrates. But these "mini-states" are of slight consequence in the world scene.

However, there are some possibilities for the augmentation of serious nation-states. With nationalism remaining strong, even pathological, especially in the Third World, there are possibilities for the breakup of the existing nation-states into smaller units. Given the virulence of nationalist feeling in the world, any state that does not have a single culture, race, religion, history, or especially language may be considered as having a potential for internal conflict, civil war, and possible breakdown. The greatest possibility of this is when there are two or more large language blocs. This situation is particularly dangerous because language is the tool of young intellectuals and the vehicle for entry into government bureaucracies. A large language-minority group must be necessarily discriminated against by the dominant language group, and the would-be bureaucrats of the minority are a destabilizing influence. Different cultural backgrounds of the various ethnic groups within a state leading to the unequal apportionment of government jobs and/or economic success are also bound to bring resentment and friction. Some of the most obvious candidates for nationalist disorder and potential breakup were discussed in Chapter III.

In the given context of the world system, each state is more or less the judge of its own cause. The internal affairs of a state are held to be its own business, and it is not considered appropriate for outsiders to meddle. Old and new movements, such as traditional religion, liberalism, and Marxism have been successful in the world in the twentieth century insofar as they have associated themselves with nationalism. People have shown themselves willing to die for the nation, but for little else in the contemporary world. Now, it is not to be expected that the nation-state system will last forever. No system does. But we can see no movement in the future which could replace nationalism and the nation-state in the affections of the masses and leaders of the world.

This is not to say that there will not be some limited authority over these states. Most of them are engaged in some sort of significant world trade, so they are like the idealized capitalists operating in a laissez-faire system, restricted in their actions by international "market" forces. The United Nations and other international authorities will have important, if limited, effect on them. Moreover, because most of these states are relatively weak militarily and internally unstable, their need for support against invasion, subversion, and insurrection will give leverage to those other countries which can provide such support. Also, because most of the leaders of nations have a remarkably similar culture and outlook, almost to the extent that they can be viewed as an international Westernized ruling class, they are subject to pressures from the rest of their class—that is, they are subject to "world public opinion" which is, in effect, expressed through the vehicle of the major newspapers and periodical publications of the Western world. If *The New York Times, Le Monde, Newsweek,* and the *Economist* disapprove of a regime and its internal policies, this is usually of some long-term effect—witness, the boycott against Rhodesia. Of course, nations which are in a very strong position can disregard world public opinion and prosper—witness, South Africa and Indonesia. Finally, and perhaps most important, is the number of ad hoc groups of great influence in various limited areas (e.g., the Group of Ten in monetary affairs, sometimes the EEC, NATO, COMECON, Warsaw Pact, etc.).

Another basic element in the existing world system is a mixture of bipolarity and multipolarity. The bipolar system is nicely exemplified by those maps which paint part of the world "Communist" and the other part as the "free." Despite the great differences which can and will exist between states within each of these alleged blocs, the bipolar model is accurate to the extent that it does reflect the sentiments of people on both sides. The people of each bloc have a feeling of cohesiveness, and the sense that they should rally together to oppose the other side, as in the support given by both China and Russia to North Vietnam. But it is unwise to exaggerate this. Multipolar elements are very strong, and perhaps are getting stronger. The Third World feels a stronge sense of cohesiveness against the industrial West, perhaps as strong as against the Communists. Latin America feels some sense of unity against the *Norte Americanos.* The white English-speaking world feels some sense of community. The Western states see themselves as a unit, but there is within this a feeling of Europeanism, versus both the Soviet Union and the United States. These sentiments will have some effect upon the actions of states, but in almost all cases they will act, or at least believe they are acting, purely in their national self-interest, despite the fact that one of the central elements of a healthy nationalism is the belief that the national well-being is also the well-being of the human race.

Although there will be much self-restraint and self-deterrence, based upon moral grounds as well as a weighing of costs and benefits, the need for military systems and the possibility of settling disputes and achieving national interests by use of armed force, will continue intact. War and the use of armed forces across national frontiers in general will increasingly be considered abnormal and unusable, yet it will always be there. In any case, the rhetoric, the legal or illegal possibility, and actual examples of the use of armed force will be around for a long time to come.

If we consider the three-fold increase since the end of World War II in the number of nation-states, that is, in the number of units capable of waging war, it is remarkable how few wars there have been. Indeed, most of the armed conflicts have not been wars between separate nation-states, but civil wars for social or political ends. Wars between separate states for classic ends of defending sovereign rights or expanding national territory have been extremely few—El Salvador/Honduras, India/Pakistan, Indonesia/Malaysia, Israel/Arab League—almost all of the remainder have been civil wars of one sort or another. Also, it is very important to note that none of these wars has been driven to a final conclusion. International or great power authorities have intervened in these disputes and stopped the war before either side was required to sue for peace. Since the founding of the United Nations, not a single one of its member nations has been destroyed. Force and military calculations seem increasingly less relevant to the foreign affairs of most nations. Therefore, the traditional justification for the maintenance of standing military forces has been considerably eroded. Still, of course, the possibility of war as a means of resolving international disputes remains, and the need for military forces for internal reasons will remain strong, and perhaps even become stronger than before in many states.

Discussions of changing strategic issues since World War II customarily stress the important role of the new weapons of war—nuclear bombs, long-range aircraft, missiles, Polaris submarines, and the like. However, the issues shown in Chart 2 may be equally important, and in some ways more important. Moral, political, and economic changes since World War II have made a huge difference between then and now. These changes have gone a long way toward making the use of force between nations, or even military calculations about the potential use of force, seem largely irrelevant to many people even when serious issues are at stake. More significant, plausible situations in which force would be relevant or useful have become very difficult to imagine.

Perhaps the most striking change since World War II is an

unprecedented sense of world community. All people are now regarded as fully human, and every nation as having more or less equal sovereign rights. An adventurer or imperialist no longer "discovers" a new geographical area and legally or morally displaces the indigenous rulers as if they had no rights. Almost no group is considered as outlawed, barbarian, or *Untermenschen*— as "objects" whom others have the right to enslave, kill, or plunder. (Indeed this tolerance is sometimes extended to individuals and groups such as terrorists or ordinary criminals who once would have received harsh treatment in the name of justice.) The exploitation of other societies by open chicanery, unfair treaties, or the use of force is condemned by almost everybody—including the domestic public of almost any developed nation which attempted such tactics.

Soviet attitudes toward counterrevolutionary elements that challenge the Communist system in Russia or threaten its control of Eastern Europe may provide some exceptions to this generalization—but even here new attitudes play a most important role. The terms of trade between the Soviet Union and Eastern Europe in the first post-war decade were indeed generally onerous and favored the Soviet Union greatly. With the exception of East Germany this does not seem to be true today. The other five satellites might often get better terms elsewhere, if they were free to do so, but the Soviet Union is itself often a high-cost producer and does not really gain very much by forcing the satellites to trade within the bloc. The Soviet Union as well as its satellites could gain economically by trading more freely with the outside world. The basic reasons why trade is encouraged within the bloc today are political and autarchical, rather than exploitative in simple economic terms.

Today power and influence tend to be based on the wealth and technology of a nation. Internal economic and technical development, perhaps combined with peaceful trade and overseas investment, rather than imperialism or aggression, seem today the more efficient as well as the more acceptable techniques for achieving most national objectives. To desire to improve national power, influence, and wealth through expansion was easily justified in an economic world in which the geographic distribution of wealth was fixed. The simple way to add to wealth, population, prestige, and power was to annex territory, treasure, and subjects.

This sort of thinking was valid in its own terms up into the nineteenth century and survived in many people's minds well into the twentieth. But it is clear today that the road to wealth, prestige, and power is not so much through external expansion as through internal development. Vast areas of territory and population are desperately poor, weak, and contemptible, whereas small nations—such as Sweden—with few significant natural resources are rich, prestigious, and relatively powerful. The World Wars demonstrated that gains in national territory did not justify the expenditure of treasure, materials, and manpower. If Germany had won World War I, nothing it could have gained would have justified its cost. As it was, the German colonies that Britain gained or the lost departments of Alsace and Lorraine that France regained were a trivial return on their material and human investment. Wealth and advanced technology are better acquired by developing existing national assets and resources, rather than seizing a neighbor's property.

Modern technology and recent political developments have lessened, made transitory, or even eliminated the strategic value of many geographical areas. An oil-powered navy does not need coaling stations and a nuclear-powered navy does not need overseas refueling at all. Developments in artillery and tanks have seriously lessened the value of strategic positions—passes, river or mountain lines—that once were so important to the geopoliticians. Airpower has converted the battlefield to three dimensions and seriously limited the value of any land position. To be sure, there are many important exceptions to this (Israeli policy is largely based on the desire to get acceptable frontiers); but overall, it is much less important to most countries than in the past. As a result, to a degree which seems almost incredible by comparison with the nineteenth century, national strength, power, and influence today depend mostly on technology, gross national product, and a host of imponderables and hardly at all on the possession of critical geographical areas. As a result there is less desire or pressure to occupy strategic territory for its own sake.

Thus today, most of the *old nations* at least, no longer look for ways to use force to gain plunder, slaves, population, foreign territory, commercial advantage, or power. (Old nations here are defined as ones that go back to the nineteenth century. Within this definition China is a *newly integrated* nation, and India, of course, is a newly decolonized state.) They seldom think of using armies to collect debts or avenge insults, or of imperial expansion to furnish employment or to relieve other internal pressures. On the contrary: for these nations foreign war and foreign possessions seem a good way to devour up resources without compensating material gain. For example, a facetious proposal has been made that all of Vietnam could have been purchased and all of its inhabitants transported to the French Riviera with a generous life-time pension for a fraction of what the Vietnam war has cost the United States. Wars are seen as creating or exacerbating internal strife and other domestic pressures and strains, rather than the opposite.

Not only have the classical reasons for going to war either diminished or vanished, but political pressures deriving from charismatic patriotism, militant or proselytizing religion, dynamic ideology, or even the simple desire to seek glory (on the part of a head of state, a general, even the individual soldier) today seem much weaker than in almost any historical period. There is a real diminution of crusading urges. Ideological and religious pressures to use force have been weakened, at least relative to many past eras. The once great crusading religions, Christianity and Islam, no longer believe in the holy war as the supreme moral act. And the Western states no longer have sufficient confidence in the superiority of their way of life to engage in the *mission civilarise*. Revolutionary Marxism remains much more vigorous, but apparently not as strong as it was in the last few generations. Missionary impulses, whether peaceful or aggressive, are a good deal weaker today in all areas of human endeavor. This can be viewed as a mixed blessing, in that people do not care as much about each other's well-being, or value their own systems as much, but still it must be recognized that the beneficial side of this relaxation is a slackening in ideologically aggressive international behavior.

Although any of these factors could effect a sharp decrease in the use of force and the role of war, they are augmented by various formal and ad hoc institutions and practices. The United States is often criticized for thinking of itself as a world policeman, and it may be argued that the United States has sometimes intervened too easily, too quickly, or too automatically; but few criticize the United Nations for acting to maintain the peace.

And the influence of the United States, the United Nations, and other powers and institutions in maintaining peace is important. In addition to their direct roles, the mere existence of these institutions helps keep the peace through an ultimate political and psychological effect. Even if they do not stop an initial aggression, their influence and action is likely to limit the extent and ultimate success of the aggression.

Finally, one of the main reasons for war in the past, an intense desire to recover lost territories—to rectify frontiers in order to redeem some historical injustice or error—has largely disappeared in Europe (with the possible exception of Germany), North and South America, and Japan. Irredentism is no longer a live and burning issue. Of the 135 nations in the world, about sixty may be thought of as meeting the definition of old nations. An examination of these old nations reveals that only three are deeply concerned with frontier issues today: West Germany, Ethiopia, and Thailand. And, at present, none of these governments is outwardly advocating aggression.

The traditional cockpit of ferocious irredentism, the Balkans, has had its principal problem greatly reduced by the liquidations and population transfers accompanying and immediately following World War II. Nearly twenty-five years of Communist rule must have, to some extent, weakened the desire of these countries to achieve "historic" frontiers which were based upon traditional concepts of national rights. (However, the large Hungarian minority still in Transylvania is a major exception to this rule, as is the ethnic composition of Yugoslavia.)

To most observers, the Soviet Union also seems no longer seriously interested in increasing its sovereign territory (as opposed to maintaining a sphere of influence in Eastern Europe, or creating new Communist nations elsewhere) and despite the Czech crisis, even spheres of influence are not what they used to be. The same comment might be made about China, whose military adventures have been almost as cautious as her rhetoric has been aggressive. Indeed many scholars feel that even China's aggressive ambitions are limited to traditional Chinese territory, e.g., the Manchu boundaries.

Some new states exhibit irredentist and expansionist tendencies, but by and large, with the exception of Communist China, they are materially weak. There are, of course, very large areas in Afro-Asia where territorial changes may yet be accomplished by force over the next ten or twenty years. But the rulers of most of the world's people—and an even larger proportion of the world's effective military strength—are not much concerned today over their country's frontiers. While nations maintain large defense forces, these forces do not have any simple or direct relationship to the defense of frontiers or to any obvious economic interests (with some obvious exceptions, most notably Korea, Vietnam, Israel, and Pakistan).

How many frontiers have been revised by force since 1945? India seized Goa; China grabbed some Himalayan territory claimed and partly occupied by India; Israel now holds some Arab territory—a few thousand square miles containing less than two million people—that is all in an entire generation. In fact, it doesn't even pay to win a war "fair and square." El Salvador clearly won in its "Soccer War" with Honduras. However, the Organization of American States did not permit it to gain any territory. Perhaps the present widespread demand that Israel withdraw from the territories it overran in 1967 is also partially based on a feeling that no one should be permitted to benefit from military victory.

A general fear of extremism by the ruling elites of most states must also be recognized as important. This is waning, and will probably continue to wane, but nevertheless, it is presently a subtle but important limitation on the use of international force.

Related to this are the relatively high standards of behavior in international relations. Violations of international law and such things as attacks upon foreign nationals, foreign ships, border incidents, trade wars, and even deliberate subversion may be striking. But they are striking because they are relatively rare. Almost all states recognize the desirability and utility of international law, and the right of almost all other states to exist with their current boundaries and internal political, economic, and social system.

Unlike the period of, say, 1880–1940, when most nations had certain ideological and theoretical systems which advocated and glorified the desirability of war as a means of improving the human and national stock, today most systems of thought prevalent glorify peace as the desirable end of human and international activity. Those who advocate having a war do not glorify war as such, but usually justify having a war (or revolution) in order to achieve "peace." Pacifist propaganda is widespread throughout the world and is encouraged by most national states. Resorts to war or preparations for national defense must always be justified on the basis of choosing the lesser evil or "waging peace." Under these conditions all-out war (and therefore to some degree any war) is nearly unthinkable and perhaps unbelievable as a practical alternative.

These pacific factors give an air of extreme hypothesis, even of unreality, to discussions of the future ultimate limits of national power, of future national capability to use force in extreme situations, or of future military tactics, analyses, and calculations. As a result, many people find it difficult to take discussions of war seriously. In addition, the world lacks actual experience or observation of most of these potential new uses of force. Who has fought thermonuclear war? The air of unreality which surrounds discussion of the future roles of national violence seems justified by the increasing length of our experience of nonuse of the most modern military technologies.

Of course, the mere fear of nuclear weapons makes "rocking the boat" a most dubious enterprise. This last factor came somewhat as a surprise to the professional defense analysts of the 1950s. They often argued then that as "the balance of terror" grew firmer, nations would be tempted to experiment with aggression under the cover of the nuclear umbrella. What was not fully realized was that, in the actual circumstances of the 1950s and 1960s, the impulse was less to experiment with aggression than simply to be deterred by the general horror of the situation. Thus the "don't-rock-the-boat" impulse became stronger as the balance of terror became firmer.

This hardly means that the world is without hostile emotions. There is plenty of nationalism, racism, greed, resentment, anger, and ambition in the world. But many of these impulses have been weakened, and in any case they are more or less coerced, restrained, or sublimated. As a result, they are not likely, *under current conditions*, to burst out.

Wars of aggression, if they occur at all, will likely prove to be *limited* wars rather than all-out wars on the World War I or II scale. One factor which has been at work is a general exhaustion of the political emotions as a result of the experience of the

1930s and 1940s. Beyond that is the obvious efficiency of internal economic development as the means for increasing a country's prestige, power, and living standard. Germany and Japan lost World War II, yet are among the most prosperous economies today. Everyone knows that Europe has lost its colonies and yet is much richer today than in 1939. It seems reasonable to say that no European nation, let alone the United States, would *accept* an underdeveloped nation as a colony today—much less risk or spend much blood or treasure to conquer one. At least for the United States this would hold true even for such apparent prizes as oil-rich Venezuela or Saudi Arabia. Certainly it is true for any lesser prize. One reason, of course, is that virtually all nations understand the value—the practical value—of maintaining a relatively high international standard of behavior. Another is that classical imperialism—economic exploitation—today does not really pay. Even if it did, most powers (possibly even the Soviet Union) would not be willing to suppress native resistance with the necessary ruthlessness. Imperialism is an awful hassle, and looks like more trouble than it is worth.

Thus, one can argue that today's world knows a peace based—in part at least—on satisfaction with the status quo, or at least a general acceptance of it. In part, too, peace is based on a climate of apathy combined with the fear of nuclear weapons. Yet, the role of nuclear weapons may actually be only one small factor of this stability.

Equally important to our sense of security is the common belief that the Communist/non-Communist confrontation is largely over, at least in Europe. Few West Europeans still care about the Cold War as an ideological confrontation with the Soviets; in the former satellite states there is a parallel and growing spirit of pragmatism on the part of the regimes (though not uniformly so) and an indifference to ideology on the part of the masses. These developments in the former Soviet orbit bode ill for the future of "classical" Communism. Even in the Soviet Union (but apparently much less than in most of the world) there is a growing alienation of the elite youth, an intellectual and moral stagnation among the Communist rank-and-file, and the re-emergence of a spirit that is recognizably Russian rather than "Bolshevik."

The detente between the West and Communism does not yet

extend to Asia (although recent developments suggest there is at least a chance that it might), where the United States is engaged in a program intended to dam back Communist China's influence and has become involved in the Vietnam war. Yet it is possible to argue that America's confrontation with Peking is to some degree a conflict with *China*—with its ancient sense of world primacy (the "Middle Kingdom") and its (ever limited) expansionist ambitions—than with the ideology of Communism itself. To the extent that this is true, some of the ideological fervor may have gone out of the Cold War, even in Asia.

Of course, it is very reassuring to conclude that major war and large-scale violence have been effectively abolished, at least so far as most of the advanced and powerful nations are concerned. The attractiveness of this argument suggests that it probably includes some wishful thinking. Before the Czech crisis of 1968 most Europeans believed that deliberate war in Europe was almost "unthinkable," maintaining that any major use of illegal force was very unlikely. They also seemed to believe that this state of "warlessness" was more easily and cheaply acquired and maintained than we would judge to be reasonable. Many of them now recognize that things are more complicated and risky. Czechoslovakia provided a dramatic and concrete reminder to a number of Europeans that political and moral sanctions against the use of force *are* "political" and "moral" and not physical—and probably not as strong and reliable as they had thought. The Czech crisis clearly showed that at least one European nation (if Russia is as European as Europeans hope it is) is willing to use force to preserve the status quo. The Czechoslovakian intervention raised the possibility—again dramatically and concretely (as opposed to hypothetically and abstractly)—that almost any crisis, whether deliberately sought or not, might, if sufficiently intense, lead to the use of force. Political and moral sanctions against the use of force today remain, in most circumstances, remarkably strong and reliable, but given the all-too-human propensity for wishful thinking, these sanctions are likely to be overestimated.

Such were the fundamental elements of the stability of the world system in the 1950s and 1960s. Most of these still apply today, some of them even more so. The chart on page 118 lists specific reasons for thinking the world to be relatively safe. First, and most important, is the economic and social recovery of Europe and Japan. The kind of recovery Europe and Japan actually achieved was not expected at the war's end. A gloomy view was held of Japan's prospects, and only a somewhat less pessimistic view of Europe's. Most Marshall Plan technicians and planners believed that it would require two or three times as much money as the United States was willing to allocate to assure the recovery of Europe. Yet the continent made a spectacular recovery, with imposing political consequences. Japan has not only experienced an economic "miracle" but has successfully converted to a liberal-democratic political system.

Yet, both Germany and Japan are still militarily weak. This is a cause for confidence to those who fear that German, or Japan are inherently revisionist, or even imperialist. The argument can certainly be made that the logic of their circumstances as the defeated in World War II inclines at least some elements in these nations to a "revisionist" point of view. Even if this is true, for the next decade or so, neither state is likely to be able to pursue a truly aggressive military policy, though their foreign policies might become increasingly assertive.

Similar in its effect on world stability is the military weakness of the underdeveloped nations. At present the New York National Guard has more military strength than two-thirds of the sovereign nations of the world. But if nations such as the U.A.R., Indonesia, or Pakistan possessed three or four Polaris submarines each (as may well be the case by the end of this century), together with reasonably large numbers of land-based missiles, one would probably find nuclear war scenarios relatively easy to write.

The seventh item on this chart is critical, even though it expresses what many people think is a simplistic or chauvinistic notion: so long as the United States has strategic superiority over the Soviet Union, the Soviet Union is likely to act with restraint. Or, more relevant, in any serious crisis the Soviets will be more likely to back down than the United States, and this is a good thing. But this aspect is changing or has already changed, which is *not* a good thing from the point of view of world stability. We will discuss the meaning and implications of the changing strategic balance later, emphasizing that the seventies will be the first postwar decade in which the Soviets are likely to be freed from the political and psychological inhibitions of strategic inferiority. While few may be concerned today about this development, because of the widespread sense that the Soviet Thermidor has arrived (see page 135), a prudent observer of the world scene must take it into account.

Today, a high level of confidence that no attacker will have great competence in central war (i.e., war involving strategic attacks on enemy homelands) seems warranted. It should probably be added that if an attacker did appear competent, it more likely would be due to the clever use of intra-war deterrence and post-attack blackmail rather than sheer technological and numerical superiority. In the 1950s, U.S. strategic forces were relatively accident prone. This factor has been reduced by making the forces invulnerable, and improving the technical and administrative controls of weaponry, thus enabling each side to relax and lowering the risks of "trigger-happy" situations.

Another past source of danger, an unrestricted arms race, appears less dangerous today because of the development of implicit and explicit arms controls. Thus in the mid and late fifties the U.S. spent about 15 billion dollars per year on central war forces. This figure fell in the early and mid-sixties to about half this value. It now is rising again, but the United States and the Soviet Union now spend a great deal less on strategic forces than was predicted in the fifties—in terms of a percentage of the gross national product, about one-third to one-fifth of most predictions.

Line 11 makes the point that any given crisis—or even war—is much less likely to escalate because of the adoption of prudent crisis management and controlled response policies. Line 12 repeats the point that escalation may be made less likely if people simply do not take "crisis-induced" or other alarms seriously.

There seem to be few "power vacuums" in the world (line 13) because most of the areas which could easily come under foreign control and influence are already in that situation. The two conspicuous exceptions may be the Indian Ocean periphery and the Middle East. And in both areas, while local military power is slight, nationalism is intense and a cultural and religious xenophobia exists. Even though the United States and Soviet Union have, of course, the ability to intervene in both places by force, they would seem unlikely to do so if there were potential resistance or the possibility of a countervailing intervention.

In the strategic area (line 15) most current calculations indi-

cate that while United States and Soviet forces are probably invulnerable, there is always some doubt. During the 1950s, numerous technical defects existed in our strategic weapons systems,
unknown to their designers, which would have nullified the usefulness of the systems. Appropriate modifications have since been
made in the systems. There is no certainty, however, that all of
the defects have been found, or that newly discovered defects
could be overcome in a way that will not nullify preparations.
Most analysts argue that sea-launched ballistic missiles are secure
from attack in a "sixty-minute war," but they tend to overlook the
possibility of sixty- to ninety-day wars. These "wars of harassment" might see the gradual attrition of Polaris-type submarines
while land-based forces were left untouched.

On the technological side, the sophistication of "state-of-the-
art" strategic weapons systems make it implausible that such systems will be widely proliferated. Their high absolute costs, and
relatively high demands on the resources of the medium-level
countries, tend to make them unreasonable options for these
countries (see Chapter VII).

Finally, line 16 refers to developments tending to discredit
the predictions, commonly made in the fifties and early sixties,
that famine would inevitably spread throughout much of the
underdeveloped world giving impetus to international conflict.
Because of the development of new strains of rice and wheat,
revolutionary technological changes in the acre-yield are now
feasible. Perhaps equally important is the current understanding
and stress on the importance of agricultural development and the
subsequent economic and political requirements. Famine, of
course, may still occur regionally, but wholesale starvation seems
unlikely to characterize the 1975–85 period.

The following chart discusses the notion of a Soviet *thermidor.**
The passions of the Bolshevik revolution begun in 1917 seem
spent. The succession of Stalin to power in 1928–36 created a
new reign of terror following the relaxations of the N.E.P. era.
The Stalinist "second revolution" attained the manic intensity of

---

* Thermidor was the French revolutionary name for the month of July,
1794, when Robespierre and his colleagues fell from power. The austere
and bloody "reign of terror and virtue" then ended, and the consolidation
of the Revolution began. Thermidor is a common metaphor for a loss of
revolutionary elan and a return to "normalcy."

the original revolution itself; but today the Soviet Union has lost a good deal of the millennial enthusiasm of the old Bolsheviks and the Stalinists. First, and possibly the most important cause of the waning of revolutionary zeal, has been the Soviet Union's *disappointing* economic and political performance since 1958, both relative to the West and in absolute terms. Sputnik marked the high point of Soviet post-World War II prestige. During the 1960s the general trend was down, especially since the Cuban Missile crisis.

Soviet Thermidor?

Loss of Enthusiasm:
1. Disappointing performance since 1958—both relatively and absolutely
2. Experience of China—a *Communist* enemy
3. Experience of Cuba—a *Communist* crackpot
4. General disarray of international Communism
5. Internal changes
6. Growing nationalism

And Even of a Loss of Nerve:
1. Yugoslav and Chinese challenges
2. Rumanian challenges
3. U.S. challenges
4. Czech challenges (?)

Most striking is the disappointing performance of Soviet foreign and domestic policy since the late 1950s. In the foreign policy field the Soviets have had an almost uninterrupted series of defeats and disappointments. They have failed to extend their influence in Europe. In fact, with the loss of Albania, there has been some regression. Their attempts to ingratiate themselves with India and other neutralist nations have gained them little. They have not penetrated Africa. Their major effort, in the Congo, came to naught. Their support of various national liberation movements has cost the West little and gained them nothing. For fifteen years the Soviet Union has been supporting the Arabs against Israel in the Middle East and all they have to show for it is the humiliation of their protégés and the capture and destruction of their equipment by Israel. The Arabs have shown no inclination toward Communist ideology and their oil continues to flow to the West. (The only other choice for the Arabs is to leave their oil in the ground.)

The major setback the Soviets have experienced has resulted from the Sino-Soviet split of 1958. For the first time, the Soviets have a serious Communist enemy. In fact, China can be said to be Russia's worst enemy, in the sense of the likelihood of war and of a threat to the national territory of the Soviet Union. The Chinese attacks against the Soviet leadership as being "revisionist," of selling out the international revolution, and of tacitly cooperating with capitalist powers have done serious damage to Soviet morale at home and its reputation in international revolutionary circles abroad. The emergence of Chinese hostility has obliged the Soviets to divert a major portion of its defense potential to guard its eastern frontiers and will encourage the Soviets to seek some sort of accommodation with the Western powers, if it has not done so already.

The Sino-Soviet split seems to have come as a great shock to the Soviets, shaking the ideological foundations of their belief. The split made clear that a strong Communist nation, far from being an ally, could still be an opponent or even an enemy. One good conjecture is that the Politburo today would not *accept* a program for reuniting Germany, even or especially if this were to lead to a Communist Germany, since a Communist Germany would, no doubt, still be nationalist and revisionist and, additionally, find itself free of the burden of Hitler's legacy. All kinds of mischief-making opportunities would be open to a Communist Germany.

Castro's Cuba, also, has proved a dispiriting lesson. The Cubans are reliably estimated to have cost the Soviets about $350 million dollars a year since 1960–61. Yet report has it that a good deal of this Soviet economic aid is wasted; but since Cuba is an "equal" socialist power, sovereign in all respects, little can be done about this state of affairs. Four hundred million dollars is not a great deal of money to the United States; but it is not trivial from the Soviet point of view. The Castro regime indicates that even a friendly Communist state is not an unmitigated boon to the Soviet Union. The peculiar nature of the Castro government—its "guerrilla" economics, its anti-urban policies, its irresponsible attempts at exporting the revolution to other Latin American countries where the objective conditions are decidedly unfavorable—all of these must have somewhat disillusioned the Russians with the idea of promoting revolution abroad. The Soviets may be experiencing the same lesson as the Americans— that allies and supporters may be more trouble than they are worth.

The appearance on the scene of China and Cuba, each of which had their own native revolution and consequent theories of revolutionary strategy which are at variance with those of the Soviet Union, has contributed to the general disarray of international Communism. Since the Chinese see the Russians as corrupt and revisionist, they have made every effort to organize their own Communist movement throughout the world. Communism in Asia, Africa, and even Latin America and Europe has divided along Soviet/Maoist lines. The Cubans add a third faction in some countries of Latin America. Partially this has come about because of the de-Stalinization campaign of the mid-1950s. The revelation of the abuses of Stalinism had the effect of discrediting the moral authority of Moscow to lead and control the international Communist movement. Also, Stalin's successors have been unwilling or unable to maintain the discipline of the Communist International. Local Communist parties in the Western world have taken positions independent of the Soviet Union in both domestic and foreign policy without reprisals. The Soviets are no longer willing to purge outside the bloc to maintain international discipline. Except in those countries where the local Communist party is weak and reliant upon Soviet directives and funds (as in the United States) the national Communist parties more and more promote their own interests rather than of international Communism as determined by Moscow. Also, in the Western countries the 1960s have seen the rise of splinter Communist groups of the type which once would have been described as "Trotskyite," that is, promoting "permanent revolution" and accusing the Soviet Union of being "bourgeois."

The waning of Soviet enthusiasm is also evident in its internal policy. Increasingly, the Soviets have been emphasizing the importance of improving the material lot of their subjects, almost in Western capitalist terms, rather than the moral importance of the achievement of equality and justice. Just as the Soviet leaders have been unwilling or unable to maintain discipline in the extra-Soviet Communist parties by Stalinist methods, they have also had a weakening of such discipline at home. Particularly notable have been the expressions of disillusion and protest among elements of the intelligentsia—most especially those intellectuals who are the offspring of distinguished Communist leaders. The managerial and scientific communities have also been increasingly restless and the political authorities have not been willing to engage in Stalinist-type purges to keep them in line. The open protests, at first by minuscule groups of intellectuals, but more recently by disaffected Jews, would have been impossible and unthinkable in the early 1950s.

Perhaps the most serious cause and effect of the Soviet lack of enthusiasm is the rise of nationalism throughout the Communist movement. Nationalism has always been a major and obvious force in Soviet Communism. However, the Soviets expected that extra-Soviet Communist parties would not subordinate international Communist interests to their own nationalism. But today Communist parties both within the Soviet bloc, such as Rumania, Poland, and even East Germany and Hungary, as well as in the Western world, such as France and Italy, openly express their interest in promoting the development of Communist theory and policy as conditioned by and in the interest of their respective nations. This is also evidenced in the Soviet Union itself, where the Communist regime seems to rely more and more upon being the Russian regime rather than a workers' regime. As far as the Communists are concerned this has very dangerous potentials for inciting the latent nationalism among the non-Russian elements of the Soviet population.

The question of a possible Soviet "loss of nerve" is more controversial. The Rumanian regime's public humiliations of the Soviets suggested to many that there was little "bite" left in the Soviet bear. The Czech affair showed that bite remains, yet its political disarray and current appearance of inconclusiveness confirmed (at least to some) a picture of Soviet confusion and indecisiveness. Similarly, United States actions in Vietnam have often implied a certain disregard of the Soviet ability to retaliate. The estimate of Soviet "loss of nerve" can be misleading if it is taken to mean that the Soviet Union is inevitably passive or effectively powerless. The hegemonial imperatives of the Soviet international position and the tradition of recourse to force and repression in Soviet policy must never be discounted. But some still argue that there is reason to ask if the Soviet leadership any longer has a clear and confident belief in where it is going.

Many people's faith in a Soviet thermidor was shaken by the unexpected vigor of the Soviet response to the growth of revisionism in Czechoslovakia. Possibly more significant is the relative mildness of that response. Although the Russians have made their firmness of purpose clear to the Czechs and other satellite nations, little use has been made of the well established and very successful Communist techniques of dealing with "counterrevolutionary elements." The prisons are not full; packed trainloads of deportees were not shipped to Siberia; deviant political leaders did not get a bullet in the back of the head. Even the arch-"opportunist" Dubcek is quietly managing a small enterprise in Prague, taking the bus to work (the equivalent of Dean Rusk teaching at the University of Georgia). Under Stalin, Malenkov, or Khrushchev, he and his colleagues would have long since been liquidated.

INSTABILITY

Let us turn now to the set of charts giving reasons why the world remains unstable and unsafe despite the favorable developments already discussed. The first chart on page 116 to some extent parallels and overlaps the first chart on page 117, but it looks less favorable. Many of these items bode well for international stability, but they are less firm than those discussed above.

Widespread alienation from and contempt for the "system" and the rise of anarchistic and nihilistic impulses may be of great importance. Although its roots can be traced to the nineteenth century, this phenomenon is relatively new to the twentieth century. These movements usually assume that a new and superior form of "government" can be successfully achieved by an affluent and peaceful people through eliminating virtually the entire apparatus of government as it exists today. As the major credible external threats to a nation erode, as the economic system improves to the point where starvation and economic disaster no longer seem plausible threats to the population, as the size and influence of government come to seem onerous at the same time that it abjures oppression in the classical sense, the growth of anarchistic reactions to the existence of formal government becomes more possible. There will, at least, be a certain contempt for the government. In many parts of the world today this attitude is confined to the young, but to a surprising degree it is increasing among older people as well. Government is now widely regarded as a major source of human folly, illusion—or even entertainment.

A cursory glance at recent events, however, will emphasize the fact that the nation-state system not only is in a state of vigor in most parts of the world, but that the nation-state system is becoming stronger in most areas of the world. From the point of view of internal order and development in Afro-Asia, this often is a progressive movement. Although the nation-state system in Europe seems in a state of flux, it is becoming increasingly difficult to find evidence for a belief in the idea of an "inevitable" movement toward a United States of Europe. To call the recent behavior of France, Rumania, China, Cuba, etc., extreme and nationalistic is exaggerated, but they have been more nationalistic than most Americans in the 1950s would have expected. This kind of conduct may spread to other nations in the 1975–85 period, causing new and unexpected problems for the international system as well as the U.S. and Soviet Union.

How safe will the world then be? Despite some obvious difficulties, most of the world might still feel relatively safe. In principle there could be a parallel growth of international law and perhaps an increase in the authority of the United Nations—although this seems unlikely. The prestige, capacity and authority of the United Nations are unlikely to increase in the next two or three decades to a point where it will play much more of a role in great power or European security issues than it does today. However, it is likely to play a lesser role since the Security Council will probably continue to be blocked reasonably frequently by the veto of one or more of the permanent members and the General Assembly will remain dominated by a negative consensus of less developed countries.

Many old hostilities have been suppressed or sublimated in various ways, contributing to the present stability. Yet they still exist—Balkan irredentism, German nationalism, etc.—and they could arise again. For a relevant, if only half-serious example, about one-third of U.S. territory was taken from Mexico, and

Mexican nationals still live in those areas. Weakened or low morale in the United States could kindle a renewed nationalist zeal among Mexicans, thus creating an issue which has, for all practical purposes, disappeared. This kind of revival of a suppressed hostility could arise in many parts of the world in the 1975–85 period.

The pressures of worldwide technological and social change could also release a variety of new hostile emotions. While many of these would be focused on specific issues, others would at least start off unfocused. Many of these still have great potential political importance, particularly if they are suitably exploited by individuals or movements to serve their own ends.

As the second chart on page 116 points out, the technological revolution in transportation and communication has succeeded in compressing the world. One result has been the creation of remarkable social, political, and economic similarities among nations. The trend toward the welfare state (almost without regard to the capitalist or socialist orientation of the economy itself), the alienation and indifference of urban dwellers, and the disappearance of the "safety factors" which in the past provided refuge for those displaced by technological change, are all examples of such worldwide phenomena.

This compression, or "spiritual constriction" is only one of many forces frustrating the expectations created by technological change which may reopen some previously settled social issues between 1975–85 (among them, the equity and legitimacy of the socio-economic hierarchy within the United States and its general "leadership" role in the world). The tendency toward loss of domestic cohesion may create a crisis of confidence among the establishments of most Western nations, opening the established system to significant attack and giving the humanist left and other revolutionary and pseudo-revolutionary movement:: (including some completely crackpot ones) many opportunities for exploitation and amplification.

Such terms as the *worldwide community, the global village,* and *small world* have meanings which depend on the context in which they are used. But they clearly suggest the technological revolution in transportation and communication that has succeeded in compressing time and space. Many people have conjectured that just as it is no longer tolerable to have poor people in a wealthy nation, the world will feel it is no longer tolerable to have poor nations in a wealthy world. In fact, some have suggested that something like an income tax, voluntary or semi-compulsory, might be used to redistribute income among nations more effectively than foreign aid has succeeded in doing. There is a possible, although extremely limited, first step in this direction in some currently functioning agencies and activities of the United Nations where the figure of one percent of the gross national product for such aid has been suggested.

By 1975–85 it is possible that mankind will have matured to the point where our leaders (and the people they lead) have attained a relatively high degree of constructive political realism. It is equally likely that continuing frustrations and disappointments will produce a prevailing climate of despair and alienation, and some previously settled issues may be reopened. Again, contradictory tendencies are almost assured.

One can argue that, roughly since the Enlightenment, whenever the requirements of social order have come into conflict with the requirements of social justice the latter has tended to win, so that social justice has been increasingly regarded over social order in the short run. However, some of the problems mentioned earlier—perhaps in particular the need for development, the control of arms, and the control of anarchist/imperialist movements—may bring back a sense that social order needs new emphasis.

On the other hand, the fact of enormous wealth in the world, and an increased feeling that the "Establishment," the "Government," the "System" is responsible for social injustice, may make the claims of social justice seem paramount. Both domestic and international divisions could be exacerbated and lead to small organizations and individuals resorting to terroristic and anarchistic techniques, in particular to what the nineteenth century called "propaganda by the deed," individual terrorist acts of symbolic value such as burning conscription records or kidnapping high government officials. Overall, there could be a serious conflict between those who regard the status quo as generally satisfactory and equitable and those who regard it as the dying manifestations of an order that is and should be passing.

Conflict between revolutionaries and the status quo will be promoted if there is a continued tendency toward a lack of assurance on the part of the established forces in dealing with "progressive" and/or humanist revolutions, agitation, and criticisms of the existing systems. The principal cause of this factor is that the Western "Establishment" is to a large extent motivated by the same values expressed by its critics. Since the Western leadership itself believes in peace, justice, freedom, etc., it is vulnerable to claims that these ideals have not been achieved. The conventional answers that "we're doing the best we can," and "well, we're not as bad as the other fellow," are weak and unsatisfying.

We call this *ancien regime morale*, using the metaphor of the old regime of France just before the Revolution. The French government was an autocratic, though very mild and fairly liberal, despotism. But most of the functionaries of the government accepted at least partially the criticisms of the regime made by the radical reformers of the day—the *philosophes* or intellectuals —who measured the regime according to the then new principles of "Reason," (essentially, the principles expressed in the U.S. Declaration of Independence, which was a product of the same ideological environment). The government of France was devoted to maintaining the monarchy, the existing class system, the privileges of the nobility, and the Roman Catholic Church. But among the highest officials of the government were persons who accepted the philosophical ideas of such thinkers as Voltaire ("Mankind will be free when the last king is strangled with the entrails of the last priest") and Rousseau ("Mankind was born free, but everywhere he is in chains"). The most extreme case was the Baron d'Holbach, who was charged with the duty of censoring literature to maintain church and state; he was an atheist and a republican.

The ruling classes of France no longer believed in their system or in their right to their positions and privileges. When the revolutionary outbreak came, they were unable to take steps to suppress it. We see this tendency throughout the Western world today, especially in the recent disorders involving universities. The weakness of university officials in dealing with disrupters has been principally caused by the belief among educated Americans that in a lot of ways the "kids" are right. The condition is exacerbated by the fact that in most cases the progressive and/or humanist left enemies of the system are of the same social class as the Establishment, in some cases the very children of persons in high places.

To a large extent, the political milieu to which we have become accustomed over the past generation is the political, moral, and morale legacy of World War II and colonialism. In Europe, the Soviet Union, Japan, and the United States, the central historical event in the minds of people of high position *circa* 1972, most of whom were at the junior or field grade officer level in World War II, has been that great war. The experience of National Socialist occupation of Europe and the atrocities of the Nazis had a tendency to encourage Europeans to be extremely skeptical about the concept of the natural goodness of man or the desirability for revolutionary upheaval. In Germany, Japan, and Russia the great destruction made the idea of war extremely unattractive. In central Europe, the failure of fascism discredited that movement and its well-publicized excesses made it odious throughout the world. But in the United States, World War II was in some sense a great national epic, an example of national unity and success, and the occasion of the propulsion of the United States into the position of world supremacy. However, all of these factors are fading from the memory of the various nations, the examples are being forgotten, and the possibilities for repeating various mistakes become less and less unlikely as time goes by.

To a similar, but much lesser degree, the same may be said of the Cold War and anti-Communism. To a large extent, the Communist threat and the Cold War were viewed in the Western countries, especially in the United States, in terms of World War II propaganda. There was an evil dictator (Hitler—Stalin) with a totalitarian party (Nazi—Communist) that had a secret police (Gestapo—NKVD), concentration camps (Auschwitz—Vorkuta) that exterminated large numbers of people (Jews—Kulaks), was swallowing up its weak neighbors (Czechoslovakia—Czechoslovakia), and sought world domination. Munich was the central metaphor in the minds of Western policy makers. Another World War would be averted by a firm stand against aggression. With the fading of the memory of World War II, this concept also fades. It is now nearly twenty years since Stalin died.

A similar, though quite separate effect, can be viewed in the Third World. Most policy makers alive today can remember when an atlas showed almost all the world painted in the colors of the European colonial powers. To them, de-colonization and the breakup of empire is a new and revolutionary condition in the world. But most of the new nations are now more than ten years old. The first countries to be de-colonized, Syria and Lebanon, have been independent for twenty-five years. Indians who have reached thirty years of age have no memory of the Raj. As these people move up into policy-making positions (and generally persons in power in the Third World are younger than in the industrial states), their outlook is less and less molded by their memories of colonial rule and the struggle against it. This has several effects. They cannot remember the rule of law imposed by colonial powers, nor the principles of constitutional and parliamentary government that most of them attempted to transmit to their colonies. Neither can these young leaders in the Third World remember the methods of political action which in most cases led to independence—the organization of trade unions, strikes, agitation, and parliamentary opposition. They have been raised in the more vigorous and sometimes vicious polity of the new states—corruption, nepotism, intrigue, insurrection, *coup d'etat*, expropriation, one-party government, dictatorship, and assassination. Also, they have lived all their adult lives as citizens of an independent state. They feel no vestigial deference to the former overlords, have less reason for a sense of inferiority, and consequently less need to react against these feelings through ferocious hostility. Few people in, say, Burma are still mad at the British. They can now deal with them on more or less equal terms, free from the hostilities of the past.

The bottom chart on page 116 lists some of the ways that serious crises may still plausibly occur. After examining the chart one can see why the general confidence in peace exhibited today (even though not always verbalized) and in the actual degree of stability in today's world is probably exaggerated.

Most people are worried about issues in the first two points on this chart, but relatively few worry about the third point—that major violence, perhaps involving the actual use of nuclear weapons, would ever be initiated deliberately and rationally. One can, however, write entirely plausible scenarios for the 1975–85 period where nuclear violence could deliberately be committed. Moreover, political value systems could change so that the relaxed world described previously will erode or disappear. We today can see some renewed taste for violent ideologies, and it is possible that an ideological movement might come into power in some critical area.

The later points of the chart specify dramatic types of movements. These dramatic movements might inspire racial, class, or regional wars. Such possibilities are widely feared today—if not for the immediate future, then for the longer term.

Countries still retain the will, means, and theoretical justification for the defense of their status quo, or some other vested interest, from real or perceived foreign threats. With a few minor exceptions, every nation retains armed forces to oppose aggression. However, there are other forms of violence, particularly domestic violence, which are more likely than international conflicts. Large areas of the world are terribly poor, undergoing serious and dislocating economic turmoil and social change, and have important disaffected political elements in them which, given the internal political conditions of most countries, have no means to achieve their ends short of violent behavior. The political state of the underdeveloped and, to a lesser extent, the developed world can, might, and very likely will, lead to some shocked, hysterical or irrational behavior on the part of some individual or group which feels that its national interests have been thwarted or betrayed in some crucial way by the opponent. Such disputes within states over any number of matters may lead to periodic crises and confrontations, which, through miscalculation and/or unintentional escalation, could lead to war.

We cannot but note the taste for at least verbally violent ideologies which are appearing in the Third World and among the young people of the Western nations. These are usually expressed in some sort of unorthodox Marxist or crypto-Communist terms, but also use, to some degree, anarchist as well as crypto-fascist terminology. Many people are bored by the peaceful, middle-aged, "bourgeois" society in which they find themselves. Among the lower classes, this boredom and desire for action takes the form of individual or gang criminal acts, for "kicks" and gain; but among the educated upper classes young people feel the need for an ideological justification for their activities; hence, the adoption of ideologies which seem to justify their drives on high moral grounds. In the Third World these tendencies will be much more pronounced and dangerous to society as a whole. In most of these countries, violence seems to many to be the only means of getting any type of short-term desirable change. Now an excellent case can be made for most of these countries that peaceful continuous development is likely to have better results in the middle and long run than any type of revolutionary activity; however, this argument is not likely to persuade the aggressive and frustrated elements of their young people, particularly the unemployed young intellectuals, which an inflated Westernized educational system is creating in large numbers for positions which do not and will not exist in the near or foreseeable future.

In Afro-Asia, the glaring and growing disparity in economic growth and general material well-being between the developed and underdeveloped countries is likely to create increased agitation for revenge against the ex-imperialists. The theoretical basis of most movements of national liberation held that the colonial powers were exploiting the colonies; exploitation was responsible both for the debased condition of the colonies and the prosperity of the dominant powers. But with colonialism gone, the ex-colonies remain poor, weak, and despicable, and the former colonial powers become more and more wealthy. Some citizens (mostly white) of the ex-colonial powers smile, and this infuriates the intellectuals. Much resentment must come from this continued condition.

Also destabilizing is the continuance of some vestiges of colonial/colonist domination in Southern Africa. The existence of South Africa, Portuguese East and West Africa, and Rhodesia is intolerable to black African and other non-white former colonists. Leaving aside the racial question, the ex-colonies are infuriated that these areas are internally stable and economically prosperous, that the "oppressed" natives are in many ways better off than the "liberated" residents of the black African states, and that tens of thousands of workers from the free states regularly migrate to the white-dominated areas to enjoy the benefits of what are relatively high wages and a generally improved material and cultural level. Indeed, if the white-dominated areas did not prohibit it, they would likely be overrun by permanent black immigrants. Worse, in order to maintain some economic growth, many of the black African states find it necessary to engage in covert economic relations with these white-dominated areas. Given current conditions, the three million white Africans are capable of dealing with the two hundred million black Africans. The exacerbating effects of this situation are clear and will likely intensify. To whatever extent possible, most black African states are likely to at least advocate military action against the white-dominated areas.

Exceptions to the general rule that there are few irredentist pressures in the world are another possible source of instability. China, West Germany, Japan, North and South Vietnam, North and South Korea have unfulfilled national structures and territories. They all feel bound to rectify this situation, which, to the extent that they act upon those desires, will cause trouble. Now it can be argued that these claims will fade into memory as these national divisions are prolonged. The divisions of the countries and their establishment as separate states each claiming a separate loyalty will mean the gradual fading out of virulent irredentisms. Still, in each of these divided countries, the existing states do not recognize the situation as permanent. They claim the right and the national duty to unite the country or reclaim lost territories. And irredentism or the nationalities problem can always be exploited by local politicians to counterbalance social divisions within the society by focusing attention on an outside condition as the source of national difficulties.

TURNING POINTS

The following chart lists a number of possible turning-point issues. It is included here because of its value as a commentary on the present stability and because it is a warning not to take this stability too seriously despite all that we have noted about its seeming strength and permanence for at least the short run. Almost any one of the items could change our estimates for 1975–85, either before the decade begins or during the decade itself.

Some Possibilities in the 1970s for a Basic Dramatic and/or Revolutionary Change in the International System and/or its Stability

Relatively Unlikely Events But Almost Certainly Turning Points

1. Major or minor nuclear war
2. Widespread nuclear proliferation (as opposed to an initial breakdown of the current five-power nuclear monopoly)
3. Other basic changes in the strategic balance
4. Collapse (as opposed to erosion) of Western morale—or the opposite
5. Collapse (as opposed to erosion) of Communist morale—or the opposite
6. Revival of an intense Cold War
7. A new ideology sufficiently dynamic to make a dramatic impact on world politics
8. Major reversal of alliances
9. Worldwide catastrophic food deficit
10. Sustained worldwide depression and/or collapse of world trade
11. Major revolution or other change in China or the Soviet Union completely changing prognosis for the country

Relatively Possible Events But Less Likely (By Themselves) to Be Decisively Destabilizing

1. Certain outcomes of the Vietnamese War
2. A major successful rebellion in East Europe
3. A real entente or rapproachement of any two vertices of the U.S.-Soviet-China triangle
4. The outcome of the current Middle East confrontation
5. A partial reversal of alliances
6. A Soviet take-over of the Indian Ocean
7. Early or very accelerated Japanese nuclear armament
8. Castroite or other revolutionary-success throughout Latin America
9. Extreme United States or Soviet neo-isolationism
10. A real slowdown (or great increase) in the rate of growth of either (gross world product) or world trade
11. Some aspect of "1985 technological crisis" both materializes early and proves unexpectedly difficult to deal with

The difference between the two charts above is that the first chart specifies *relatively unlikely* events which would necessarily cause very fundamental changes or raise fundamental issues, while the second chart deals with the range of normal political or economic events which may be *relatively fortuitous or accidental.* In most cases, events on the second seem unlikely to have a big impact on our surprise-free projection even though they could; while the events on the first list might not have a great impact but most likely would. Some of these turning point items are obvious, others require some discussion. The major effect of a nuclear war of whatever size is among the events having an obvious impact, but also of vital importance would be widespread nuclear proliferation.

In the 1970s the most likely shift in the strategic balance is an erosion of the U.S. superiority over the Soviet Union. The present stability has been based on more than U.S.-Soviet choice, though this is clearly important; it has also been based on U.S. political/military and economic/technological dominance of the nation-state system. This dominance has been generally accepted and is largely taken for granted. Soon it may no longer be real.

Today it is popular to argue that because both sides have "overkill" the notion of strategic superiority is meaningless— being only a useless superiority in number and/or quality of weapons which provides no intelligible advantage. But this was not true until 1968 or 1969. U.S. strategic forces were relatively well protected and more numerous than Soviet forces. In a crisis a Soviet attack on U.S. strategic forces could not be decisive. But the contrary was not true. The U.S. could destroy the greater part of Russia's forces. What Russian forces survived a U.S. strike would be relatively limited in effectiveness, whereas the U.S. would still have a residual force sufficient to destroy Russia. Both the American and Soviet governments seem to have had some inkling that the above outcome was possible. The implicit *bargaining* advantage this perceived imbalance provided was probably more important than the actual threat. Even a pro forma and operationally meaningless superiority may lead the "superior" nation to feel it is entitled to political advantages for its extra strength and that the other government should back down.

In the 1970s the American strategic advantage either will have disappeared or come close to disappearing. For the first time since World War II the Soviets will have a justified sense of strategic parity with the United States, and conceivably even a sense of superiority. We know that the last time the Soviets acted out of a feeling of parity or impending superiority (during the so-called missile gap period of the late 1950s and very early 1960s), they tried to gain immediate political advantage. Should they do so again, and particularly if they should achieve some tangible success, the impact on the other major powers could be decisive. If, for example, the "Nixon Doctrine" is interpreted, correctly or incorrectly, by America's allies as a general move toward isolationism and an American backdown during crisis is interpreted as evidence of strategic inferiority, it would be surprising if the other major powers did not make serious efforts to arm.

The point here is that the *nation-state system naturally lends itself to individual alliances and actions*, to multi-party balances of power. The bipolar world under American dominance, which has provided the current stability, has for all practical purposes obviated this characteristic on a political/military level in the post-World War II period. As this era ends, a multipolar political/military world once again becomes a realistic possibility.

The collapse of Free World and/or Communist morale as well as the great augmentation of the morale of either bloc is also unlikely but certainly would create a turning point—a major shift in the moral balance could have just as serious an effect as a major change in the strategic balance. In fact, either of these basic changes could lead to the revival of an intense Cold War. And there are still many other events and/or tendencies which could have the same effect.

Another factor threatening stability is that the Soviets might overestimate or misinterpret the importance of the "counterculture." In the Soviet Union, according to the official Marxist ideology, these new values are interpreted as "bourgeois capitalist decadence." Marxists believe that a socialist form of government is a necessary and an inevitable outgrowth of capitalist society. According to the Marxist scenario, the last stages of capitalism will see a moral breakdown of the system—capitalist youth will become disaffected from the system, and their better elements will turn to Marxism, others to corrupt hedonism. In this decadent phase, capitalism will no longer be able to count upon the confidence of the people who live under its sway. According to

Marxist ideology, this will be a particularly dangerous phase for the socialist states because the more perceptive elements in the capitalist world will recognize this impending collapse and their immediate absorption into the socialist system; therefore, they will be tempted to make a preemptive strike to destroy the socialist states which will inevitably supplant them. The socialist states must be on their guard and well armed. However, basically the capitalists are morally bankrupt and getting continuously weaker. Sooner or later they will collapse.

In order to promote the revolution to socialism, the socialist states have a historical obligation to continue to put pressure on the capitalist states, probing for the weak points, and accelerating their decay. American phenomena such as the rising use of drugs, the spread of pornography, upper-class alienation, hippies, peaceniks, widespread strikes, terrorism, demonstrations, and public disorders of various kinds could indicate to the Soviet Union that capitalism is in the state of dissolution long anticipated by Marxist science. Given this interpretation of U.S. events, it is sensible and correct for Soviet policy makers to get tough with the Americans, knowing that toughness will likely pay off in the speedier achievement of worldwide socialism. Of course, Soviet policy makers must be somewhat cautious for fear of a last gasp strike at the Soviet Union. Note that this conjectural Marxist analysis does *not* require that the Soviet Union attack the United States—such an attack would be pointless because the socialist victory would already be in sight. The Soviet Union must only prepare to defend itself from capitalist aggression and to continue to put pressure on America in order to expose the "internal contradictions" of capitalist society. Up to certain limits, it will be safe to put such pressure on America, because the Americans will no longer believe in their system and will not fight for it.

From a Marxist point of view, therefore, an America in which humanist left values are spreading is a tempting target for Soviet pressure. From their point of view it would be their duty—to Communism or to history—to hasten the collapse of the West. It would be immoral not to take advantage of such an opportunity. Such a Soviet interpretation of events in the United States (and the rest of the West) could contribute to a Soviet decision to move away from detente.

Also, of course, there are possibilities of new forces arising in the world which cannot be identified at this time. Many people are disillusioned with existing systems of thought and are search ing almost desperately for a new ideology. In the unlikely event that one should appear, this could make a dramatic impact, par- ticularly if it promoted the establishment of an important new political entity such as a European political community, an inci- pient world government, a real third force, etc. And a new politi- cal entity from some other source would also be a major turning point, as would a major reversal of alliances caused by ideology, political innovations or other factors. A major reversal of alli- ances, such as Western Europe adhering to the Soviet Union, China adhering to the United States, or U.S.-Soviet de facto or de jure alliance against China, are all extremely unlikely but cer- tainly would have radical effects upon the world scene.

In the mid-1950s, General de Gaulle's Eastern policy seemed to be trying to set up a new "little entente" among France, Poland, and Czechoslovakia, which presumably would have eventually been integrated into a Franco-Soviet agreement or under- standing. If this had been achieved, it would have been some- thing between a major reversal of alliances and a partial reversal of alliances, though approaching the former. Clearly, it could have made a great deal of difference. However, France would be willing (and able) to do this only if there were no great threat of Soviet aggression and probably no great threat of other drastic developments in Europe. Thus the conditions under which France would have been willing to—and could have achieved—a reversal of alliances are almost exactly the conditions under which a reversal of alliances would not have made a great deal of difference.

For another example, what could be called a partial reversal of alliances (but could be more): consider the current attitude of many West Germans towards closer relations with China. Their attitude derives from an exaggeration of likely Chinese power and a more general expectation among Europeans that China will continue to put pressure on the Soviets and that this can only benefit Europe. Thus the Germans toy with the idea of a tacit Sino-German collaboration directed at weakening or con- taining Soviet power. The Soviets tend to share the common European estimate that China will be very powerful in the future, and they can envisage a close alliance between the Germans and the Chinese—conceivably even one backed by the Americans. Yet the only circumstance which an important degree of Sino-German cooperation seems at all likely to develop is one in which both the United States and West Germany have confidence in preserving a relative stability in relations with the Soviets. There might then be a modest degree of cooperation between the Germans and the Chinese which Americans are perfectly willing to live with but are unlikely to encourage. But the only plausible circumstance for serious Sino-German collaboration is a modern *Rapallo*, or an alliance between two "outlaw" powers —in the past, between defeated Germany and Bolshevik Russia; today, between a newly "outlawed" West Germany and China.

Some non-political events would almost certainly be turning points. Many people have projected a worldwide, catastrophic food deficit, resulting in famine, upheaval, and possibly a food war between the rich nations and the poor nations. However, the people who are making these catastrophic projections do not have a very good case. This is because of pressures by the United States on India to place priority on food and fertilizer rather than on steel and industry, and because of the development of the new Philippine "miracle" rices, new Mexican wheats, and new Mexican sorghums. As a result, we can confidently predict a world food surplus rather than shortage for the mid-seventies. A moderate world agricultural depression due to overproduction is much more likely than a Malthusian famine caused by increased population outstripping agricultural land.

Of course, local food deficits may be caused by combinations of crop failures, poor distribution, and bad government policies. And it certainly is true that a worldwide deficit caused by some factor that we cannot now recognize, like a new sort of food plague, would have a catastrophic effect. A similarly disastrous impact would be realized by a sustained worldwide economic depression on the order of the Great Depression of 1929–1939. The impact of such a depression would likely be even greater than that of the model—there are very few people in the world who are willing to accept the laissez-faire explanation of the inevitability of depressions anymore, and everywhere in the world government action to deal with severe economic problems would be demanded. Governments that did not appear to be moving fast enough to restore economic prosperity and stability would probably have grave difficulties in holding power against democratic and/or revolutionary political movements which offered alternatives. Again, the economic conditions of today probably are not such that a worldwide depression can be expected, but if one should occur, we might very well expect to see the appearance of very exotic and angry political revisionist movements throughout the world, perhaps even new Hitlers and Stalins.

While all the above items are extremely unlikely, the second chart lists some events which are relatively possible. In fact, any one of these could occur, although any one item is more likely not to occur than to occur. In terms of probabilities, each item has between ten and forty percent chance of occurring. There is almost no chance of all of the items occurring, but it is possible. While these effects could create a major crisis and greatly disturb the world political scene, each one is relatively unlikely to be decisively destabilizing by itself. However, several of these together, or in series, or combined with some other event could conceivably have disastrous effects.

The most obvious destabilizing event would be an unfavorable outcome of the Vietnamese War; that is, unfavorable to the United States. Many writers have talked about the ill effects if the United States should be (or appear to be) defeated in Vietnam, or if it should appear that it has abandoned its allies. Without getting into the issue of whether or not these possible losses from a Vietnam defeat outweigh disadvantages of the United States continuing the war, even patriotic "doves" should recognize that there are some disadvantages of a Vietnam defeat. A Vietnam defeat could seriously injure the credibility of the U.S. foreign and military policy abroad, casting doubt on United States ability to defend its allies. An apparent abandonment of the South Vietnamese would certainly cause many nations to doubt the credibility of a U.S. guarantee. A V.C. victory would likely give new spirit to those who would promote wars of national liberation elsewhere in the world, while a Vietnam victory by the U.S., within the limits of the war now being fought, would merely re-enforce the status quo.

The Soviet equivalent of Vietnam is Czechoslovakia, and the final outcome of this Soviet intervention is not yet clear. It seems that the Soviets have reestablished order, on their terms, in

Czechoslovakia; however, they have not made any fundamental changes in the Czech social and economic sphere to prevent a new "liberal" movement from arising once the Soviet army slackens its grip on this country. If the Soviet occupation of Czechoslovakia turns out to have been reasonably successful in meeting Soviet objectives, tendencies toward demoralization in the West could be reinforced while Communist-bloc liberalizing movements are effectively suppressed. On the other hand, if the Soviets have a serious failure in Czechoslovakia, Eastern Europe and the Soviet Union could well experience further ferment. While the West might applaud the latter trend, the world might become considerably more dangerous.

The future stability of the Soviet bloc must be assessed with great caution. The renewed reactionary course of the Soviet Union could impose a surface stability while provoking potentially uncontrollable impulses beneath the surface of events. From this point of view Czechoslovakia's orderly transition toward an internal system closer to Western European standards, while attempting to respect Soviet security interests, may have been a great opportunity that Russia threw away. The desire for change may have been suppressed—at least for the decade of our interest—or it might also have been intensified so that it will find more and more desperate methods of expression. Indeed, something like the popular spirit of nihilism sometimes detected in the contemporary West may become a deadly serious matter inside Eastern Europe—not only in Czechoslovakia, and not simply among students. In any case, the present situation is certainly highly unstable, as the workers' riots in Poland demonstrated. The crisis latent in this situation is perhaps more likely to take shape before 1975 rather than within the 1975–85 period, although it will affect the latter decade.

Today, Russia and China appear to be in a period of transitional leadership and intra-party conflict. Conceivably, the outcome could produce dramatic new leadership. A progressive leadership might prove a greater threat to world stability than a reversion to old-style Soviet and Chinese dictatorships—to essentially isolationist Stalin-type regimes. A new and dynamic—and presumably younger—Soviet leadership might even accomplish a successful modernization of its relations with the East European states and project a magnetism and dynamism which would attract, once again, the left-wing revolutionary movements of the Third World.

A successful and charismatic leadership in China could reopen the fear of recent years that China might become the political leader of a variety of Third World revolutionary movements. We are inclined to discount the possibility that this could happen in any simple way. There is a lack of real common interests or perceptions between China and the Third World rebels, as well as a seeming lack of the talent, and perhaps the material competence, for serious Chinese worldwide interventionist action. But we can imagine—particularly if the West were in economic crisis or serious political disarray—a sizeable revival in Third World revolutionary activism which China might support without being able to control. The threat would not be a coordinated assault on the West or a disciplined hostile bloc, but a spreading anarchical condition or an economic breakdown engulfing large areas of the world, perhaps infecting the West, driving it back into defensive isolation, or bringing about a new period of attempts—cooperative or competitive—by the advanced states to police the Third World.

Or there could be a limited but important new threat to a specific area in the Third World. Many U.S. Navy analysts worry over a possible Soviet "take-over" of the Indian Ocean. The usual concern is that the Soviets might replace the British as the provider of the local balance of power "East of Suez," which could have ominous implications for the United States. These concerned analysts point out that at least thirty nations touch on or are within five hundred miles of the Indian Ocean. Moreover, there are several suitably located island groups (e.g., the Chagos Archipelago or the Aldabra Islands in addition to the British base already established in the Maldives) that could serve as naval and/or air bases. In the past, the British presence in the area has been decisive in achieving a favorable resolution of conflict situations in Kenya, Kuwait, Malaysia, and elsewhere. With the British leaving, the Soviet Union might choose to maintain a permanent naval presence. Or—far more serious—they might actively intervene in the Persian Gulf and Arab coast principalities in an attempt to find allies and to influence the supply or control of the region's oil. This would obviously represent an adventurous Soviet policy since an American (or British) response might be expected. An entirely new zone of Cold War competition would be opened up, involving the Soviets rather than their proxies. However, while such an event would be annoying and unpleasant to the West, it would not in itself be decisively destabilizing.

Another of our "outcome" items is that of the current Middle Eastern confrontation between the Arab states and Israel, each of which is supported, overtly or covertly, by outside powers. The fundamental political conditions of the Middle East are such that a "final" settlement of the Palestine problem within the next fifteen years, or even within our lifetime, cannot be reasonably expected. In politics, as in physics, two objects cannot occupy the same space at the same time and neither the Israelis nor the Arab refugees are going to abandon their right to occupy the Holy Land. However, there are many other outcomes of the current struggle, short of final or total solutions, which could have important effects although they are not decisively destabilizing. For example, it is conceivable that some or all of the Arab states could come to some sort of acceptable terms with Israel, or, on the other hand, that a new war could break out at any time, indeed at any hour, and might, theoretically at least, involve not only the Middle Eastern states, but the Soviet Union and even the United States. This last possibility, leading to a direct confrontation between U.S.-Soviet forces in the Middle East and the Mediterranean, would obviously be extremely destabilizing.

It is difficult to write plausible scenarios which support the notion of a U.S.-Soviet central war over Middle East issues. However, a localized U.S.-Soviet confrontation following renewed Middle East hostilities and the deployment of a substantial naval presence in the area by both nations is easier to envision. Other escalation scenarios could be written if Israel acquired a nuclear weapons capability for possible use against the Arab states in the region.

There could be other political reversals than Sino-Soviet rapprochement. "Reversal of Alliances" covers several such possibilities, any one of which could occur in the period of our interest, breaking up the configuration or power which has dominated the international system for the last twenty years. Among the possibilities are a Franco-Russian (or West European-Russian) alliance. The Czechoslovak invasion put at least a temporary end to this possibility—at least creating a "road accident" on the way toward a Europe extending "from the Atlantic to the Urals." But in the years to come the possibility of independent West European deals with the Soviet Union, particularly if such a deal appeared to offer the chance of European reunification or some form of solution to the German problem, will continue as a serious possibility.

Sino-Soviet tension provides an additional motive for Soviet "reinsurance" in the West. Presumably the Soviets would prefer to reinsure with the United States rather than with the European powers—or an individual European state—but they might not have that opportunity. The Sino-Soviet situation also has been interpreted by some as opening the possibility of a West German-Chinese alliance, an arrangement designed to put pressure on the Soviet Union. This obviously presupposes a much more adventurous or desperate Germany than now exists, but it must be taken into account in considering the 1975–85 decade. Even today from the business, commercial, economic, and technological points of view there are reasons for a West German-Chinese alliance. One crucial factor obviously standing in the way of such an alliance is that it might easily jeopardize U.S. support and would not likely be strong enough that, in the absence of U.S. opposition, the Soviets could not take very strong and effective actions against it, at least against the West German member. Hostile reactions might also be likely in Western Europe.

A further Castroite success in Latin America would bother the United States very much and would create great concern among U.S. policy makers; however, we should remember how little effect the Castroite regime really had on the total world picture. Of course, the existence of the Castro government led to the Cuban missile crisis, but this can be seen as a separate event which was in addition to the establishment of a Communist regime in Cuba. It would not be decisively destabilizing if, say, Chile or even Nicaragua should fall to a native Communist movement. The same can be said of a radical, Black Power government taking hold of some Caribbean island or Guyana.

Of course, the growth of U.S. "neo-isolationism" has been one of the already obvious results of the Vietnamese War. In the unlikely event that this trend should accelerate to the extent that the United States becomes a "hermit" kingdom, cutting itself off from the world, taking a "Fortress America" position, this would constitute a major reversal of alliances which would certainly be a turning point. However, it is unlikely that neo-isolationism will spread so far, and even an improbable widespread tendency in this direction together with a policy based upon neo-isolationist premises would not in itself be decisively destabilizing. However, this, combined with some of the other events such as, for example, a Soviet takeover in the Indian Ocean and a defeat of Israel as a result of direct Soviet military assistance to the Arab States, would have important effects on the international scene, not to mention the U.S. domestic situation.

The growing neo-isolationist movement as it exists today is an odd phenomenon. The old isolationism was based on the assumption that what happens in Neville Chamberlain's "far away country . . . of whom we know nothing," cannot concern us very deeply. Today, of course, there are no "far away" countries or people of whom we know nothing. Although it is possible not to intervene in the affairs of others (e.g., Biafra, Bengal, Ulster), few Americans are really prepared to take the position that United States' policy should be almost totally indifferent to the rest of the world. Few are willing to take this position because they are unwilling to live with the arms race or the new alliance structures which would follow upon an explicit or implicit U.S. disengagement from world affairs. The very smallness of the world is a threat—a threat which might prove overwhelming even if we were to act as world policemen.

Japanese nuclear armament and the creation of an effective European defense community are two versions of the "rise of a Third World Power" theme. Both seem reasonable possibilities for the 1975–85 decade. A breakup of the Western alliance system could ensue from some substantial American retreat from responsibility. Or, alternatively, the Europeans might find new American interventions—new "Vietnams"—or other American policy moves deeply disturbing or destabilizing. Either case could create pressures in Japan and Europe to seek security through nuclear autonomy (in Japan's case) or the creation of a new and independent European nuclear defense grouping. If this happens, the world of the 1975–85 decade might have four or more major nuclear power centers with competitive foreign policies.

It may be that if the present nuclear powers do not in the

next few years make additional political use of their possession of these weapons, non-proliferation efforts will succeed and the possession of the weapons will remain limited to those states which have them now. But if the existing nuclear powers in the next few years dramatically exploit their nuclear capabilities—particularly if it were by means of specific and dramatic threats or blackmail—the outcome by 1975–85 might be as many as ten to twenty nuclear states.

VI

Alternate U. S. Futures–
Scenarios and Branch
Points

IN considering how the United States might develop through the 1985 time period, a large range of possibilities must be taken into account. We could construct alternative futures which would range from the most glowingly optimistic to the most horrifying. For example, a rather grim future can be constructed from an extrapolation of the accelerating tendencies of violent civil defense, demonstrations, riots, and terrorism of the late 1960s. Starting from the first important overt act of civil disobedience— the "sit-in" by Greensboro State College students in 1961—this movement, at first among Negroes, but later spreading to other elements of the population, built up by the end of the sixties to a quite high level, and could reasonably have been projected to continue into the future, with increasing numbers of Americans repudiating the democratic process itself and the country becoming ungovernable by 1975. Even if the tendencies increase at the current rate, without acceleration, their intensity and scope might still reach a level which made governing exceedingly difficult. But naive extrapolation, of course, ignores both the countervailing trends in American society and the development of the issues that lie behind contemporary unrest. Many processes that suggested a topping out phenomenon, or even a reversal of these particular trends were already beginning to operate in the late 1960s. This example cautions us to beware of such naive extrapolation, because as we see now, the tendencies toward violence began to "top out" after 1968, and, although we by no means have the level of domestic peace of the 1950s, most Americans seem able to tolerate the existing level of public and political disorder (although private lawbreaking, i.e., crime, is much less tolerable).

Taking this into account, the three alternative contexts described in this chapter are of particular interest in considering the range of possible U.S. futures. These contexts represent a range of surprise-free projections for the United States, particularly emphasizing phenomena which will have a major impact on the future of the entire society. There are no fundamental differences between these contexts. The "modestly optimistic" and "modestly pessimistic" contexts present more or less of the same tendencies described in the "neutral" context, their main differences being matters of degree. And many of the individual items in the neutral context are part of the other contexts as well.

A NEUTRAL CONTEXT

1. Vietnam has been settled. The domestic effects were unfavorable, but not disastrous, and have largely vanished or been absorbed by 1975. (It is very important to assume this—a disastrous outcome of the Vietnam War could have devastating effects, as we shall discuss later.)

2. There is a further extension of the sensate technological and affluent society—perhaps with some development of a mosaic culture.

3. Partly as a result of a parallel development of late sensate culture, vice, dissent, anarchism, and nihilism become very visi-

ble but are concentrated among relatively small groups. However, the growth of these tendencies has stopped or slowed. They are considered a normal part of the political and cultural landscape and create little or no intense concern. Disaffected elements turn more to "dropping out" or sullen conformity rather than radical activism. However, because these "late sensate" tendencies are concentrated in large metropolitan centers, faculties of prestige universities, various artistic and political movements, and elements of the media, they have a visibility and impact far out of proportion to their numbers.

4. While life is extremely good for the overwhelming majority of American people by almost any of the classical materialistic, cultural, or political standards, and to some degree even from the moral and morale points of view, both the upper classes and the various kinds of dropouts prefer to emphasize the defects of American civilization.

5. Domestically, many of the "great society" problems are being alleviated, particularly those that are susceptible to money and physical engineering.

6. There is less success with the problems that correspond to "social engineering." Indeed, there have been some regressions. Nevertheless, by most objective standards, poverty, racism, etc., have been greatly reduced. As in the 1960s, this progress is hardly noted by academia or the media.

7. Despite great technical advances, physics, mathematics, and engineering steadily decline in prestige and charisma, but there is sufficient quality and quantity of technical manpower. On the other hand, life sciences, psychology, and sociology flourish.

8. Despite its enormous productivity and effective financial success, business has also lost some prestige and charisma. It attempts to recoup its prestige by trying to be a "good citizen," participating more fully in community life as a patron, engaging in "social responsibility," and being a serious innovator in various areas. This will not enable it to recover fully the ground lost, but it does prevent precipitous erosion.

9. The gross national product (in 1967 dollars) reaches 1.1 trillion by 1975, 1.6 trillion by 1985. Unemployment fluctuates between three and five percent. Most additional jobs are provided by government, particularly state government, or by private organizations with government contracts.

10. Labor force participation rates by women continue to increase. By the late 1970s, for the first time in history, a majority of married women are employed outside the household. Married women with grown children are the backbone of the suburban "white collar" labor force, but even women with young children are more and more employed. Employers prefer to hire these women rather than the traditional urban source of single work-ing girls, who are increasingly from minority groups and increas-ingly less competent (of course, with millions of exceptions).

11. There is continued moderate inflation, increasing real wages, and standard of living.

12. There is a gradual leveling of income and advancement opportunities between big cities, smaller cities and rural areas. However, large metropolitan area residence remains a necessity for top positions in certain industries—e.g., finance, advertising.

13. Some erosion of work effort is evident. Absenteeism and turn-over climb. Life is centered around weekends and vacations. But technological advance and steady (and cumulatively revolu-tionary) substitution of capital for labor keeps productivity ris-ing.

14. "High culture" lags behind in the quality of new produc-tions and in the quantity of live performances because of high labor costs and the diffusion of the markets into the suburbs. Spectator sports and individual sports are more important.

15. Expanded government services are principally funded by the "fiscal dividend" created by increased productivity and infla-tion. At first, working people are angered by their increased taxes, but gradually accept middle-class resignation. Needless to say, the expanded services satisfy few.

16. The spreading out of cities, particularly in the South and West, continues, together with population decline in older areas. The free-standing, owner-occupied, single-family house remains the predominant American ideal, but small and growing minori-ties prefer either rural or high-density urban residential styles.

17. Continued social and economic gains by minority groups continue, but non-whites do not close the "gap" with whites. Prosperous Negroes move out to the suburbs, but there is little residential integration. Several large U.S. cities are Negro-domi-nated and controlled.

18. Despite the social and economic gains of most black Americans, there will remain a hard-core bloc of black urban

poor, highly represented by fatherless families, which will be recognized as a major social problem.

19. As it becomes clear that Negroes are not especially interested in social and residential integration, white liberals press less for it. The large numbers of prosperous Negroes relieve white guilt. Radicals, white and black, curse the "black bourgeoisie," which is more concerned with black crime than with white repression.

20. Police, courts, prosecutors, public opinion get tougher on criminals within the present legal framework. The slowdown of growth rate of youth has an inhibiting effect on the crime rate. People have become accustomed to lower levels of security. There is less toleration of extremists.

21. Despite myriad squabbles and prophecies of doom, pollution control begins to pay off.

22. A gradual extension of government regulation of business and personal activity (on grounds of pollution, safety, consumerism) is evident, but private property and individual freedom remain the national ideals.

23. Pornography, promiscuity, drug abuse continue to spread, although more slowly. The public at large becomes more tolerant and marijuana, homosexuality, abortion, fornication, and blue laws are rarely enforced. There is more contraception and more divorce.

24. The birth rate continues at a relative low level (approximately 2.5 children per couple). Despite more divorce and fewer children, nuclear family remains dominant form.

25. There is somewhat less sex and race segregation, but more age and class segregation.

26. More, but still limited, concern is created by the growing mutual alienation between the United States and the rest of the world. On the one hand, the fund of goodwill that the United States built before, during, and after World War II is gradually exhausted and forgotten—partly because of a relatively bad press and partly because of many "necessary" and "unnecessary" U.S. actions that struck foreigners as irritating, immoral, unwarranted, and/or outrageous. Much foreign and domestic comment focuses on and emphasizes these acts and their actual and imputed consequences. Also, "puritan" Third World countries see the U.S. as a corrupt society. On the other hand, there is a grow-

ing frustration and indifference—even hostility—in the United States because of foreign ingratitude, envy, misinterpretations, intransigence, and seemingly unreasonable hostility. U.S. alienation from the world also increases because of the failure (or at least seeming failure) of many made-in-America foreign aid and intervention programs.

27. The military establishment is supported adequately at about six to seven percent of the gross national product (or about two-thirds of the current rate and about half of the rate of the late fifties). This is about ninety billion dollars in 1980 (in 1967 dollars). Despite cancellation of the draft, it also manages to find enough competent recruits for all ranks. However, it has only minimal political support among the intellectuals, "respectable press," universities, and even the upper-middle class in general.

28. NATO continues but with a continually decreasing esprit, elan, and charisma. It becomes relatively clear that the active, in-being defense of Europe against a land attack by the Soviets is basically furnished by a U.S.-West German working alliance, possibly with significant British participation, which is legally and politically imbedded in a loose cooperative effort of nations. However, various fringe activities of NATO, such as information exchanges, continue to be important. Participation in them is greatly prized by the smaller nations.

29. There is increased polycentrism and diversification in the international arena. The United States retains a position of leadership, but in part by largely emphasizing a responsible low-keyed diplomacy (despite the irritations, etc., mentioned earlier)—even occasionally adopting a "low posture" that is perilously close to neo-isolationism. In effect, it preserves a veneer of hegemony by not trying to exercise it too often or too heavily. This hegemony is very loose and allows for much independence, dissent, and even outright opposition by its members.

30. Gradually, the concept of an area of responsibility rather than an area of influence or "world policeman" has become widely understood—both domestically and abroad. Under this concept the United States feels more or less obligated to defend nations that are in its area of responsibility from external attack, even if these nations are relatively hostile and unfriendly to the United States

31. Despite some modest reforms (such as creation of special drawing rights), international monetary and internal inflationary problems continue, but at a relatively low level. Thus, no international monetary crisis occurs but many continue to think that there is one in the offing, and they may be right.

32. U.S. productivity advantages over other industrial nations gradually erode and foreign (and some domestic) markets are lost to competitors, particularly Japanese. A less favorable balance of payments condition is partially relieved by the reduction of overseas garrisons, but there is increasing agitation among affected industries, especially unions, for more protectionism. This is bitterly fought by the finance community and international corporations. A hidden protectionism is imposed by safety and pollution requirements for U.S. market.

33. U.S. foreign aid rises over current absolute levels but is less than one-half percent of the gross national product, or about five to eight billion dollars per year (as opposed to the one percent attained during the late fifties). A good deal of this aid is given through multilateral bodies (especially U.N. regional and technical assistance agencies). While this aid is not successful in largely dissipating the demands of some of the "poor" nations and has many U.S. critics, the fact remains that while the developed nations are no longer "listening guiltily" they are still listening. There is no widespread food deficit and massive starvation, largely because of improved agricultural technology promoted by the United States.

34. The international north/south problem (rich versus poor or white versus colored) is gradually being perceived as far more serious than east-west tensions—but even this problem is seen without hysteria or intensity.

35. A partial "failure of nerve" occurs, particularly among the philosophers, intellectuals, theologians, and so forth. This is very similar to the failure of nerve which occurred in Athens and Hellenistic Greece in the fourth and third centuries B.C.* Various fin de siècle ideologies such as anarchism, syndicalism, neo-racism, and crypto-fascism proliferate among these people.

36. However, this failure of nerve does not affect the great mass of people who participate relatively fully and heartily in the

---

* Gilbert Murray, *Five Stages of Greek Religion* (1951).

three major establishment life styles, which we label *neo-material-istic, neo-epicurean,* and *neo-gentleman.* Another important and prominent life style from the point of view of the masses and the establishment is the *neo-stoic.** There are also many small groups which "drop out," or oppose the Establishment (though some-times only in a rather passive and pro forma manner), that is, become hippies, New Left revolutionaries, investigators of "inner space," participants in esoteric religions, participants in various kinds of neoclassical religious movements, and the like. The nation becomes accustomed to a more or less permanently disaffected left intelligentsia. And there are vocal and dissident elements on the right also. Politically, America has become somewhat Europeanized, but more on the model of France than England.

37. There is some loss of national vigor and a vague sense of malaise with the potential to respond to the call of "get the country moving again."

A MODESTLY OPTIMISTIC CONTEXT

1. In an optimistic context the various Hellenistic syntheses we call the neo-materialist, neo-epicurean, neo-gentleman, and

---

* We defined these terms as follows: a neo-materialist is simply an in-dividual who is very advancement-oriented because he is very interested in gaining and spending a rather large income. Alternatively, he might be an extremely consumption-oriented individual who uses his income to enjoy life in various ways. The neo-epicurean might bear some resemblance to the epicurean of Greek philosophy in that he is oriented towards home, towards family, towards friends, towards a decent and humane life, but he does not have the same kind of discipline and asceticism. In many ways the current Southern California barbecue culture exemplifies this neo-epicurean life style. The neo-stoic is quite similar to the stoics of imperial Rome who in fact tended to staff the civil service in the first two or three centuries. These again have American characteristics and possibly are some-what more interested both in personal success and in success in their efforts than their classical prototypes. (The neo-stoic analogy might be more that of an ambitious soldier doing his duty rather than the actor in the play—the analogy of the Roman stoic.) A neo-gentleman would have a rather large number of diversified skills and pursuits, all of which would require great effort. On all of these he would achieve a very high level of performance, but none of these skills would be put to any economic use. (*The Year 2000,* pp. 189-193.)

neo-stoic life styles prove to be unexpectedly attractive. Many more people participate enthusiastically in them and in other healthy social movements than one expected in the neutral context, and the morale and self-confidence of these participants is high.

2. There is less erosion of the traditional U.S. work-oriented, achievement-oriented, advancement-oriented values than is envisaged in the neutral context, so that the American society and economy are more vital and dynamic than might have been expected. The society has little difficulty in withstanding the criticism and attacks of the cynics, the alienated, and other critics and "dropouts." Indeed, these American life styles are obviously fairly full and satisfying, and thus it is the morale and confidence of critics that has a tendency to erode.

3. Poverty and student dissidence have been substantially overcome, in part because of intelligent and well-run reforms by government which produced useful short-, medium- and long-term impacts.

4. In particular, various "reverse discrimination policies" prove successful. Tens of thousands of Negroes are either at the top levels of U.S. society or clearly on their way. Everywhere—in both personal contact and in the media—there is visible proof to the Negro that he can "make it" (and even more visible proof to the white man). This spectacular increase in the status of upper-class Negroes reduces tolerance, both within and without the black community, of illegal or unreasonable acts by destructive and extremist protest groups. In particular there is little or no implicit (much less explicit) encouragement of such demands or behavior. Increasingly, successful Negroes—despite their protestations of solidarity with Black Nationalist sentiments—are co-opted into the "Establishment" and suburbia and find that their major concerns, satisfactions, and psychic income come from much the same kinds of rewards as those of the whites they work and live with. In addition, there is a burst of creativity among Negroes which shows up in almost all aspects of culture and in many political, business, commercial, technical, and governmental areas. This also gives Negroes self-confidence and a feeling of pride and participation in "the system." When combined with the fact that they do not feel forced into the system—they all know they have the opportunity to opt out—their allegiance is to the liberal system. There are, of course, many hard-core problems

and much alienation among the Negroes, but the problems are now regarded as soluble and the protests mainly "rhetorical."

5. Non-white, non-black minorities also advance. Attempts to mobilize them, as well as ethnic groups, for radical action fail.

6. Community control agitation has the effect of making decision-makers, public and private, a great deal more sensitive to local public opinion in policy-making.

7. Americans of recent European (and Asian) ancestry are more closely assimilated into conventional U.S. family and economic patterns, but many of them find satisfaction in maintaining various superficial "ethnic" customs, such as national holidays, foods, and traditional religious observances.

8. There is some return to religion, but it is motivated by a need for continuity and values, rather than a deep-felt religious faith. In Jewish terms, the revival is conservative rather than orthodox or reform. Orthodox sects continue to lose communicants, but the rate slows. Some reform sects stand pat (e.g., Unitarians) and others continue to experiment with radical religious forms, but most of them move toward more conservative positions. Middle-aged radical clergy are seen as somewhat anachronistic by their younger brethren. Seminaries promote pastoral care rather than social activism.

9. Upper-middle-class youth—white and black—also participate actively in society, regaining interest in government and private programs, particularly action-oriented social welfare programs. They therefore have a heavy stake both in society and in reforming it. In most cases, after a burst of energy into pursuing altruistic and/or public service objectives, they end up by putting most of their energy into living well and succeeding in their careers (i.e., being good citizens, neo-epicureans, and neo-gentlemen). There are, moreover, sufficient competent and motivated leaders to sustain strong and innovative government.

10. With the gross national product reaching 1.1 trillion (in 1967 dollars) before 1975 and 1.9 trillion by 1985, there is sufficient investment in new housing and urban redevelopment to maintain historical rates of improvement in housing quality. However, poverty pockets remain in old cities and rural areas, and municipal finances remain a problem, though the predominantly suburban electorate and legislatures are more sympathetic to them.

11. Multi-channel cable television and cheap transmitting

equipment permit a full spectrum of cultural, educational, political, and entertainment programs, mostly commercially sponsored. Public television continues to appeal to the "lowest common denominator" but competitive pressures push its rates and its number of commercials down. Children demand and get their own TV. The great variety of TV offerings promote mosaic cultures and have gradually replaced uneconomic live performances. Live audiences at public events are present primarily to improve the TV show.

12. Excesses by environmentalists have provoked a "backlash" leading to a more balanced approach to pollution. Severe environmental contamination is well on its way to being cleaned up. Pollution control has become just another parameter in the design of systems.

13. While the most important single recreational activity is the cheerful hedonism of lying near-naked on the beach, the overrunning of the shore by the lower classes drives the upper classes inland to more active leisure. Ski resorts proliferate wherever the climate permits, and artificial snow-making equipment drives that climate south. Ice skating and hockey also spread south (but restrictive regulations limit the use of snowmobiles). American campers are increasingly found as far afield as Alaska and Central America and mountain climbing and hiking are important. Hunting remains for rural and small town people, but more and more urban people find it distasteful; in conflicts over the use of recreational areas, hunters begin to lose.

14. The American presidency and the political and business decision-makers are largely in the forty to fifty age bracket but with enough thirty-year-olds so that one can argue it really is not a "middle-aged system." The most prized political and business characteristics are: style, pragmatism, optimism, moderation, innovation, and expertise. The most successful politicians are, in effect, members of what can be called the technocratic and/or responsible center.

A MODESTLY PESSIMISTIC CONTEXT

1. We assume here a degree of stagnation within at least the non-technical and "square" sectors of intellectual life, and, in general, diminishing satisfactions and élan in most elite occupa-

tions. While nominal participation in U.S. "square society" and its goals, aspirations, and activities is still high, pride and monetary reward for such participation have diminished.

2. The prestige of physics, mathematics, engineering, and the life sciences has eroded more rapidly than was suggested in the neutral prognosis. Political activism by social scientists and psychologists has given them very low credibility among the public. The failure of economic theory to reflect the real economy has discredited economists. There is a widespread belief that science and reason have failed, and even educated people feel free to admit to being "unreasonable" and advocate moral nihilism and/or raw dogma. Political and even academic debate is highly polarized, emotional, and filled with invective.

3. Much of the population is suspicious of and hostile to the military-industrial complex, big business, and big government. (In this scenario the military-industrial complex exists as an important and relatively unified political and economic pressure group and plays an increasing role in American political life, though still not as much as has often been typical in continental Europe.) While the United States is, generally speaking, a low-morale country, many of its elites and pressure groups are, at least in some cases and on some issues, relatively touchy. Thus, while they lack confidence and assurance, they can still act resolutely on occasion, even provocatively. In particular, they may not always consider it important to observe the kind of constraints, precedents, and various unilateral limitations which now function in American society.

4. The gross national product fails to reach 1.1 trillion (in 1967 dollars) by 1975 and falls short of 1.6 trillion by 1985. Unemployment is at least five percent on the average.

5. Drug use, alcoholism, pornography, gambling, promiscuity, abortion, adultery, and other forms of vice and crime spread. Fundamentalist preachers compare America with Babylon as a matter of course, and millions of Americans agree with them.

6. There are bitter fights over pollution vs. production and pollution vs. power.

7. A striking feature of the society is the spread of *syndicalism*, a "gang" society wherein groups responsive to only their own self-interest compete for economic and political advantage.

8. Increasingly militant trade unions, particularly in gov-

ernment, take a "public-be-damned" attitude toward the common interest. Mostly in self-defense, white-collar workers (perhaps even executives) organize.

9. Labor indiscipline makes it advantageous for employers to retain older workers. Forced retirement rules are relaxed. There is agitation to change social security employment regulations. "Old Power" slogans are heard.

10. Despite economic gains, Negroes remain alienated. Successful blacks accept their rewards as partial payment for the sins of whites. Militants may move away from Marxist-Leninist and African nationalist ideologies toward radical black movements in the West Indies.

11. Increasing militancy among Indians and Mexicans is evident, as well as early 1960s-style activism by ethnic groups.

12. Black nationalism spreads to the South, leading to a confrontation with white militants. The Ku Klux Klan revives. The South has three-party politics: Negroes and progressives—National Democrats; urban traditionalist and business interests—Republicans; rural traditionalist and lower whites—Wallace-style demagogues.

13. Nationally, polarization is seen as the prime social and political issue. In the industrial states, three (and even four) party politics becomes the norm rather than the exception.

14. The estrangement of America from the rest of the world, and most important, from the liberal democracies in Europe, is much greater than in the neutral context. Increasingly, America's actions are perceived as unilateral (or arbitrary) definitions of the international as well as the national interest and as unnecessary or provocative violence (or threats of violence). The United States condemns or threatens from a posture essentially that of a beleaguered "Fortress America." But America, justly or unjustly, is widely believed to have become a major destabilizing factor in international affairs, and perhaps a dangerously unpredictable one. This reinforces the American sense of isolation, contributing to the low morale of American elites and to the intensity of domestic political dissent.

15. Existing American alliances, and certainly NATO and the Japanese alliance, have been ended or lost their significance; and there is a growth in economic protectionism, paralleling the breakdown of political cooperation in the Free World.

There is a falling off of world economic growth and a realignment of trade patterns. There may be an economic crisis, and a severe drop in world trade. If this did occur, America's domestic problems may well find echoes in other countries as well as being reinforced here. Or, the crisis might produce a political reaction in the United States sharp enough to revise many of the tendencies described here.

16. America's relationship to the world community has undergone important change. The general high regard for America in much of the world, historically a matter of respect for America's domestic political and economic accomplishments, has in considerable measure been supplanted by hostility or distrust.

17. By almost every historical measure of national well-being, the United States remains the most powerful, the most free, and the most prosperous country in the world, but most Americans perceive that things are getting worse, not better, and are discontented. Thus there is a continuation and predominance of domestic division and controversy, of international isolationism as well as American isolationism, and possibly of arbitrary or authoritarian action by political elites within the United States.

BRANCH POINTS

Within the range of surprise-free projections described above, there are some important events whose outcome cannot now be predicted or whose probability may be very low. Therefore, these events are not a part of any of the three contexts. However, if they should occur, they would have obvious and crucial effects upon the national environment. These events, called *branch points*, are located by examining a series of contexts or scenarios (see page 163) of the future and attempting to find out where there are major turns or choices which would make a big difference. Many branch points are obvious. However, it often turns out that events which appear important at first glance, at least to the people directly involved in them, turn out to be relatively insignificant. On page 149 there is a list of major events which could occur on the international scene but would not make a very big difference on the whole world; a similar list could be made on the domestic level. For example, it probably does not matter very much who is elected President of the United States in 1972 (provided he is a candidate of one of the major parties—the election of Governor Wallace certainly would make a big difference—although the likelihood is too low to be worthy of detailed consideration).

Generally, the branch points most easily identified are those which are or lead to disasters. A surprise-free projection is usually a disaster-free projection. There are necessarily only a limited number of national disasters possible; indeed, in recent times these can only be: a natural calamity (which because of the continental nature of the United States would not have a serious national impact as one could in the Netherlands or Pakistan); an economic debacle (the Great Depression was the best example); or a political debacle (that is, a serious insurrection or civil war or a military defeat). Of course, there are many other disasters which could occur in a country, but these often take the form not of a single event or clusters of events limited in time, but a long, drawn-out, gradual, evolutionary process which is normally identifiable through ordinary trend analysis. The steady erosion of the U.S. international economic condition would be a good example of this type of drawn-out, negative occurrence. It cannot be said to be a branch point.

Normally, the favored means of probing possibilities for the future is the use of scenarios. A scenario is a hypothetical sequence of events, usually in the future (but sometimes in the past—reconstructions of past events, as in criminal court cases, could also be described as scenarios). A scenario is not a prediction—it does not represent what *will* happen, only what might possibly happen. Nor is a scenario a normative forecast—it does not represent what we want to happen.

Scenarios and the term "scenario" have been employed since the early 1950s. However, the nature and purpose of scenarios is still often misunderstood. An article in *Izvestia** accused the Hudson Institute of planning the liberalizing movement in Czechoslovakia for the CIA and "Zionist" elements. Apparently, the Russians had seen a scenario written in the mid-1960s which had a remarkable resemblance to the events which occurred in 1967–1968. This was pure coincidence. A scenario is not a plan

---

* Reported in *The New York Times*, February 20, 1971.

for future events, but more a suggestion of how they *might* occur. (And to the best of our knowledge, no staff members at Hudson have been moonlighting for any "International Zionist Conspiracy.")

Another recent misunderstanding of scenarios appeared in the reporting of the "Pentagon Papers" in *The New York Times.** Reporters chose to interpret scenarios which were being written in the U.S. government in late 1964 as normative plans for escalation of the Vietnam War. Actually, of course, those scenarios were hypothetical constructions of future conditions which could occur which might lead to escalation, not normative plans for widening the war. If this tendency to interpret scenarios as plans spreads, a new term must be found to describe this form of intellectual activity.

Since we have ruled out the possibility of natural calamity being a branch point for the United States, let us consider economic and political disasters. The worst thing that could happen to the United States economically would be an internal and international economic crisis. Because our standards of economic performance are higher, and because we now expect direct government action to prevent adverse economic conditions, it is not necessary that an "economic disaster" reach the proportions of the Great Depression, or the German inflation of 1923. Unemployment or inflation reaching ten percent would probably be serious enough to set off major changes in the U.S. system. Under such circumstances a scenario for an American social democracy follows easily.

Now let us turn to a specific version of a political disaster interesting not only in itself but as representative of a class of scenarios in which some major failure of foreign policy produces a harsh public reaction against the administration in power and to some extent against the established apparatus of government— the political establishment.

A VIETNAM "DEBACLE"

The most obvious case of a political disaster would be a Vietnam debacle; that is, the United States is defeated or is perceived

* *Loc. cit.*, June 13, 1971.

as defeated in the Vietnam War. This scenario assumes that the administration's present efforts to develop an honorable negotiated settlement or form of American disengagement take a dramatic and discrediting turn. A settlement is negotiated—perhaps over the objections of the Saigon authorities—who are overthrown by the Communists as soon as American power is withdrawn. Extensive reprisals against non-Communists or a clear terrorist program against the population ensues. The North Vietnamese overrun Laos and Cambodia. Or, Communist aggression against Thailand quickly and provocatively follows what was supposed to have been a neutralization of the area. The American government would then be judged by the American public—and perhaps by many abroad, even including many who had been critical of the original American intervention—as incompetent, unreliable, and even immoral. The alleged folly or crime of Vietnam intervention would be seen as compounded by folly or failure in ending that intervention. The generation of policy makers who have dominated the Republican as well as the Democratic administrations of the last twenty years—internationalists, generally liberal in terms of the American political spectrum—are then repudiated by an angry American population.

From this point another branch point is apparent, which is unpredictable because it depends upon the quality and calibre of individual political leaders. The reaction could be to both left and right: on the left there could be a condemnation of this leadership as immoral and incompetent even by its own standards, and on the right there could be either a rise in aggressively interventionist attitudes (possibly including a heightened willingness to make use of nuclear weapons) or a developing Fortress America outlook.

Even though a left liberal reaction is possible, a rightist ideological renewal government is probably more plausible under this scenario. If the "liberal establishment" leadership did nonetheless continue in office, it would function within wholly new constraints and in an atmosphere of radicalized controversy. If it was ousted, the successor administration might represent a coalition not only of politically conservative forces largely denied national office in recent years, but possibly of populist reactionary groups or groups alienated by the cosmopolitanism and sensate qualities and devoted to the "ideological renewal" of this country. One can obviously imagine these last forces assuming a politically repressive stance, although it may be more difficult to see them overcoming the resistance of the major population groups which have been in the ascendance in American society (and in the Western nations generally) over the recent decades. Whether the reaction were to the left or to the right, one would expect an America that is reacting against a foreign policy debacle to be much more bitter in its divisions and inner struggles than at any period since the Civil War. The consequences for government and for the health of the social organism could be crippling.

The immediate question that most people are going to ask is· Why was the United States defeated? There will be several answers: Many professional analysts of the war would prefer to say that there were technical failures in waging the war by the politi cal leadership, the civilian military and diplomatic bureaucracy, and by the uniformed military. We to some extent share the view of many dissident civilian and military analysts that there has been a failure to understand the nature of the war and an inability to perceive and effectuate the available means of achieving victory in Vietnam.* However, this answer is not very satisfying —it says that many of our leaders have been less perceptive and competent than they ought to be. Many people find such a banal explanation unsatisfying, particularly when results are disastrous. There is a tendency to attribute debacles to conscious evil intent.

Another answer is already visible among the more extreme elements of the antiwar movement: that the United States was fighting a vicious, immoral, and criminal imperialistic aggressive war and our policy, strategy, and tactics were so thoroughly evil that the people of Vietnam (and to a lesser extent the rest of the world including the United States) rallied to solidarity. Moreover, the rank and file of the American forces in Vietnam perceived the war in the same way, which had definite effects on their fighting capabilities and morale. They knew it was a "bad scene" and they took it easy and hoped for a Viet Cong victory.

From this point of view, the basic questions of why Vietnam was lost are: why did we get into Vietnam in the first place, why

---

* These views are discussed at length in Frank Armbruster, *et al., Can We Win in Vietnam?* (New York, 1968).

did we fight the war the way we did, and why did we continue it after its evil results were made apparent? The answer, of course, is found in the military and political leadership. There were evil men at the top who plotted this war out of their fundamental depravity. Such men are by definition "war criminals" and should be brought to the bar of justice in some sort of American Nuremberg to answer for their felonies and through their punishments to purge the American people of this stain upon their honor, reputation, and character. If these people with this point of view come to power, it could be very nasty for people like Dean Rusk, Walt Rostow, and William Westmoreland.

The preceding two paragraphs form a very bad scenario. It is implausible; there is not a prayer of people holding such extreme left positions achieving power in the United States in the next fifteen years, although continued agitation from this group could have important effects upon the American polity, particularly in promoting what we call "polarization" and in bringing other elements to power. This is particularly important because there is another explanation for the defeat of the United States in Vietnam.

The following argument would be much more persuasive to the average American: The United States has a population of two hundred million people, a gross national product of one trillion dollars, and armed forces of more than three million. All of Vietnam has a population of thirty million, a gross national product of six billion, and armed forces of one million. Even if the extreme dove position that all the Vietnamese are against us except a few puppets is true, how could the United States possibly be defeated by Vietnam? (Indeed, most Americans tend to think of war in national terms, which is at least partially responsible for some of the problems in waging the war. The average trooper believes that we are at war with the Vietnamese and finds it extremely difficult to discriminate between the "good gooks" and the "bad gooks.") There is another important element involved in the popular perception of the war, independent of the relative power of both sides: the average American knows that America is good and that America does not lose wars. Period. How could the United States possibly be defeated by the Vietnamese? There is only one answer—treachery. Our boys in the field, brave as they were, could not possibly win because they were stabbed in the back. It does not require much imagination to conceive of a *dolchstoss* myth spreading throughout the American masses. Now, who are the back-stabbers? Almost certainly not the Jews, certainly not the Negroes, certainly not the generals, nor the military-industrial complex, but the press, the doves, the liberals, *The New York Times*, Walter Cronkite, Eugene McCarthy, William Fulbright, Edward Kennedy, and on and on. And what is treachery in wartime? Treason.

Following this line of reasoning, it is not difficult to write a scenario of some sort of resurrection of McCarthyism in the United States, possibly in a much more virulent and nasty form. And since so much of the national media has been involved in antiwar agitation, the scenario could be extended to include serious attacks on the freedom and autonomy of the press. It is also likely that civil libertarians and the judiciary, particularly the federal judiciary, would attempt to protect individuals and groups from attack because of their political views, thus perhaps bringing even the courts under attack.

This is an extremely ugly picture, but it is one that people should keep in mind as the early part of the seventies progresses. Now, short of some sort of credible victory, that is, the establishment and maintenance of a fairly secure South Vietnamese government, there is probably only one way that the United States can extricate itself from Vietnam favorably without some sort of very serious or even disastrous domestic outcome. The Administration's current "Vietnamization" program has the possibilities of finding such a way out of the war.

In that case, the United States will have achieved its stated objective in Indochina, to defend a non-Communist state—so the United States has won the war, and there is no problem. If Vietnamization does not work, and the United States does not re-intervene in great strength (which is highly unlikely) and then the Saigon government falls eventually, then the United States has lost the war. The issue here is how long it takes. If we gradually pull out and then the position of the anti-Communist forces in Vietnam slowly erodes and Indochina in effect reverts to the situation in the early 1960s, then it can at least be said that we gave the South Vietnamese ten years of our time, treasure, and lives; we built them up but they just couldn't "hack it"—too bad. Such an explanation is not very pretty but it is reasonable and could be accepted by the majority of Americans (although, of course, many will feel that it is a shameful and disgraceful outcome of the war). Nevertheless, such a policy position is the only credible rationale for Vietnam defeat and therefore the only one which could prevent a serious domestic repercussion.

Scenario writers are often accused of being "paranoid" because they seem to write more scenarios of perverse or disastrous outcomes than positive or cheerful ones. There may be something in this criticism, because it certainly seems more interesting to write a disaster scenario than an optimistic one. Recently, Arthur Schlesinger, Jr., wrote two scenarios following a Vietnam debacle;* it is interesting to note that the right reaction was much more interesting and drawn with much more careful and loving detail than the "left" reaction which he obviously would prefer. Perhaps this has something to do with the tenor of our times— historically, writers of science fiction or fictional representations of ideal societies drew up Utopias; but twentieth-century writers have concentrated their attention on anti-Utopias. In the discussion above, it was noted that the American social democracy outcome of the Great Depression is a favorable and cheerful scenario for people who appreciate those values, even though they certainly would prefer that their programs be achieved without the cost of a Great Depression preceding them; the right-wing reaction to a debacle in Vietnam is also a favorable scenario to persons who hold to a certain amount of traditional martial, religious, and other values. The following scenario is a "pipe dream" for a member of the existing responsible center or governing liberal establishment. Although we would estimate the possibilities of this occurring in any way similar to that described as extremely low, nevertheless it is a possibility, and for persons who adhere to this group it might make a useful program for normative forecasting.

A DYNAMIC AND COMPETENT RESPONSIBLE (OR HUMANISTIC) CENTER REESTABLISHES ITSELF

The Neutral Context assumed a continuing prominence in political leadership and a continuing influence of intellectuals

* *Playboy,* February, 1971.

and, more generally, of the highly educated upper-middle classes. However, internal or external developments may operate to discredit the values and methods of this cultural stratum before or during the decade under consideration.

A "shameful" settlement in Vietnam could have this effect. So, too, could a protracted period of negotiations during which American military casualties continued to mount. In the former case, popular discontent might be intensified by increased militancy and arrogance on the part of New Left students and black separatists, and also by the Populist Right. In the latter, the malaise and unrest born of governmental ambivalence and vacillation could be fortified by the persistent problem of inflation.

Even a satisfactory settlement in Southeast Asia does not, however, preclude the possibility that "the middle Americans" will become an increasingly important and possibly decisive force in our politics and culture. Among the domestic factors aiding instability in our present apportionment of political power and cultural influences are: (1) rising violent-crime rates; (2) rising tax rates, afflicting especially the urban middle class; (3) school-district problems, including soaring costs, crowding, integration issues, and curricular reforms; (4) campus violence; (5) the confusing and perturbing results of the anti-poverty programs; (6) the breakdown of traditional barriers regarding sexual behavior, dress, drug use, the arts, etc., and the erosion of "establishment" support for religion, patriotism, and private business; (7) the penchant of parts of the liberal press for gratuitous denigration of the values and behavior of the "lower-middle classes"; and (8) comparative governmental indifference to the middle-American's "side" of the racial problem, as well as to such problems (including psychological ones) as are peculiar to him in a period of rapid change.

A scenario which stresses the potential of these factors would entail rhetorical (and some legal) reassertion of "official" support for traditional religious, patriotic, sexual, and private-business values and practices. Among political candidates and administrative appointees, practical men would have a clear edge over academicians. Governmental social welfare programs would be designed and administered with a different—possibly more effective—set of attitudes and approaches than today's fashions permit. It is likely that programs specifically designed to reduce inequities of opportunity and to stimulate enterprise would be encouraged. Support for tax reforms and for meeting the nutritional, medical, and educational needs of the children of the poor could be stronger and more effective than today. Education in general, as our traditional means for class mobility—and class definition— could receive increased attention, although one would suppose that today's educational philosophy would undergo modification in the direction of stressing competition, vocational training (possibly), and moral training also.

A reestablished responsible-center government would be compelled by the reasons for its ascent to power to devote considerable attention to the law-and-order issue directly by monetary and advisory aid to police, expediting court procedures, and prison and parole system reforms; and indirectly by its functionaries' personal examples of commitment and resolution to protect the constitutional system of orderly conflict and dissent and the conditions set for receipt of federal grants or loans by universities, anti-poverty groups, etc.

In foreign affairs, this type of government might tend toward interventionism or a fastidious "holier-than-thou" policy of disengagement, depending upon circumstances and the mood of its constituents. It might, of course, follow these opposite policies simultaneously, since both express the middle American's preference for unilateral actions—reducing international cooperation.

Variants on the theme of a responsible-center resurgence derive from the variable strength of its opponents. In addition, it is possible that what appears, from a present-day perspective, a reestablishment may seem different in hindsight. One possibility is a prelude to authoritarianism. A second possibility is that emphasis on the middle Americans may serve to stimulate the development of a new and militant "populist" movement in much the way that emphasis on the American Negro has borne unexpected fruit in the sixties. Such a movement of the "people" could play as seminal a role in responsively restructuring our social philosophy to "post-industrial" conditions as the populism of the 1890s played in catalyzing public response to industrialization and urbanization.

One must, finally, take into account the vigor of existing American political leadership elites well within the established "center" of American politics. A satisfactory Vietnam outcome and new successes in domestic policy by the Nixon Administration could, for example, produce a reconstituted establishment of somewhat more conservative cast than in the recent past. Or, the Democratic Party might bid successfully for the presidency on the basis of new domestic reform proposals and with new leaders, again within the responsible center range and drawing on the same establishment sectors of big business, the academic world, and the professions as the other Administrations of modern times. In either case, the present alienation of significant minorities in American society from a leadership constrained by the imperatives of America's world position and the social demands of technocratic society would be substantially reduced—possibly with a new degree of power decentralization, or of participation through new political or economic mechanisms. With international stresses lessened through a Vietnam settlement, and possibly by a general international trend toward "inward-looking" or neo-isolationist policies, domestic controversy could lose some of its present intensity and the major domestic issues of racial relations and poverty become more susceptible to remedy.

Certainly a reasonable (and historically warranted) scenario for America lies on this scale of moderate, incremental change, accompanied by intense creative controversy, rather than the starker alternatives feared by many people. But the less favorable scenarios must also be taken as possibilities for this period of history.

VII

Military-Technological Possibilities in the Seventies and Eighties— Technological Forecasting

TECHNOLOGICAL forecasting is probably the most sophisticated and highly developed form of futurology. This is true principally because more effort has been put into this type of forecasting than any other (with the obvious exceptions of attempts to predict the outcome of horse races and the fluctuations of securities and commodities). Many books on this subject go into methodology in considerable detail and seem very impressive. But, viewing technological forecasting by how successful it has been in forecasting technological innovations or developments of existing technology, its track record is not as good as some of its proponents would suggest.

Excepting individual works of art and genius, there appear to be only two really important methodologies. Other methods have great potential, but, as far as we can tell, they have not yet demonstrated general usefulness to planners. The two methods that interest and impress us are *delphi* and *envelope forecasting.** A delphi as developed at RAND Corporation is operated thus: a panel of experts is selected; they are sent a questionnaire asking them what date they expect a list of technological events to occur; the returned questionnaires are returned to the experts for possible revision; and the final opinion of the experts is then calculated. The results of the delphi will say that the median of the opinion of the experts is that innovation X will appear in year Y and the range of the middle quartiles is from $Y-m$ to $Y+m$. Delphi is a particularly interesting form of technological forecasting, but it must be noted that it is not really forecasting at all, but a method of polling experts to systematize their opinions in various aspects. It could be used to poll a small group of people on any subject. For example, it would be possible to run delphi panels of historians, to find out what the consensus of expert opinion is about, say, the relationships between the Aztec and Inca civilizations.

Nevertheless, this is an excellent method for technological forecasting, but with the following important qualification: delphi work best when it polls the experts who are actually attempting to achieve the given result. Not only will they have some idea when the innovation can be expected, but they will have a large influence on programs. A successful delphi is often an exercise in a self-fulfilling prophecy. The men who are attempting to make plastic widgets are very good people to ask when plastic widgets will be achieved. For this same reason, delphi looks far less promising when it attempts social forecasting because here the experts are not the people who are making the social change but merely observers of the social scene. Typically, delphi panels have been made up of upper-middle-class bureaucrats, technocrats, and social scientists, and their predictions reflect their view of the world and how it ought to go. Although the delphi seems to be a fine method of tabulating technological forecasting, it is actually the individual experts who do the forecasting. We suspect that most of these experts use "intuitive"

* On delphi see Olaf Helmer and T. J. Gordon, "Report on a Long Range Forecasting Study," RAND P-2982 (1964); on envelope curves see Robert W. Ayres, *Technological Forecasting and Long-Range Planning* (New York, 1969).

methods, that is, they rely upon their experience, intelligence, and good sense; others use envelope curves, even if intuitively.

Envelope curves have shown their utility, particularly in indicating the rate of innovation or the effects of such innovation. Let us assume that in 1935 you were trying to predict the energy of accelerators ten years later. As a typical expert, you would know all about cyclotrons and, consciously or unconsciously, your sense of what improvement is possible will go along the cyclotron curve, which is what you know about. You're busy designing cyclotrons; you know all about next year's cyclotron. You know nothing about betatrons. If you knew about them, you would already be using them. And it never occurs to you that the crucial issue in prediction is the rate of innovation of new technology; in this case, the betatron and synchrotron.

Now, if some forecaster came along and said to you, "I've been looking at a three hundred year record, or a twenty or ten year record, and there ought to be at least two inventions by 1945, and these two inventions ought to give you a factor of improvement of ten each," you would reply, "What do you mean by two inventions; will you please describe these inventions to me?" "I can't describe them, but there is a kind of track record here; there is a process going on." There are some hundreds of envelope curves like this which are used regularly and those that are based on the rate of innovation are remarkably accurate. Indeed, these curves are so good at forecasting the progress of technology that sometimes attempts to exceed the performance projected have been duds, as in the attempted IBM Stretch computer on the following graph.

There was a startling demonstration of its effectiveness at the RAND Corporation in the late 40s and early 50s. The most important single number in American military planning was the energy yield per pound of nuclear weapon. A weapons system designed around a specific number could magnify changes in that number by, say, a factor of five. Thus, an increase in the yield/pound by ten percent could improve the efficiency of the weapons system by fifty percent. But this number did not change by ten percent—it changed by a factor of two or so every three years or so. In the design of weapons systems one is generally looking ahead five to fifteen years, or even ten to twenty, yet the systems were sensitive to the assumed value of this rapidly chang-

TRENDS IN COMPUTER CAPACITY

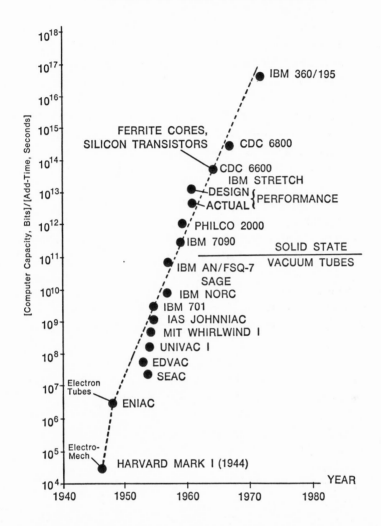

ing number. As you can imagine, a major effort was put into pre-
dicting this number.

At that time the Scientific Advisory Board to the Chief of Staff
of the U.S. Air Force was composed of the top American scientists. Every year they put out a ten-year prediction. Sam Cohen
of RAND also put out a ten-year prediction every year. He
generally predicted that the labs would achieve in two years

what the Scientific Advisory Board thought they would do in ten. That is a very big discrepancy. Cohen was right for many years in a row, to the great chagrin of the Scientific Advisory Board, which had put first-class brains to work using highly sophisticated thinking. Finally they asked him, "Sam, how do you do it?" And he answered, "It's very simple. I put a straight line on a piece of paper. I use a ruler." (That is, he used simple envelope curves.)

Needless to say, this concept infuriates scientists and engineers. If you are engaged in working these things out, you consider it a triumph of intelligence, dedication, organization, allocation of resources, and creativity to come through with these breakthroughs. Imagine yourself slaving in a lab, having brilliant ideas, and when you emerge proudly with your innovation, someone like Sam Cohen says: "Right on schedule."

Of course, many other techniques are used more or less systematically, or more often in an ad hoc and/or intuitive manner. An important one involves major analogies to the idea of the biological analogy of conception, gestation, and birth. Once a conception has been noticed, the projection of the rest is fairly straightforward. This is particularly easy in fairly large technological projects where the gestation period necessarily takes many years, perhaps even decades. In the late twentieth century, such long periods of gestation are typical of major military weapon systems, although the problem is spreading to other technologies as well. In the past, a decade was a short period in military systems. Even today, one can forecast most of what will be available within that time frame on the basis of what is being worked on now. Another method is the identification of "challenge and response"—new technology will respond to perceived need and demand.

This chapter sketches a range of technological possibilities that may be of importance in the 1975–85 period. We are mainly concerned with weapons possibilities, but some areas of non-weapons technology with likely military significance are also included. We comment below on the spread of advanced military technology to new countries because we wish to "flag" this as a major problem in the 1975–85 period. We are not attempting any exhaustive or detailed discussion of future military technology; this should be regarded as a survey of material that can be gleaned from unclassified technical publications and the press.

A separation between the military/technological possibilities of the 1970s and those of the 1980s must be made because the weapons possibilities of the 1970s can be foreseen much more clearly than those of the mid-1980s. One reason for this is that it is unlikely—though not impossible—that qualitatively new weapons development based on the discovery of new knowledge will play a significant military role in the middle or late 1970s. The same statement cannot be made for the 1980s; for this period we are obliged to think more in terms of relatively "far out" ideas. Weapons possibilities can be discussed with reasonable assurance for the mid-seventies, but not for the mid-eighties.

POSSIBILITIES FOR THE SEVENTIES

Ballistic missiles will continue to be the delivery system of principal interest in strategic warfare. MIRVs (multiple independently-targeted reentry vehicles) are coming into the operational inventory of both the United States and the Soviet Union and will remain operational for the rest of the decade, in lieu of firm arms control agreements.

Certainly, in the mid- or late-seventies ICBMs with (or without) MIRVs can be deployed in a manner limited only by resource allocation (i.e., budgetary) choices. Qualitative improvements may also be expected: MIRVs and their associated technology will probably lead to greater accuracy and a greater range of choices among warheads and advanced penetration aids devices. But while advances in MIRVs and missile technology in general could upset the strategic balance—possibly even to the extent that a counterforce first strike by either side would prevent retaliation at an unacceptable level—this is not likely to occur. In practice, the threatened side is likely to take compensating measures reasonably early. If warhead accuracy reaches the point where hardening (the fortification of missile launch sites to prevent or reduce damage from a near-miss) no longer seems to be an effective means of insuring ICBM survival, then other options can be expected. Among these possible options are an increased emphasis on submarine-launched missiles, active defense of selected missile silos (including, perhaps, a strengthened U.S. "Safeguard" ABM system), hidden launch sites, and perhaps mobile land-based ICBMs to be added to the U.S. arsenal.

We do not foresee any ASW (anti-submarine warfare) developments in the 1970s that could negate the present heavy U.S. reliance upon submarine-launched ballistic missiles, unless some innovation such as a supersonar makes it possible to, in effect, make the oceans "transparent," although this situation could change in the eighties. But it is important to note in connection with this forecast that the role and effectiveness of ASW, at least as regards strategic war possibilities, depends critically on the scenario of the war. If the actual use of strategic nuclear missiles by one side against the other is preceded by a period of extreme international tension and conflict to the extent that one or both sides tries to sink ("attrite") the other's submarines, then of course the effectiveness of the U.S. Polaris/Poseidon force might be substantially reduced. Similarly, in a stretched-out strategic war, attrition of missile-launching submarines could make a major difference. But we do not consider either of these to be particularly plausible scenarios (although they are perhaps much more plausible than the sneak attack case). The deterrent or retaliatory effectiveness of each side's submarines could be *increased* if a period of tension provided time for the best deployment of the submarines.

The United States and the Soviet Union can be expected to put greater emphasis on ballistic missile defenses, both in strategic thinking and in actual operational capabilities in the 1970s. Today the generally prevailing view in the military/technical community seems to be that the offensive vs. defensive competition has shifted in the last seven years in favor of the defense, although some might dispute this statement. However, even if technological developments in the seventies continue to favor the defense, *at least so far as the two superpowers are concerned*, the concept of a reliable balance of terror is unlikely to be disturbed seriously. We make this caveat even though we expect to see more BMD* deployment by the United States and the Soviet Union.

We will not attempt to predict how effectively the BMD systems will be deployed by either the United States or the Soviet

---

* Ballistic Missile Defense (BMD) is the generic term for all means of preventing a ballistic missile from reaching its target after it has been launched. ABM is a particular form of BMD: a missile system configured to intercept an incoming missile.

Union in the 1970s. But, at a minimum, missile defenses deployed by the superpowers may be quite effective *for the period of the seventies* against missile attacks from China or any other country. Even primitive BMD could offer the advantage—to the superpowers—of keeping the strategic arms race more of a bilateral competition by excluding lesser powers, who lack the technical or financial resources to keep up. An emphasis on defensive systems may also be a means of limiting the qualitative and quantitative race in offensive systems, and thus can have advantages from an arms control point of view.

New developments in manned strategic aircraft probably will not affect the strategic balance between the United States and the Soviet Union in the 1970s, although some possibilities seem worth brief comment. Although it is hard to say for certain which way the technological competition might go *if the competition is pushed* by each side, it seems likely that strategic air defense systems can be made substantially more effective in the 1970s than has been the case in the 1950s and 1960s. Advances in detection techniques, especially airborne and other advanced radars useful against bombers traveling at low altitude, are likely. Interceptor aircraft and missiles will probably be improved at a similar pace. In favor of the offense, however, we may note recent developments in avionics, as exemplified by the sophisticated systems now in use in the F-111 and the possibilities embodied in a B-1 fitted with such missiles as SRAM. Air Force pilots who have flown F-111's are enthusiastic about its terrain avoidance capability for accurate bombing by radar. These avionics developments will probably be especially valuable in tactical warfare, where we think in terms of relatively short-range missions and attacks on targets heavily defended by anti-aircraft guns or missiles. However, even though advanced avionics may facilitate the penetration of bombers on strategic missions, the problem of high fuel consumption at low altitude will probably continue to limit the range of strategic bombers in the 1970s.

Except for possible developments in counter-insurgency warfare (see page 196), the role of CBW (chemical and biological weapons) is likely to remain limited by their "unfashionableness," their relative military ineffectiveness as controllable weapons, and the tacit mutual restraint which has limited their use since before World War II. At least this should be the case for the United States and the Soviet Union. However, chemical and biological weapons do offer one means by which a small power can cause a larger power concern. A small power could threaten to use CBW, which they may or may not in fact have. Probably this is one reason why President Nixon's unilateral disavowal of CBW by the United States explicitly excluded research in defensive applications.

Turning away from the area of strategic weapons—but still confining ourselves chiefly to U.S. and Soviet technology—the possibilities of very large transport aircraft deserve particular attention. Development of C-5 type aircraft (or "growth" versions thereof) by the United States and the Soviet Union in the 1970s may have military (and political) implications that are not yet fully recognized. One frequently mentioned and perhaps valid possibility is the prospect of substantially reducing the number of U.S. troops now stationed overseas, especially in Europe. Also, qualitatively new airlift capabilities make possible U.S. or Soviet intervention on a sizeable military scale in relatively remote parts of the world, and may thus afford a range of options for military action that U.S. planners are not yet considering sufficiently.

There is also another possibility worth noting: the use of very large aircraft might help to ensure not only the physical survival but also the *economic viability* of West Berlin, in a way that was not possible at the time of the 1948–49 Berlin land blockade. Although very large transport aircraft are a technological option available to either the United States or the Soviet Union in the seventies, the still relatively limited range of these aircraft (similar to present jet transports of the 707 class) means that the United States, with its relatively extensive complex of overseas bases, should have substantially greater worldwide troop deployment capabilities than the Soviet Union even if both sides had an equal number of similar large aircraft. Related to large transport airplanes are concepts such as the FDL (fast deployment logistic) ships. These could be built without major technological advances, although innovations in ship design could possibly result in striking performance improvements.

There probably will be significant improvements in strategic command and control systems in the 1970s. These improvements may be stimulated by greater sophistication in strategic thinking, particularly when it comes to the management of central nuclear wars. It seems fairly likely that both superpowers will recognize increasingly the need to be able to manage crises, and control and terminate wars—and that they will then make sure that they have the physical means for doing so. In addition to unilateral command and control systems, the superpowers may recognize a need for being able to communicate certain types of information to each other even while a central nuclear war is in progress. As a first step in this direction, we may note the often suggested possibility of "hardening the hot-line." This would be done more to increase survival from accidental or third-power attacks than from attacks by the United States or the Soviet Union.

Two technological areas which will probably take on growing military significance in the seventies are applications of satellites and lasers. Military satellites can, of course, be either manned or unmanned. The seventies could possibly see important military applications of manned satellites, although it is not yet clear exactly what these might be.* (It has been suggested in the aerospace press that manned satellites could be valuable in detecting and pinpointing ICBM and SLBM launchings.) Satellites seem certain to be used extensively and increasingly for military communications, navigation, tactical weather information, and surveillance. Other advanced space systems might also have important military implications.

The progress of laser technology since its invention in 1960 has been phenomenal. The development of laser systems for many diverse military applications will almost certainly be pushed energetically in the seventies. By the end of the seventies lasers will likely be playing a significant role in military (and perhaps commercial) communications. What other military applications of lasers may be possible depend on technical questions that are probably not yet resolved, such as the size, power, and the cost of laser systems of different types, optimum laser frequencies for different purposes, beam pointing and propagation, etc.

Laser rangefinders will be used extensively on tanks and on various kinds of aircraft and will be integrated into fire control systems. Laser designators have been successful in increasing the accuracy of gravity bombs in Vietnam, and one of the significant improvements in general purpose weapons will be the increased

---

* Most Western analysts do not see military applications for the present Soviet Salyud "space station" program, but second-generation systems might have more martial capabilities.

accuracy of air-delivered weapons made possible by the utilization of lasers and related electro-optical devices. The possibilities of using laser radiation weapons on aircraft and ground vehicles to defend against missiles, as well as the more remote possibility of laser BMD using aircraft or satellite basing, have greatly increased due to the steady upward trends of laser power and efficiency. It seems that the availability of laser weapons for use against land vehicles, ships, and even people ("death rays") depends largely upon commitment and the level of funding.

In the broad area of tactical weapons we may expect the United States and the Soviet Union to make continuing progress in the 1970s, although we do not foresee any developments that would revolutionize tactical combat. A very likely possibility is significant qualitative improvements in helicopters and V/STOL aircraft. We have seen the large impact of helicopters on the Vietnamese war and we may expect specialized helicopter developments (e.g., gunships) to continue. Hybrid aircraft types, involving features and advantages of both helicopters and fixed-wing aircraft, will introduce significant new tactical operational capabilities by at least the end of the seventies.

The Vietnam War focused attention on future developments in counter-insurgency warfare. Developments in the techniques and equipment of counter-insurgency will probably outpace progress in insurgency. Because of this, the capabilities of insurgents and terrorists—however effective, unpleasant, and currently difficult to counter—are not likely to improve very much, while capabilities for counter-insurgency are expected to steadily improve. Among the more specific technological improvements in counter-insurgency capabilities we may include *barrier technology* (means of detecting and/or preventing physical access to large and small areas), improved tactical aircraft including helicopters and V/STOL's, new techniques for identifying and keeping track of people (including the use of computers and sophisticated identification techniques—a particularly nasty form of technology which could help to create an electronic police state), and various kinds of sensor improvements. There may also be improvements in counter-insurgency tactics, both extremely advantageous in themselves and also developed to complement technological advances of the sort just mentioned.

But we should not overlook the possibility that insurgent groups may find it possible to obtain relatively sophisticated equipment—the "insurgents" in Vietnam, and reportedly in the Middle East, have large Soviet-built rockets—both to give themselves qualitatively new capabilities (including, for instance, helicopters for mobility) and to counter technologically advanced counter-insurgency techniques. From the counter-insurgent's point of view it will be more important to make sure that advanced equipment capable of being effectively used by unfriendly insurgents does not fall into the wrong hands. Increased security at depots, armories, and ranges will be necessary.

THE SPREAD OF MILITARY TECHNOLOGY

Fashion is important in weapons technology. Weapons which seem economically and technologically possible, and from an overall military standpoint perhaps most valuable to a country, may not be the weapons that the country chooses to build, buy, and deploy. The importance of weapon fashions is now a generally well-recognized phenomenon. The latest manifestation of this is the aspiration of a number of countries to build or obtain ballistic missiles, which certainly make more sense as showpieces for parades and propaganda and similar purposes than as cost/effective delivery systems—especially for countries that do not have nuclear warheads.

Some smaller but advanced countries may equal or surpass either of the superpowers in some areas of technology with military applications, even though they lack the economic resources to approach the superpowers' scale of military effort. Thus Sweden currently has a Mach 2 jet fighter that can operate effectively from a five-hundred-yard stretch of public highway. The British can claim world leadership in some areas of V/STOL aircraft and jet engine technology. British and French military aircraft (fighters at least) are as good as U.S. and Soviet machines. Although its military significance in the seventies is not so clear, the Anglo-French *Concorde* is the first Western supersonic transport (SST) plane to fly. (Even in the unlikely event that the American SST project should be resurrected in the early 1970s, it could not be operational before the 1980s.) Among many other things, we might note the current French leadership in some areas of high power laser technology.

There are one or two misconceptions about command and

control systems that many Americans seem to have accepted rather uncritically about the lesser powers. It is often assumed in connection with the nuclear proliferation issue that smaller countries with nuclear weapons will lack both the military sophistication and the technical means for controlling these weapons with skill and restraint. The notable example is, of course, China, so often labeled "irresponsible." On this score two points should be noted: (a) Propaganda notwithstanding, the Chinese Communists have on the whole practiced restraint in their military actions. (b) Since the Chinese have the technical capability to develop nuclear weapons—and at this point they may lead France in thermonuclear development—they can also develop very adequate command and control systems for these weapons, irrespective of delivery systems. Interpreting "command and control" broadly, we may note, for instance, the superb "surgical" skill of Israeli military operations. Even though many small countries may have nuclear and other advanced weapons, there is no reason to assume (almost a priori, as some Americans seem to do) that they will use these weapons irresponsibly or that they will lack the technical means for their control. But this is not to deny that the worldwide strategic situation may change greatly in the next ten to twenty years, or that we should seriously reckon with the possibility of irresponsible use of advanced weapons by "small" countries.

We must also consider the chance that other countries may not follow the military/technological fashions set by the United States and the Soviet Union. Weapons that are disadvantageous for the superpowers might, for various reasons, look more desirable to some smaller countries. For instance, chemical or biological weapons might be produced cheaply by a small country and used to threaten its neighbor or even the superpowers.

Many other weapon options are open to smaller countries in the seventies and eighties. Any country with nuclear weapons and a modest space program can put at least a small nuclear weapon into orbit. Any country with nuclear weapons can threaten to use (or actually use) them in a variety of ways—"suitcase" delivery, ships in port, etc. Also, any country that can make a thermonuclear weapon can, where size and weight do not matter, make weapons with enormous yields; and these weapons could be placed on the ocean floor, for instance, and used for "terror" or blackmail. A related possibility is that smaller countries may try to make up for deficiencies in vulnerability and perhaps in command and control by devising ways to hide its strategic capability so that it will be relatively safe from attack. A country could, if it chose, probably find ways to hide its strategic capabilities by siting nuclear weapons on the ocean floor or on a barge floating on a domestic river or lake, for instance. We can even conceive of hiding them outside of national territory. A "sneak" power might not reveal the existence of its capabilities until a crisis or when it wanted to confront other nations with a sudden and startling threat.

In the area of counter-insurgency warfare, many of the techniques and equipment available to the superpowers should also be available by the end of the seventies to many smaller countries. These countries might not be able to operate the equipment on the same *scale* as the superpowers but, as the United States has painfully learned in Vietnam, equipment or weapons used even on a very large scale (compare, for instance, the bomb tonnage used against the VC and North Vietnam with that used in the most intense bombing of Germany in World War II) do not necessarily solve the problems of counter-insurgency. Much effective counter-insurgency potential has already been exported, as the shattered would-be-Castroite guerrilla movements in Latin America have learned. Rural insurgency is looking more and more unpromising. Revolutionaries are turning to urban guerrilla warfare, where counter-insurgency techniques are less effective.

While it would be unpleasant if the smaller powers of the world gained more military technology, the world could easily live with more countries having jet fighters, tanks, short-range rockets, etc. But the spread of nuclear weapons is another matter. One of the worst nightmares of the late twentieth century is the vision of dozens of countries armed with thermonuclear weapons, so that the smallest war or the most rabid gangster dictator in the most insignificant mud-hut republic could unleash a nuclear holocaust. Actually, in terms of economic capability and technical availability, any country with competent physicists, a nuclear reactor, and willingness to invest a few tens of millions of dollars could obtain at least primitive nuclear arms. Some eight or ten countries have the potential, by perhaps 1980, of building

ICBMs with thermonuclear warheads that are technically as advanced as those of the United States and the Soviet Union today. Although the deployment of ICBMs by smaller but advanced countries may be limited by resources, it should be noted that the cost of weapon technologies drops with time. A nation as small as Israel could, by the 1980s, have some hundreds of Minuteman-type—or even more effective—missiles.

We have no guarantee that many countries are not already nuclearly armed. We know that all but five countries *say* they do not have nuclear arms, that most of them have signed the nuclear nonproliferation treaty, and that they have not exploded nuclear weapons. But that does not necessarily mean they do not have weapons. But let us assume that nations with untested, or practically completed weapons are not nuclearly armed. The following table illustrates one possible scenario for nuclear proliferation.

Scenario for Nuclear Proliferation

1945-1960: Five victors of World War II either initiated programs or achieved a blast
1960-1975: Gestation for proliferation to non-victors
1975-1985: Japan in the late seventies or early eighties, West Germany about five years later soon followed by Italy; other possibilities are India, Australia, Sweden, and Switzerland

Another scenario, a "worst-case" scenario, is possible if the United States should, as many articulate commentators and politicians have advocated, adopt something resembling a neo-isolationist position and largely withdraw from the world, including a withdrawal of the U.S. nuclear "umbrella" over the free world. One of the major costs of the United States giving up the role of world policeman is that the areas that it was policing must then begin to police themselves, and because they will feel "naked" against nuclear threat, they may see a necessity to obtain similar equipment for their national "police." A U.S. withdrawal from Asia could provoke Japanese nuclear rearmament and/or a Japanese alliance with one or the other of the Communist powers. If the United States withdrew from the Middle East, Israel would certainly prepare itself for the contingency of a Soviet nuclear threat in support of the Arabs. And if Israel acquired nuclear weapons, Egypt would feel obliged to follow. The same can be said for India and Pakistan. It is very unlikely that the United State would withdraw its so-called nuclear umbrella from Latin America, but if it should, Argentina or Brazil would likely arm nuclearly. If one of them arms, the other will almost certainly follow suit both for self-protection and for purposes of national prestige (unfortunately, nuclear weapons carry an awful lot of prestige in the political world) and Mexico could follow for the same reason. A very similar situation exists in regard to Africa, where the South African Republic might feel itself subject to Soviet or Chinese threats in support of the black African governments and liberation movements. A U.S. withdrawal from Europe could lead to similar problems except that there are already nuclear forces in existence which could provide something resembling a cover. However, if Sweden did not wish to be involved in general European security or if for some reason it did not trust or place reliance upon a credibility of support by France and/or the United Kingdom, it might obtain its own nuclear weapons. The same is possibly more true of West Germany, and the Soviet Union's fear of Germany's rearmament is stark. Similar factors apply on the other side of the Iron Curtain as well, if the Soviets should (and we recognize this is extremely unlikely, if not impossible) withdraw their cover from Eastern Europe, Poland might obtain weapons to protect itself from Germany. As stated before, this is a "worst case" scenario and we expect that consideration of it will go a long way toward preventing it from occurring. Faced with these possibilities we would think that most decent Americans would want to carefully consider how much U.S. influence it is safe to withdraw from the rest of the world. Being a world policeman is a dirty and unrewarding task, but it is probably less intolerable than living in a world bristling with nuclear powers.

POSSIBILITIES FOR THE 1980s

The discussion of military/technological possibilities for the 1980s is brief, partly because we can speak with much less specificity and confidence than for the 1970s. Events in the decade of the seventies could force the United States, the Soviet Union, or other countries to develop new strategic offensive options. Some of these options would be clearly possible in the seventies, although they now seem unnecessary or too costly for consideration. The siting of strategic missiles on the ocean floor is one of these options. Another is very large nuclear weapons in orbit. For instance, rockets with thrusts on the order of Saturn V (7.5 million pounds) or even substantially smaller rockets could place into low earth orbit satellites carrying nuclear warheads with yields of perhaps one thousand megatons (or one gigaton). Such weapons, detonated at altitudes in the vicinity of one hundred miles, could effectively destroy unprotected people and property over tens of thousands of square miles. (The deployment of orbital weapons would of course violate the present treaty banning weapons of mass destruction in space.) We cannot rule out the possibility that, by the decade of the 1980s (or any time, for that matter) pure fusion nuclear weapons may have been developed. This means, of course, that some technique will have been found to eliminate the fission trigger with U-235 or plutonium, upon which all known fusion weapons presently depend. If this were to be achieved by a method that did not require expensive materials and techniques, especially if it did not entail expensive capital plant, it would radically alter the prospects for nuclear proliferation.

In the eighties, there may be means for the development, deployment, and possible use of chemical and biological weapons. It is theoretically possible to develop chemical and biological agents that are controllable, both in their geographic dissemination and in the nature and seriousness of their effects on people.

Ballistic missile defense may also have new possibilities even though, as noted earlier in this chapter, we do not care to predict in the long run which way the offensive-defensive technological missile competition may go. New BMD possibilities include: (1) Currently existing possibilities which now seem unsatisfactory from a cost/effectiveness standpoint, such as space-based interceptors, but which might become more attractive because of technological advances; (2) entirely new BMD possibilities that depend on new discoveries in basic knowledge.

One item perhaps worth investigation is the possibility for the implications of nuclear-powered aircraft. The apparent success of very large aircraft of the C-5 type means that we now *know* that aircraft large enough to carry nuclear reactors can be successfully built and flown. This was not the case until recently, and it was certainly not the case in the late forties and the fifties when nuclear aircraft engine development was receiving quite substantial funding. Given reasonable estimates about the rate at which necessary parallel developments might occur, nuclear-powered aircraft are not likely to be flying, at least in any signifi cant numbers, until the 1980s. But such aircraft would open up several interesting possibilities. They could fly indefinitely as mobile missile launchers, approximately as Polaris submarines cruise now. The present limitation on the low altitude penetration capability of strategic aircraft would be entirely removed (although there might, of course, be good reasons for preferring to use other types of delivery vehicles). Nuclear power might permit the development of truly enormous aircraft—by present standards—with weight in the ranges of thousands or tens of thousands of tons, and these in turn would permit extremely low ton-mile costs for transportation of military and other materials. Presumably, nuclear-powered planes would have speeds similar to those of present jets. So we could think of such planes as having the weight-carrying capacities of ships and the speed of present jets and unlimited range; this would present revolutionary possibilities for the rapid worldwide deployment of armed forces and equipment, not to mention commercial potentials.

However, even though such aircraft are technically possible, we doubt if they could get funding in time to be operational in the early eighties. This raises a very important issue in military and other forms of technological forecasting that is now coming to the fore. Previously, forecasters were mainly concerned with technology more or less independent of the rest of society, and then with the effects of *technology* on *society*. In the milieu of the 70s, the principal issue is the impact of *society* on *technology*. The disillusion with progress could have seriously inhibiting effects on technological development. (Military technology has some other obvious problems in a hostile milieu.) The scrubbing of the American SST by the Congress demonstrates there is no longer a necessary correlation between technological potential and technological advance. An excellent case can be made that the advanced materials, improved propulsion systems, and other advanced technology necessary for the B-1 are now within reach, and that achievement of the B-1 will further advance aerospace technology; but the real issues which will determine whether or not the B-1 flies are political, economic, and even social, but not technological.

Some knowledgeable members of the defense community have recently stated that the Soviet Union is spending significantly more money on military research and development (R&D) than the United States (eleven billion dollars to eight billion dollars). It is argued that the continuation of present trends in R&D expenditures will increase the vulnerability of the United States to "technological surprise" and will constitute an irrevocable loss of technological superiority. Clearly the entire process of threat assessment related to military technologies and the associated interpretation of intelligence data is quite difficult and highly controversial. The evaluation of relative R&D spending depends on how one measures Soviet R&D expenditures relative to American. The R&D gap is an important issue for the early 1970s. Whether or not this turns out to be a spurious issue—as did the bomber gap of 1955 and the ICBM gap of 1960—will be determined as new Soviet prototypes of advanced weapon systems appear and are evaluated.

Contemplating the decade of the eighties, one can think of many kinds of R&D results with both non-military and military implications. Thus for instance: Control of the geophysical environment by various means could bring great benefits to mankind, and also revolutionary weapon possibilities, perhaps even hand-held laser "blasters." Pharmacology could improve the ability of soldiers and others to maintain peak performance for long periods, enhance learning ability, etc.; or lead to the effective "weaponization" of mind-influencing drugs. Advances in the behavioral sciences could lead to solutions of cross-cultural problems, and importantly affect political-military relationships. Developments in sensors, computers, control systems, power supplies, transmissions, etc., could lead to diverse types of "automata" capable of doing many tasks now performed only by humans. The list of possibilities is virtually endless.

The very enormity of these possibilities suggests the need for a technological approach to arms control. A very good case can be made for arms limitation through constraints on offensive and emphasis on defensive systems.*

* See J. J. Holst and W. Schneider (eds.), *Why ABM?* (1969).

VIII

The 1985 Technological Crisis—The Social Effects of Technology

A favorite subject of forecasters is the effect of technology on society. Certainly this is an understandable result of the technical education and background of so many forecasters. A glance at world history, particularly within the last 150 years, provides beautiful examples illustrating the importance of technology in promoting social change. In individual cases the impact of technology may be exaggerated; however, forecasting of this type frequently does not go far enough. Let us take the example of the social impact of the introduction of the privately owned motor vehicle at the turn of the century. A perceptive forecaster writing in 1900 might have forecast the demise of the horse and the vast networks of highways, gas stations, and garages which have spread across the nation. If he had watched the living patterns of the rich, he might have picked up the inevitability of suburbanization. And if he had been very good, he might have seen the immense effect upon the lives of people in previously isolated rural areas of the country when they were brought within easy reach of the cities. But would he have guessed at the revolutionary effect the automobile had upon the courting and sexual habits of young America?

More fundamental basic changes also may elude the forecaster if his analysis is not sufficiently wide in scope. As an exemplar, we will present our concept of the 1985 technological crisis in which we hope to demonstrate that technological advance, particularly cumulative technological advance, is likely to begin undermining value belief that has been fundamental in Western society for the last three hundred years—the idea of progress.

In popular usage, the justification, "Well, that's progress," has long been a virtually unanswerable argument. Since the Renaissance, and most strongly since the nineteenth century, progress has been seen as desirable, inevitable, and beneficial. This notion of progress has been very closely tied up with a view of technological and material progress. It was assumed that the world would be better off with better and more technology and machines and that there would be a forward movement of mankind based upon science, technology, and material improvement. But, in the United States the class that has historically been most committed to progress (the upper-middle classes and especially their children) is becoming disillusioned with technological and even economic progress to a growing degree. Advancing technology and economic growth, once thought of as desirable goals and signs of achievement, are coming to be regarded as villains. In the past the attack on progress has generally come from conservatives and reactionaries interested in preserving feudal, heroic, religious, or humanist relationships and values. Some who have joined in the revolt against progress have adopted such perspectives; but the basis of the current attack arises directly from negative reactions to modern technological change and economic growth. Partially because of social factors, but also because of the very real problems that have been raised by the accumulation of modern technology, many no longer see science and technology as basically beneficial.

Today, most people would to some extent agree that the blessings of progress are not unmixed. For example, the development of short-cuts to gratification has caused a partial but increasing loss of meaning of many traditional activities. Traditionally men spent most of their time at means rather than ends. They needed to eat, so they were forced to spend twelve hours a day laboring in the fields. They wished spiritual salvation, so they had to travel thousands of miles on pilgrimages. They wished entertainment, so they laboriously had to teach themselves to sing and dance.

But modern industrial society permits us to obtain these ends with very little effort. We do not work so hard; medical advances have made our continued survival more predictable, and make us less reliant on the solaces of religion; we can have entertainment by turning a knob in our living room. We seem to be having some trouble adjusting to this situation. Many people do not like it and even though few of them would really like to return to previous conditions, there is a good deal of verbal nostalgia for this return.

Another consequence of technological and material progress is that we have created some things we would simply prefer not to have. An obvious example is the accumulation, augmentation, and proliferation of weapons of mass destruction. Very few people would argue that the progress represented by the atomic bomb was a good thing for the human race.

Furthermore, advances that seemed (and were) beneficial and/or necessary at the time have often had pernicious side-effects. For example, better methods of communication are also potential methods of surveillance and manipulation. Consider the relative power of a modern, "constitutional," "liberal" president such as Richard Nixon with that of a traditional "absolutist," "tryrannical" ruler such as Louis XIV. Louis, the history books tell us, was an "absolute" monarch; that is, he could do pretty much as he pleased with any of the persons or property in his realm. But how much could he do before there was the telephone, radio, teletype, typewriter, and computer? His "absolute" power did not extend beyond the persons in immediate contact with him. As you receded down the political hierarchy from the king, his power was diminished. He could not keep sufficient records to keep track of people. He had difficulty in collecting taxes. In the provinces, his writ hardly ran at all. Furthermore, he could not address his subjects directly, nor manipulate public opinion, save through the pulpit. On the other hand, Nixon can lift a telephone and within a few minutes find out about any American, where they are, who they work for, what they do, how much they make, how much they have, how much they owe, what kind of vehicles they have, where they have traveled, and, within a few days, if he pleases, he can find out who they sleep with, who their friends are, what are their personal tastes in books, furniture, and anything else. Nixon can speak directly to everyone in the country and has the technical potential at least to try to control public opinion. The fact that Nixon does not exploit all these potential powers lies in his own convictions that he ought not to, as well as those of the nation which does not permit him to do so; but this is not up to the individual citizen.

All we are saying, perhaps, is that technology can be put to bad as well as good use; but as technology becomes more and more advanced its pernicious ramifications may become more and more pronounced and may come to outweigh the benefits. Many who remain strongly committed to technical and material advance think that objections to progress are fuzzy-minded, wrong-headed, and/or reactionary. This may be true in some cases, but not uniformly. The charts on pages 210-213 list some possibilities that could be achieved by the end of the century, and some are likely to occur. They are not "far-out" science fiction.

Furthermore, it is not just a matter of advancing technology itself being troublesome. Advanced technology can force us into increasingly undesirable moral dilemmas. Take, for example, an immediate problem which may arise from the combination of our increasing propensity to use social engineering and technological advances: despite the opposition to abortion by most Americans, "enlightened" public opinion favors permitting easy abortions on the grounds that "a woman has an absolute right to do as she pleases with her body." As a result legislatures and courts, perhaps more sensitive to the moral values of "the classes" than "the masses," have been easing abortion laws. But to our knowledge, no one involved in the abortion debate has volunteered the information that Israeli scientists claim to be on the verge of being able to identify the sex of fetuses very soon after conception. Now it is easily discovered by polling or casual conversation that more people prefer boy babies than girl babies, at least for the first child. This preference plus early sex identification plus abortion on demand may give us a substantial disparity of boys over girls in a generation. What will this do to society? Will we have widespread homosexuality or matriarchy or polyandry or perhaps collective property in women, or will we have some complex means of regulating who can abort what and when? Many people would rather not have to deal with such questions.

Or consider an only slightly more bizarre case. In the late 1950s a study was done with rats. The pleasure center of a rat's brain was located and wired to a stimulator which was activated by a lever that the rat could operate. The rat was given the choice of the stimulator lever, or similar levers which would provide him with water, food, sex, or rest. Some six thousand times an hour the rat pressed the pleasure lever and ignored the others. If the rat had to suffer an electric shock when he pressed the pleasure lever, he would endure an unbelievably heavy shock before stopping. But if the rat was forced to take food, water, and rest, he would lead a longer, and as far as we can tell, happier and healthier life.

Scientists believe that human beings have many more pleasure centers than rats—perhaps ten. Imagine a human being with his pleasure centers wired to a console fitted on his chest: just begin to think of the moral questions this would raise. Would it be necessary to be married to play the console of a member of the opposite sex? Would playing the console of a member of the same sex constitute homosexuality? Perhaps society would agree that any two consenting adults could play each other's consoles, but this might risk perversion: "Have you ever tried one and five together?" If you were really "square," you would be disgusted by the idea of playing your own console. We don't know if this will occur, but with "advances" in drugs, electronics, and genetics research, people may well be presented with extremely complicated moral problems and dilemmas.*

It is not necessary to be a "hippie" or a hysterical academic to recognize that our much-vaunted technological advance may soon lead us to disaster. Remember Faust's bargain with the

* Some of these issues are discussed in Herman Kahn and Anthony J. Wiener, "Faustian Powers and Human Choices," in William P. Ewald, Jr., ed., *Environment and Change: The Next Fifty Years* (Bloomington, 1968). A forthcoming book by Wiener will probe these issues in depth.

Disillusionment with Progress

Some Mixed Blessings of Progress

1. Defunctionalization—partial (but increasing) loss of meaning of many traditional activities through the development of shortcuts to gratification: erosion of "traditional societal levers"
2. Accumulation, augmentation, and proliferation of weapons of mass destruction
3. Loss of privacy and solitude
4. Increase of governmental and/or private power over individuals
5. Loss of human scale and perspective
6. Dehumanization of social life or even of the psychobiological self
7. Growth of dangerously vulnerable, deceptive, or degradable centralization of administrative or technological systems
8. Creation of other new capabilities so inherently dangerous as seriously to risk disastrous abuse
9. Acceleration of changes that are too rapid or cataclysmic to permit successful adjustment
10. Posing of choices that are too large, complex, important, uncertain, or comprehensive to be safely left to fallible humans

Some Aspects of Privacy Threatened by Technology

1. Right to idiosyncratic
   A. Thoughts
   B. Utterances
   C. Values
   D. Way of life
   E. Style and manners
   F. Methods of self-expression
2. Isolation or protection from:
   A. Selected aspects of the physical environment
   B. Selected aspects of the social environment
   C. Many pressures and/or other intrusions by individuals, organized private groups and businesses, and political and governmental organizations
3. Right to:
   A. Withhold information
   B. Make many family and personal decisions
   C. *Be oneself*
4. Enough elbow room:
   A. To be unobserved occasionally
   B. For aesthetic purposes
   C. To get things done
   D. *As a value in its own right*

Some Conceivable Weapons Possibilities

1. New kinds of nuclear weapons
2. Various kinds of laser and other "death rays"
3. A menu of chemical and/or biological weapons
4. New kinds of ballistic missile defense particularly effective against relatively small offense forces or against forces which use unsophisticated technology and/or tactics
5. Similar developments for air defense against airborne threats
6. Well-understood doomsday machines (or near-doomsday machines)
7. Tsunami (tidal wave) producers
8. Climate changers, earth scorchers, or other ways to modify or damage the environment on a large scale
9. Psychological, or even direct mental warfare
10. "Nuclear six-gun" technology—cheap and widely available nuclear weapons of mass destruction
11. Others even "better"

By 1985 the Following Areas Are Likely to Give Rise to Special Technological Dangers:

1. Intrinsically dangerous technology
2. Gradual and/or national contamination or degradation of the environment
3. Spectacular and/or multinational contamination or degradation of the environment
4. Dangerous internal political issues
5. Upsetting international consequences
6. Dangerous personal choices
7. Bizarre issues

Intrinsically Dangerous Technology

1. Modern means of mass destruction
2. Nuclear reactors—fission or fusion
3. Nuclear explosives, high-speed gas centrifuges, etc.
4. Research missiles, satellite launchers, commercial aircraft, etc.
5. Biological and chemical "progress"
6. Molecular biology and genetics
7. "Mind control"
8. New techniques for insurgency, criminality, or ordinary violence
9. New techniques for counter-insurgency or imposition of order
10. New "serendipities" and synergisms

Gradual and/or National Contamination or Degradation of the Environment

1. Radioactive debris from various peaceful nuclear uses
2. Possible greenhouse or other effects from increased CO_2 in the atmosphere
3. Waste heat
4. Other special wastes
5. Other wastes, debris, and just plain garbage
6. Noise, ugliness, etc., associated with many modern activities
7. Excessive urbanization
8. Excessive overcrowding
9. Excessive tourism
10. Insecticides, fertilizers, growth "chemicals," food additives, etc.

Spectacular and/or Multinational Contamination or Degradation of the Environment

1. Nuclear war
2. Nuclear testing
3. Bacteriological and chemical war or accident
4. Artificial moons
5. Projects West Ford, Storm Fury, etc.
6. Supersonic transportation (shock waves)
7. Weather control
8. Big "geomorphological" projects
9. Million-ton tankers (*Torrey Canyon* was only 111,825 tons) and million-pound planes
10. Other enterprise or mechanism of "excessive" size

Dangerous Internal Political Issues

1. Computerized records
2. Other computerized surveillance
3. Other advanced techniques for surveillance
4. Excessively degradable (or unreliably reassuring) centralized capabilities
5. Improved knowledge of and techniques for agit-prop and other means of creating disturbances
6. Improved knowledge of and techniques for preventing disturbances
7. Complex or critical governmental issues leading to either "technocracy" or "Caesarism"
8. Nuclear weapons affecting internal politics
9. Excessively illusioned attitudes
10. Other dangerous attitudes

Upsetting International Consequences

1. Both new and "traditional" demonstration effects
2. Technological obsolescence of "unskilled" labor
3. New synthetics—e.g., coffee, oil, etc.
4. Forced modernization
5. Growing guilt feelings by many in wealthy nations—particularly among the alienated or young
6. Inexpensive and widely available "realistic" communications and physical travel
7. Accelerated "brain drains"
8. Cheap (synthetic?) food
9. Cheap education
10. Control and exploitation of the oceans, space, moon, and even the planets

Dangerous Personal Choices

1. Sex determination
2. Other genetic engineering
3. Psychedelic and mood-affecting drugs
4. Electronic stimulation of pleasure centers
5. Other methods of sensual satisfaction
6. Excessive permissiveness and indulgence
7. Dropping out and other alienation
8. Excessive narcissism or other self-regard
9. Super-cosmetology
10. Lengthy hibernation

Bizarre Issues

1. Generational changes; e.g., extended longevity
2. Mechanically dependent humans; e.g., pacemakers, diabetics
3. Life and death for the individual; e.g., artificial kidneys, etc.
4. New forms of humanity; e.g., "live" computers
5. "Forcible" birth control for "impossible" groups or nations
6. Other external controls or influence on what should be a personal or even institutionally private choice
7. Life and death or other control of "outlaw" societies which, however, have not yet committed any traditional crime
8. Even the continuation of the nation-state system
9. Controlling and limiting change and innovation
10. Radical ecological changes on a planetary scale
11. Interplanetary contamination

Devil—worldly knowledge and power in return for ultimate damnation? Satan may soon collect. On the other hand, it is also worth remembering that Faust got into trouble only when he tried to stop the process—to halt further progress because he was satisfied (or satiated).

Like Faust, those people who today have two cars, a dishwasher, a washing machine, and so on—who are satisfied or even satiated—are those who are most upset about the need to reduce consumption, to protect the environment, to preserve living space, and so on. Most still wish to enjoy material progress, value such progress greatly, and will fight to get it. In effect, only people who have grown up with the fruits of material progress and have never seen serious deprivation are arguing for some equivalent of asceticism. However, those who have not yet achieved material goals may be overvaluing what they are missing.

A negative attitude toward further technological progress and economic growth may well become increasingly relevant and forceful as our society becomes post-industrial. We may come to see—some already see—our situation as similar to what appears many times in nature when the limiting factor to further growth is pollution, the problem of getting rid of waste products. This is what limits the size of a colony of bacteria on a nutrient surface—not the availability of air, food, or space. It can be argued that our situation is similar, that Western capitalist industrial growth in technological and economic terms is limited by its unavoidable waste products. A respectable case can be made that the threat of catastrophe is real enough so that we must control and limit technology even at the cost of progress and growth.

We reject this position (and think most people will) at least for the next ten to twenty years. Technological growth and economic progress will be able to make the rest of the world rich; and with advancements in technology itself along with self-restraint, proper policies and designs, and the allocation of sufficient resources (mostly money), we will be able to cope with problems of pollution. Technology can often solve its problems. We can deal with electronic bugging only with electronic devices to detect and/or nullify bugging devices. Some forms of technology are needed just to cancel each other out—if there are new techniques for insurgency, criminality, or ordinary violence, we need new techniques for counter-insurgency or imposition of order. Other "mixed blessings" of progress may demand or seem to demand fundamental changes in attitude and action, and the argument that, in a post-industrial society, we no longer need nor can tolerate unbridled technological and even economic "progress" may become increasingly relevant and, in fact, restraining in the long run.

A turning away from progress and growth has been heralded for a long time, but it was only when the issues listed above became really critical that it became a strong movement—perhaps the strongest and most successful movement of the last decade. These issues can be grouped under the rubric "1985 technological crisis."

To our knowledge, the initial identification of the 1985 technological crisis was by the great Hungarian-American mathematician John von Neumann in an article in *Fortune* Magazine in the mid-1950s.*

> The great globe itself is in a rapidly maturing crisis—a crisis attributable to the fact that the environment in which technological progress must occur has become both undersized and underorganized . . .
>
> In the first half of this century . . . this safety . . . was essentially a matter of geographical and political *Lebensraum*: an ever broader geographical scope for technological activities, combined with an even broader political integration of the world. Within this expanding framework it was possible to accommodate the major tensions created by technological progress.
>
> Now this safety mechanism is being sharply inhibited; literally and figuratively, we are running out of room. At long last, we begin to feel the effects of the finite, actual size of the earth in a critical way.
>
> Thus the crisis does not arise from accidental events or human errors. It is inherent in technology's relation to geography on the one hand and to political organization on the other . . . in the years between now and 1980 the crisis will probably develop far beyond all earlier patterns. When or how it will end—or to what state of affairs it will yield—nobody can say.

* "Can We Survive Technology?" by John von Newmann, in *Fortune,* June, 1955.

Von Neumann suggested 1980 as the year in which we will really have to face the effects of the finite size of the earth in a critical way. We take this to mean a decade or two of crises—starting in the seventies, but really culminating in the eighties—and use the phrase "1985 technological crisis" to include issues other than simply those involving the finite size of the earth. As we look over this list of relatively imminent technological dangers it is hard to believe that mankind will cope successfully with all of them, though he might. Many, of course, may prove to be non-problems or non-issues. But nothing has happened since 1955 to challenge von Neumann's basic assertion—indeed most events have made his basic conjecture more likely and more deadly.

"1985 technological crisis" covers many issues, some of which are fairly self-explanatory, some of which are now receiving much publicity. But three points should be made about this crisis as a whole:

1. We are faced with the spectre of many different technologies breaking down or developing out of our control almost simultaneously.

2. Many of the crises are simply bigger than those of the past.

3. Due to the fact that both pollution and technology tend to grow exponentially, we often do not know about the problems until they are already critical, and have little time left to deal with them.

Let us present perhaps the most alarmist possible view of the first point (but one that is now believed by many). Imagine you were building a Hollywood film set, and wanted it to last until 1980. Someone points out that the paint will have cracked by 1978. So you use a better paint. Another critic points out that the concrete may begin to crumble, so more reinforcing rod and more cement and less sand is used. But he also points out that the plumbing will wear out in 1982 and the electrical wiring is going to wear out in 1988. This does not bother you; the set will be abandoned in 1980. In some ways the world today looks like that kind of Hollywood set, designed—or at least currently operated—to be abandoned at some point in the early eighties.

While we would not accept this formulation as a wholly accurate estimate of current practices, a case can be made that things are simply going to fall apart and there is a similar but different threat that we will lose control of technological progress and application. And the two possibilities are not mutually exclusive. In any case, it seems highly likely that some of the technologically threatening issues listed, if not corrected soon, will come to dominate some aspects of our lives and endeavors during the next two or three decades.

Furthermore, many of the threats (e.g., the "greenhouse effect," or a general cooling of the earth's temperature) are worldwide. Historically, most predictions of worldwide disaster have not been validated by events; but although this will continue to be true for many threats of the 1985 technological crisis, there may be a definite change in the underlying situation. Hence, the typical—and to some degree justifiable—apocalyptic language.

Not only may some of these issues be worldwide; we may have very little time to correct them. Assume, for example, that some reservoir—think of a bathtub—is filling with a pollutant at a constant rate; at some point the bathtub will run over—that is, there will be a disaster. Let us also assume that people pay effective attention to the problem when they notice that the reservoir is ten percent filled. At that point almost all the interested parties can see—or have to concede—that there is a problem. Assume that this reservoir (or bathtub) took one year to become ten percent filled. Since it will take ten years in all to fill, nine years are now left to fix the problem. That is a lot of time. But if the same reservoir were filled by some kind of an exponential process in which there was an e-folding rate* of one year to fill it to ten percent, then only 2.3 years are left before the reservoir will be totally filled. This property of exponentials—that by the time you notice that you are in trouble you often have very little time left—can prove disastrous; for it is often too late to react adequately. This is one reason for the current concentration on pollution issues. When President Nixon said in 1971 that we have a

---

* An exponential process is one which proceeds at a rate proportional to the accumulated total of the past. An e-folding time corresponds to the length of time it takes to accumulate 2.72 times as much as some original amount. An annual growth rate of 10 percent corresponds to an e-folding time of slightly more than a decade, 5 percent to two decades, and 20 percent to 5.5 years.

decade to fix these problems or it would be too late, he was not employing empty rhetoric. He was probably quoting from a report by the President's Science Advisory Committee or other expert and responsible groups which today often use this kind of language in describing the problem. Many of the processes which trouble us today are exponential processes with e-folding times of from two to twenty years.

Partly for the above reasons, everyone today is against pollution; environmentalism has become almost a religious issue. But the issue has a special radiance for the political left. In the past the left often talked about the "increasing misery of the masses," arguing the false or illusionary character of the seeming success of society in general and the benefits of modern affluence and technology in particular. In the middle and late twentieth century it has been increasingly difficult to make this position convincing. Clearly, the "masses" have been prospering under "capitalist exploitation" and loving it. But thanks to the pollution issue, the left, rather than talk about the affluent society, now talks about the *effluent* society; rather than talk about gross national product the left now talks about gross national *pollution*. As a result, a man of the left can argue that all this marvelous technology, all this unbelievable affluence created by industrialism and capitalism, has been unmasked at last: "bourgeois" progress has proven to be only a complicated way to produce garbage, to destroy the ecology and landscape, and to dehumanize the individual. The "internal contradictions of capitalism" are finally clear to all. Thus the negative picture of technical and industrial progress held by much of the left, especially by today's new left, is regarded as having been validated and vindicated.

In the past, ecology was the concern of conservative (Carlyle) and revolutionary (the younger Marx) romantics who were not overly fond of industrial society; in the United States in the sixties, it was a major concern of the counterculture before being co-opted by everyone else. Many of the critics who first became very concerned about the pollution issue a few years ago regarded it as yet another count in their indictment of and attack on modern industrial society. But what was seen originally by one radical as "a piece of the revolutionary puzzle" now seems to be accepted by society as a whole. Traditionalist Americans, particularly the hunters, outdoorsmen, and the like, tend to have an almost mystic interest in preserving historic America—including the woods, the streams, the beaches, unspoiled wilderness areas, and the like. And almost everybody would like to breathe clean air, drink clear water, and have comfortable and good-looking recreation areas readily available, as well as living space, elbow room, and privacy in normal everyday life.

The widespread adoption of the environmental issue is an interesting and important development. Society as a whole seems to be embracing an issue that has been in the past part of a broad anti-bourgeois, anti-industrial platform. The rise of a strong concern about pollution does not mean that everyone is rejecting industrialism; but everyone is not accepting it as automatically or wholeheartedly as before. This is not necessarily bad, but it does represent a big change.

The pollution issue represents only one of the possible 1985 technological crises, all of which can potentially be serious, not to say crucial. And our handling of the pollution issue represents an important change, or at least modification, of our traditional attitude toward material progress and technology, and perhaps toward modern industrial society itself. Dealing with some of the other prospective 1985 technological crises may similarly lead to or accelerate important changes in our attitudes and values.

A very strong case, for example, can be made for the creation of an "index" of forbidden knowledge, either imposed by some national or international institutional authority (like the lists of morally dangerous works issued by the Roman Catholic hierarchy), by scientists themselves operating under a code of ethics, or by some religious or quasi-religious movement simply making such research immoral. In any event there would likely be "underground" science like medieval alchemy or today's illicit drug laboratories, manned by inquisitive and dedicated men and women who think Faust made a good bargain.

IX

The Emerging Post-
Industrial Society–
Evolutionary and
Revolutionary Change

ONE of the fundamental issues facing people who are concerned
with long-term historical trends, past and future, is the question
of continuity and discontinuity. A common argument among historians goes something like this: Professor A will state that there
was a "revolution" of some sort or another at a certain time in a
certain place. Professor B will examine the period immediately
preceding the period when the revolution was said to have occurred, and will find most of the "new" elements of the revolutionary era present under the "old" regime. Then the professors
(and their disciples) will argue for some time whether or not
there was a real revolution, a qualitative change. A classic example of such a dispute can be seen in Tocqueville's criticism of
the theory that the French Revolution created a unified French
national state. According to this analysis, the ancien regime fea-

tured the same tendencies toward centralization of governmental power, and increased bureaucratic control along with many of the other "revolutionary" aspects of 1789–1799. This is more than a semantic quibble; it is a question of how fundamental changes occur, and how we recognize and identify them. "Is there anything whereof it can be said, 'See, this is new?'"

Although in most cases evolutionary development is a more accurate picture of the real movement of human history, we do recognize that changes are sometimes so rapid and cumulative as to be revolutionary, creating a new stage, a whole new ball game. Karl Marx's theory of history was based upon five distinct stages which were fundamentally and clearly different in their basic economic organization and superstructure of values, institutions, ideology, and culture. We do not accept Marxist analysis as a whole, although we think he was probably justified in calling primary attention to the fundamental difference between industrial "bourgeois" and agrarian "feudal" societies. It is worth noting that many commentators, even scholars, who today claim that Marx's system was crude, implausible, and oversimplified, often accept an even simpler system when they contrast modern, urban, industrial, mechanical civilization with traditional, agrarian, pre-industrial society, under which they group three of Marx's historical stages. The question of where you draw the line, where the thresholds between fundamentally different societies are, is difficult and important. Sometimes a mere difference in quantity constitutes a fundamental difference in quality.

Many writers today conjecture that we may be going through a period of transition, or stepping over a threshold, as vital and important in world history as the breakthrough of Europe in the eighteenth and nineteenth centuries when it moved from a feudal to a bourgeois civilization. A change from our industrial system to a post-industrial system may have as fundamental and profound effects upon the world as the change from feudalism to industrialism. This revolutionary change may affect the world, our way of looking at the world, and the way we live as much as any other breakthrough in all human history.

To drive this point home, we sometimes joke that in all of human history, all million years of it, only two events seem worth really serious note—the Agricultural Revolution and the Industrial Revolution. (Religious people might add a third event, but would not agree on what it is.*) The chart below displays a widely accepted scheme of world history.

The first important event, the Agricultural Revolution, created civilization and a new way of life. For every twenty people on the farm you had a man in the city—and therefore civilization

THE ECONOMIC DEVELOPMENT OF MANKIND

HUNTING AND GATHERING SOCIETY
(Pre-Agricultural)
Approximately $50 per capita income per annum

C. 8000 BC ——————— Agricultural Revolution ——————————

AGRICULTURAL SOCIETY
(Pre-industrial and usually "civilized")
$50-500 per capita income per annum

C. 1800 AD ——————— Industrial Revolution ——————————

INDUSTRIAL SOCIETY
(or "Modern")
$500-5,000 per capita income per annum

C. 2000 AD ——————— ?   ? ——————————

POST-INDUSTRIAL SOCIETY
$5,000-50,000 (or more?) per capita income
per annum

—for civilization means civic culture, living in cities. This did not significantly increase the per capita income. The next revolution, the Industrial Revolution—which began about two hundred years ago—changed per capita income. The British learned the trick of enlarging their population by two percent a year and their productivity by about two percent a year per capita, and that was the wonder of the age.

If projections of continued economic growth in industrial

---

* One of us is certain this third event was the Covenant of G-d with Abraham; the other is equally sure it was the fulfillment of that Covenant by the Incarnation of Jesus Christ.

societies are achieved, by the end of the century there will be another order of magnitude change in per capita income. Will this have the same fundamental effects as did the Agricultural Revolution and the Industrial Revolution? And if so, what can we do to prepare for it?

The difficulty of speculating about a society built upon an economy of $5,000–$50,000 per capita income is suggested by our adoption of the sociologist Bell's term *post-industrial society.** No one would call Babylon or Ming China a post-hunting society; and to call today's Western world post-agricultural would be equally absurd. We do not know what the identifying activity of a society after industrial society will be, but there have been some fascinating speculations.

A POST-MANUFACTURING ECONOMY?

Already in the industrial West we are seeing a topping out of the growth of that portion of the economy devoted to manufacturing, historically the principal activity of industrial society (indeed, when we say industry we usually mean manufacturing). It seems safe to project that the industrial activities that have dominated the economy for the past two hundred years will play an ever decreasing role. This does not imply that industry will decline in real terms (although it might) and it certainly does not imply that industry will not play a vital role in the society. The argument is that industry, that is, secondary industry (manufacturing) and its direct services will go the way of primary industry (farming, fishing, and mining) and its direct services. Instead of having ninety-five percent of the labor force engaged in primary industries, in the United States today less than five percent manage to do these things for us. A similar shift from secondary to "tertiary industries" (services) is taking place today. We know of no one who doubts this trend will continue.

Now it may be argued that what people do in the post-industrial society will ultimately rest upon the productive capability of secondary industry, which will remain necessarily dominant. We can counter this with two arguments by analogy. Industrial soci-

* Daniel Bell, "Notes on the Post-Industrial Society," *Public Interest*, Winter and Spring, 1967.

ety ultimately rests on primary industry and no one would claim that it is dominant in our society. Quite the contrary, the enormous productivity of our farmers is taken for granted. If they somehow failed, we would be furious at them, but we give them little credit for their performance, certainly feel no gratitude toward them, and certainly would not let them dominate our economy, society, or polity. A somewhat similar transformation could develop with respect to manufacturing activities in a post-industrial society. A smaller percentage of people may be engaged in manufacturing, and the very success of industry may make its further successes seem less exciting and dramatic. While industrialists will probably continue to be deeply occupied with their affairs, the issues of finance, investment, production, sales, and distribution that have so long been dominant concerns of Westerners could very likely dwindle in interest. Also, those who would maintain that industry would be basic to post-industrial society sound suspiciously like the physiocrats of the eighteenth century (e.g., Thomas Jefferson) who claimed a similar primacy for agriculture. We now take agriculture for granted. There is no reason why we cannot take cars, clothes, etc. for granted also.

A QUATERNARY ECONOMY?

As mentioned briefly in the multifold trend (Chapter I), the most important economic activities in 1985 will probably be quaternary activities, rather than primary, secondary, or tertiary activities. Quaternary activities are services to services or services for their own sake, such as recreation activities, the arts, etc., and most importantly, certain forms of government services. Everyone is familiar with how bureaucracies can grow to the point where they "exist for their own sake" as much as they exist for their originally intended function. As a society grows to the point where it can increasingly afford to have a larger percentage of its people working in government, so the pressures to continue to do so increase. This may be a very dangerous trend. As production becomes more efficient in traditional industries, requiring ever fewer people, the new areas of opportunity—the new services—can either be based on the efficiencies of a system privately operated in accordance with traditional market criteria or on a system where the majority of the people just "turn wheels" and accomplish very little beyond what the industrial system has already accomplished in itself. This is an important difference. It is not safe to assume that all quaternary services will be added to existing efficient industries; they may operate against present industries, reducing their potential and slowing economic growth.

A POST-ECONOMIC SOCIETY?

Another assumption about the post-industrial society is that it will be a post-economic society. Presumably there will be so much money around that people will not feel hard pressed to make a living. This idea would seem to be contradicted by the history of industrial society. As wealth grew, people did not take it easier. Most of them worked as hard, or even harder, for luxuries as their forefathers did for necessities (except the profligate son—a character of all societies). Right now, it is possible to subsist in our society with little or no work as hippies, drop-outs, and "welfare chisellers" demonstrate, but few are willing to do without what have come to be regarded as necessary luxuries. (Upper-middle-class aesthetes blame advertising for forced consumption—they may take the pretensions of their Madison Avenue friends too seriously.) Post-industrial man will likely require similar goods and services, not absolutely necessary but nice to have. Still it cannot be ignored that the development of industrial society has reduced many economic incentives and most people have responded by working fewer hours per week, fewer weeks per year, and fewer years per lifetime, and maybe not so hard when they do work.

A LEISURE SOCIETY?

It has been widely speculated that vast wealth will at last liberate man from labor and free him for leisure. Will post-industrial man hold with Aristotle that, ". . . Nature herself . . . requires that we should be able, not only to work well, but to use leisure well, for, . . . the first principle of all action is leisure. Both are required, but leisure is better than occupation and is its end?"* Certainly a post-industrial society offers the potential for more leisure time. Probably at least part of that potential will be achieved. There will be more, perhaps much more, leisure time. This will partly cause and partly reflect a decline in the traditional work ethic. Most people will probably continue to work hard and derive satisfaction from this certainly for the next generation, but the need to work in the emerging post-industrial societies will decline as the level of affluence and productive efficiency of the society at large increases. Leisure itself is not a focus for society; it is rather a focus for an individual's choice of how to use his life and indicative of an individualistic focus on life. As leisure time increases, societies should increasingly reflect this individualistic approach. There may be more mosaic cultures, where many life styles and many behavior patterns are reflected within the overall context. But we must not ignore the importance of collective leisure. Already, new stadiums and the location of franchises for professional athletic teams are burning issues in local U.S. politics. It is not difficult to project national leisure issues. When Pompidou promised the French a "Sweden with sun" surely he was not speaking only of social welfare legislation.

AN ENNUI SOCIETY?

Some writers forecast that a society rich, fat, and secure will be a "Proust-industrial society," with current tendencies toward tedium accelerated. However, the problem of boredom is grossly overstated. Peasants around the world have a great deal of leisure; farming occupies no more than about six hundred hours of their working time each year—the rest of their time is free, and they fill it rather well. It is true that most of the time is filled with rituals, with religion, with games which are "out" in the modern American sense. But they may be coming back. As far as working people are concerned, we notice that when they are given a year's sabbatical, they have the time of their lives: they visit relatives, they repair their houses, they go fishing, they play games. Time does not hang heavily on their hands.

Even the prosperous are rarely bored unless they are literary.

* *Politics,* VIII (Jowett trans.)

Carol Kennicott was probably the only bored person on Main Street. Most people have little trouble in finding enough to do with their families, their homes and personal property, and their hobbies. Travel and tourism will devour enormous amounts of time.

Boredom, or rather the thought of it, is an affliction of the twentieth century urban upper classes. The people who can have a real problem with boredom are those who have leisure without affluence, without sufficient money to spend on active leisure—students, professors, hippies, and the unemployed.

Many intellectuals and other upper-class people are worried about what will happen when the masses have a lot of time on their hands. Partially this may be a vestige of "idle hands do the devil's work," but there is also an element of rational class interest—already the recently prosperous lower-middle and embourgeoised working classes are overrunning traditional upper and upper-middle class preserves such as beaches, wilderness areas, ski resorts, and cultural or historical sites.

A related issue is that of structural unemployment of the relatively untrained individual with a low I.Q. in a post-industrial culture. A U.S. commission made a study of this problem. It went through the evidence with a very fine comb indeed, and could find no sign of the low-priced occupations (elevator operator, baby sitter, maid, cook) disappearing. On the contrary, the jobs are there but there are not enough people to fill them. People can make better money elsewhere. In Scandinavia, if you get off at a small airport, there is nobody to carry your bags for you. If you are sick, the pilot will do it, but you cannot tip him for he is making more money than you are.

It may be correct to say that the technology of the coming decades will provide work for only a small and shrinking part of the working population. In the post-industrial civilization industry becomes a small part of the social effort, but as far as we can tell there will continue to be an inexhaustible demand for people in the services, in maintenance types of work and the like. The problem is a rather different one: because there is a scarcity of people willing to go into these service industries, the cost will go sky high.

Contemporary experience suggests that the great mass of mankind will not make intelligent or creative use of its spare time. Vapidities and trivia will be with us in the future, and man's good nature will not necessarily increase with the growth of his wealth and security. It may, in fact, decrease. However, the people who indulge in these vulgarities and spawn the trivia will find them both interesting and satisfying. Certainly the quality of high culture in the last generation gives no one the right to sneer at the products of mass culture.

A NEW RELIGIOSITY?

The post-industrial society may well be marked by more leisure time; but it seems unlikely that leisure per se will be the central element of that—or any—society. What we may see, as people find more and more idle time on their hands, is a new "religiosity" answering a search for meaning and purpose. This could take many forms, as suggested by the present flourishing of both "Jesus freaks" and Billy Graham. Whether a true religious revival will occur, reversing the long secular trend of modern history, is doubtful. Religious—even fervently religious—groups may well exist and even proliferate, but it is more likely they will exist as bits of a mosaic, post-industrial society than play a central role in it.

A LEARNING SOCIETY?

It has been suggested that the post-industrial society will be, above all, a learning or knowledge society. Not surprisingly, this vision is held mainly by academics. The current trend toward a greater emphasis on education may well continue, partly because of the necessity to keep up with the information explosion, partly because of the complexity of many decisions, and partly because of the rapidity of change. Knowledge that was useful two or three years ago is outdated; concepts must be relearned, and sometimes entirely new concepts must be devised in order to deal with today's potentialities. So education and training are bound to be important in the post-industrial society. But we think it highly unlikely that education in itself will play the central role in this society. It will be a tool, and will perhaps become an increasingly useful tool, but a learning society would probably be more indicative of the last stages of an industrial society than of a post-indust.ial one. Advanced industrial societies need many technocrats, but in a post-industrial society technocrats will become routine. In fact, it can be argued that post-industrial society will be less dependent on education.

A GENTLEMANLY SOCIETY?

The most obvious model for how people will live in a world of great wealth is how the wealthy live today. Let us imagine we were trying to guess how people would live in the industrial society on the basis of how the rich lived in pre-industrial society. Imagine we were asking a man in Europe on the eve of the Industrial Revolution how a people would live on a thousand pounds a year: that was a nobleman's income. Obviously everyone would have a country estate filled with servants, several carriages, silver, foreign wines, and closets full of clothing, would travel abroad occasionally, would send their children to the university, and would be involved in politics. To a remarkable degree that is what has happened. A suburban house is no palatial mansion, but it is closer to Blenheim Palace than to a peasant's hut. The average household has no servants, but has machines which do the work of servants with less insolence. A car or two is better than a stable full of carriages. And the average wardrobe contains several suits and a dozen or more dresses. The average middle-class industrial family has silver, wines, and travels abroad occasionally. A child of industrial society does go to college or at least to a secondary school that teaches more than eighteenth-century Oxford did, and the average man is as much involved in politics as the average country gentleman of the eighteenth century—he votes.

Now let us look at today's rich for clues to daily life in the post-industrial society. Perhaps we ought not to look at the very rich but at the high-salaried, the managers and professionals. They have very large homes filled with gadgets, and often have two homes, one just for vacations. They have day servants, once or twice a week, but we do not need them in our post-industrial society—there have long been dreams of household robots or trained simians, and why not? Today's wealthy work their own hours, many very hard, others coasting. They travel frequently both on business and pleasure, penetrating all parts of the globe. When not dieting they eat well, whether the cosmopolitan food of the East or the grade A beefsteaks of the West. They have two or more cars, a Cadillac or a Mercedes-Benz, a station wagon, and a sports car for the kids. Many of them have planes or boats. Their children go to graduate school and do not start work until they damn well feel like it, and the parents do not seem to mind. Of course, they may have the mild alcoholism of too many martinis, neurotic wives popping pills, junior who is wild and undisciplined, and little Sally who is sleeping around, but despite the pretensions of the upper-middle classes, these "depraved" tendencies seem to be less intense than among "the lower orders" and in any event pale before the vice of the eighteenth century gentry. If one takes this comparison seriously, the post-industrial society doesn't look very strange or unmanageable.

But, of course, we have loaded the dice. No class in industrial society has the prestige, power, or relative wealth of the eighteenth-century *noblesse*. The formality and ritual of pre-industrial upper-class life are noticeably absent from industrial society. Will the post-industrial revolution face similar leveling? The trend toward informality and the proletarianization of manners and style would suggest so.

A WESTERNISTIC SOCIETY?

In *The Year 2000*, there are speculations about the possibility of a post-industrial society which might resemble something like Hellenistic Greece, except that virtually everyone will be rich instead of just a narrow upper class. Around 250 B.C., the traditional Greek culture of the democratic city-state and the Olympian Pantheon of gods had been pretty well discredited among the educated classes. The Greek upper classes at this time were immensely rich from the land purchased with the profits gained in trade. Formal education systems became widespread, and leisure was considered the principal concern of a civilized man. In this period we can first clearly delineate the "gentleman." (But unlike the early modern gentleman, a Hellenistic aristocrat was not necessarily genteel or snobbish, nor did he retain any vestiges of chivalric values.) Like their counterparts in later historical periods, most gentlemen were more interested in their personal lives and having a good time than in the philosophical justification of them.

The difference between Hellenistic Greece and post-industrial society will be that everyone is rich, and everyone can afford to be a gentleman, living neo-epicurean lives and enjoying rather plain (if everyone has money, there is no reason to show off) but not unsubstantial comforts.

Those who will be concerned with ultimate meanings and justifications may have—like many in the Hellenistic period—a widespread sense of their civilization as being the culmination of history, but also a sense of decadence. The managerial classes might try to adopt a philosophy of neo-stoicism, a rather pessimistic attitude that it falls on them to do their duty and keep things running, while most enjoy themselves. If, however, those who are enjoying themselves begin to ask, "What's it all worth?" and are not satisfied by material happiness and greater individual choice, religious revival movements could have great appeal. But it may be that the best bet to replace the Protestant ethic is some sort of neo-stoicism combined with neo-epicureanism. In a society in so many ways so incredibly different from that of ancient Greece and Rome the dominant philosophies may be similar. Just as Hellenistic civilization and society consolidated the Hellenic culture, we might have a "Westernistic" civilization built on Western culture, expanding its material horizons but lacking its spiritual content. As in the Hellenistic age, this society could be characterized by a widespread sense of its civilization being the culmination of history, by a sense of decadence, by monumental, but not heroic, architecture, and by great works projects (e.g., great transport systems, space exploration), which will be an exciting fulfillment of modern technology but will probably be viewed by the most highly cultured elites with a sense of ennui or even contempt.

X

The Rise of Japan—
A Case Study in
Methodology

THE most important change impacting several major areas of international concern—the political future of Pacific Asia, international trade, and many other areas—will probably be the rise of Japan to a superstate in the 1970s and 1980s. Today, most decision-makers are just becoming aware of the potential importance and significance of Japanese economic growth. Our identification, analysis, and interpretation of the rise of Japan makes an excellent case study in the methodology of future studies.*

Japan was first noted at Hudson in connection with studies of the economic and military potential of nations in the early 1960s. The method employed was relatively simple—the growth rates of Japanese gross national product were projected and it was found

* Most of the themes in this chapter are developed in detail in: Herman Kahn, *The Emerging Japanese Superstate* (Englewood Cliffs, N.J., 1970).

that if they continued to grow at these high rates (over ten percent per annum) Japan would have a gross national product per capita and perhaps even a total gross national product exceeding even the United States by the end of the century. Such a wealthy Japan would necessarily have immense economic power, which could be translated into political or military power.

A trend line in GNP growth is merely a line on a chart. Some very important characteristics of the Japanese economy, which almost require a very high growth rate, were also identified at Hudson. Some of these are:

1. High savings and investment rates (about twice the U.S.)
2. Superior education and training (i.e., American scale and European quality through high school)
3. Adequate capitalization
4. "Risk capital" readily available
5. Technological capabilities competitive to West
6. Economically and patriotically advancement-oriented, achievement-oriented, work-oriented, deferred gratification, loyalty, enthusiastic employees—probably increasingly so
7. High morale and commitment to economic growth and to surpassing the West—by government, by management, by labor, and by general public
8. Willingness to make necessary adjustments and/or sacrifices—relatively mobile capital and labor
9. Excellent management of the economy—by government, by business, and, to some degree, by labor—this results in a controlled and, to some degree, collectivist ("Japan, Inc.") but still competitive and market-oriented (but not market-dominated) capitalism
10. Adequate access—on good and perhaps improving terms—to sufficient world resources and markets
11. Relatively few and/or weak pressures to divert excessive resources to "low economic productivity" uses
12. Current high momentum of growth facilitates further rapid growth
13. Increased emphasis on research and development
14. Availability of skilled work force in Non-Communist Pacific Asia
15. Almost all future technological and economic and most cultural and political developments seem favorable to continuation of the above

Looking behind these to find the secret of Japanese performance, it can be concluded that the real "engine" of rapid growth, the key factor in the equation, is Japanese national character and Japanese leadership—both private and government.

National character is a very hard thing to quantify in general or even in relation to economic growth. Indeed, many aspects of national character are inherently subjective and all aspects are subject to change, qualification, and exception. Japanese national character is complex and subtle, and would require more space to delineate than is available here,* but briefly, in Western terms, it may be described as follows. Imagine that the idealized world of the Middle Ages was transferred intact to the industrialized twentieth century, complete with all the feudal virtues of loyalty, deference, honor, and absolute solidarity to the group. If you can imagine a crusading order like the Templars operating a factory, you have a rough idea of Japan. For example, going on strike in Japan often means just to wear an armband on the job, raturally without slowing down production, or for that matter, without skipping the daily company hymn sing.

What might this unparalleled Japanese economic growth mean to the world, particularly the United States? Happily, there is an excellent historical precedent for such an event which may shed some light on future events. In the nineteenth century, the British occupied much the same position in the world that the United States does in the twentieth. Unquestionably, the British were the most powerful political and military state; they were the industrial and commercial leaders of the world; also, they were the cultural leaders in that other nations eagerly imitated their customs and manners; most important of all, the British had a sense of national superiority. They believed that they were unquestionably the most progressive and moral people on the face of the earth. Whatever merits there may have been in other cultures, they were inferior to the British. This attitude is perhaps best expressed in the popular English slogan, "Niggers (i.e., barbarians) begin at Calais." But in the late nineteenth and early twentieth centuries Britain suddenly became aware of a powerful challenger. At first unnoticed, Imperial Germany began to rise against British world domination. The Germans were hardworking and industrious. Behind tariff walls they had built up their

---

* See *Superstate* pp. 16-74 and Ruth Benedict, *The Chrysanthemum and the Sword* (1946).

own powerful industrial plant which was in many ways superior to that of the English. Certainly, the discipline and spirit of German labor was superior to their British counterparts. After building domestic markets, the Germans began to penetrate England's export domination. At first German goods were bought merely because they were cheaper than British. They were recognized as inferior. Foreign markets, such as the United States, were inundated with cheap German toys, domestic utensils, and consumer goods of all types. But gradually German superiority in the production of major industrial goods became evident. German armaments, ships, and machine tools came to be sold all over the world.

Initially, the British were friendly to the rise of Germany. They were happy to see a strong and prosperous Germany because they still had a vestigial fear of their traditional enemy, France, and were glad to see a powerful Germany to the East. The Germans were slavish in their regard for the British, set Britain as their model for civilization, and made every effort to imitate and flatter the English. Of course, this attitude largely derived from the Germans' deep sense of inferiority to the British—which later led to a shrill and belligerent attitude toward the senior power. It would seem that the British went out of their way to be friendly to the Germans. In the late nineteenth century the mark of a great power was colonies. The Germans were late in the colonial race, but the British obligingly permitted them to grab off some of the less attractive parcels of Africa and Oceania. The British and German upper classes intermarried to a certain extent. Many German aristocrats attended Oxford and Cambridge. Indeed, when Cecil Rhodes established his scholarships he provided for Britain, the colonies and dominions, the United States, and Germany. British tourists visited Germany in large numbers. Up to the point of the death of Bismarck, we see many parallels between the relationship between Germany and Britain, and Japan and America.

But here the analogy breaks down. Under the cautious leadership of Bismarck, Germany made every effort to stay on good terms with Britain. The large German army was seen as no threat to the British and Germany's rapid economic growth, which was slowly displacing England in the world, was hardly noticed in the British Isles. But after Bismarck left, under the leadership of Kaiser Wilhelm II, Germany began to feel that its power required a higher position in the world than being England's little brother. It was felt that Germany was no longer a developing nation, but a full-fledged first line power, equal in every way to Great Britain, and in some ways superior. German economic and foreign policy became increasingly aggressive. The Germans were no longer satisfied with their few paltry colonies; they demanded more. But additional colonies could only be obtained at the expense of some other colonial power or from allegedly independent non-European states that were within the spheres of influence of other powers. The Germans began to push in China, in Morocco, and in the Ottoman Empire. The British were really awakened to the German threat by the decision of Germany to go ahead and build a first-class ocean-going navy. This, of course, was a direct threat to England's maritime supremacy and the very survival of the British Empire. Moreover, the Germans had the best army in the world, and the addition of a first line navy would unquestionably make the German Reich the first power in the world. Once it became apparent to the British ruling classes that Germany seemed bent on becoming the paramount power in the world, they began to agitate against the Germans throughout English society. Businessmen and workers were exhorted to meet German competition. For the first time since the defeat of Napoleon, the British perceived a strong outside military threat. Gradually, there were serious attempts at the militarization of British society. Military virtues were glorified in various ways. This is the period of the bellicose rhymes and jingles of Kipling. Military training was begun in the English elite public schools. The Boy Scouts were founded by Lord Baden-Powell as a means of inculcating manly and military virtues among British youth. The upper classes began to worry about the physical health of the laboring classes, from the point of view of their suitability for military service. The recognition that Germany had a larger population and much more natural resources than Britain led the English to concentrate on tighter links with the Empire to overbalance German strength. Empire Day was founded, and all sorts of institutions and public promotions were formed to create a sense of unity, at least among the white peoples of the Empire.

Since the German challenge to Britain was conceived as predominantly military, the response was military. We do not anticipate a military threat to the United States from Japan. Although it is possible, it is highly unlikely for many reasons. Rather, we see a challenge to our economic and industrial leadership. Should the Japanese gain on us, we may reasonably expect, at the very least, a good deal of breast-beating in the press and in public statements by government and business leaders to the effect that we are lazy and ought to work harder. In particular, business spokesmen will use Japanese productivity as a stick with which to beat organized labor. It is also likely that serious concern with America's growth rate relative to Japan's may work against the further growth of the ecology movement in the United States: society as a whole may be willing to pay less in terms of a loss of productivity in return for an improved environment.

There are also some much less attractive prospects. Perhaps Americans cannot or will not work harder. The threat of Japanese goods to American industry will almost certainly provoke a cry for protectionism, particularly among organized labor. The current agitation for quotas on Japanese textiles is a harbinger. Soon we may see the same effect in the automobile industry, should Japanese imports continue the advance of the past five years. Steel is also an issue, as are cameras and toys. We should not ignore the possible effects in a multitude of minor industries. For example, Japanese motorcycles are now hurting the sales of Harley-Davidson. Japanese barber chairs and dental equipment are beginning to cut into American markets. Except for primary and secondary industries, which require immediately available sources of raw materials to be economic, it could be that no American industry is safe from Japanese competition. Theoretically at least, services are not even exempt. U.S. services could be shipped to Japan to be performed, or performed here by colonies of Japanese workers imported for just that purpose. It is difficult not to see strong pressures for higher tariffs and other forms of protectionism.

Needless to say, high American protectionism will severely modify America's role in the economy of the world. Currently, we are the leading provider of banking and other services necessary to the undertaking of international trade. Like Britain before us, when that nation held the central position in international finance, we are the principal supporters in the world of liberalized trade policies, believing these to be in the interests of ourselves and the world economy. But if we feel ourselves obliged to resort to the exclusion of Japanese imports, this cannot but affect our relations with the rest of the world. The most extreme position toward which the United States could be driven is economic autarchy, that is, as near self-sufficiency as possible, and international barter of other goods. Probably the United States could operate such a system at some cost in our standard of living, but at a great cost in our international relations with other parts of the world.

On the domestic front, a sense among the public that America is no longer the number one country with the best system imaginable or operating could have undesirable consequences. Of course, to some extent the existing system would be discredited and more heed would be paid to persons who offered alternative systems.

However, it is possible to use another analogy. Instead of looking at Japan and Germany in the late nineteenth century, let us compare Japan today with Japan in the early twentieth century and place the United States today in the role of Great Britain then. The rise of Japan in the late nineteenth century was not unnoticed in Europe. Despite the fact that they were obviously (and proudly) Christian, imperialist, racist, and aggressive, the Europeans looked with pleasure and pride at the Japanese success in imitating at least the outward manifestations of Western culture and cheered at their defeat of the Chinese and even the white Russians. Of course, this was somewhat patronizing, because the Europeans did not dream that the Japanese would ever really catch up with Europe, so their feeble efforts at trying to be "civilized" were charming and in no way a direct threat to European hegemony. Nevertheless, the analogy points out that it is possible for people of one culture to adapt another culture as a protégé and support its success, without any direct threat.

At the beginning of this century, a new arms race began between Britain and Germany, prompted by the invention of the Dreadnought battleship which instantly made all previous strategic systems obsolete. England at the same time was undergoing political upheavals and the ruling classes thought it necessary to make some concessions to the masses. Lloyd George's 1908 budget proposed the first comprehensive system of social security. Immediately, there was a nasty fight over "priorities"—battleships or pensions. A characteristic compromise was reached—some guns and some butter. But the guns were not enough to maintain England's worldwide commitments. To withdraw some strength from outlying positions in order to concentrate naval forces in home waters against the growing imperial German fleet, Britain signed a naval treaty with Japan and handed over its responsibilities in the Far East to the Japanese.

The British also looked to the New World for support against the German threat. The concept of Britain and America as having a common heritage, culture, and political tradition largely dates from this period. It is very difficult for us today to understand the hatred between the British and Americans in the nineteenth century. Most of the British ruling classes looked upon the Americans as vulgar, crude, and vicious barbarians; the Americans responded the feeling in kind. Only when Britain felt hardpressed by Germany and the American upper class began more or less successfully to imitate their British counterparts was it discovered that we were "cousins."

Another possibility we cannot ignore is that America could respond to Japanese success as a sort of "economic Pearl Harbor" and turn nasty, even with racial overtones. Here there is a difference of opinion among the two authors of this book, based upon different evaluations of American national character. Herman Kahn prefers to emphasize our great resources of benevolence and lethargy, believing we will take credit for Japanese success, considering them as our protégé and ward, just as Europeans did for Japan in La Belle Epoque. Besides, it is easier to take credit for the Japanese than fight them. B. Bruce-Briggs would call attention to the clear-minded ferocity of Americans once they are aroused, as revealed in our history and expressed by General Patton: "America loves a winner. America will not tolerate a loser . . . Americans play to win . . . the very thought of losing is hateful to any American."* It is the latter view which most impresses the Japanese, because they see the world as a hierarchy of nations and find it difficult to imagine a nation being toppled from a high position without responding vigorously, just as the Japanese did when the United States attempted to curtail their hegemony over East Asia in 1941.

Many critics (in Western countries, not in Japan**) were extremely skeptical about the conclusions in *The Emerging*

---

* Quoted in Dwight MacDonald, *Memoirs of a Revolutionist* (New York, 1957).

** The Japanese were more troubled by the loss of their "low posture" position and possible reactions in the United States, a concern that seems to be partially justified by Nixon's New Economic Policy of 1971.

Japanese Superstate. Although they agreed with the principal point (i.e., if Japan continued to grow economically as was projected, this would have major effects upon the world scene) they said it was implausible that the Japanese would continue to grow at present day rates. However, many of them failed to notice that these projections were not derived from projecting the highest possible growth rates, but assumed lower growth rates, and even took into account the fact that the Japanese might have to divert large resources for pollution control, defense, and improving their infrastructure. Even with these investments, and lower growth rates, Japan still would achieve a gross national product of 650 million dollars by 1985.

We could maintain that it is unnecessary to prove that these growth rates will continue, but rather for skeptics to prove that they will go down, but that would be insufficient. Japanese growth rates are so startling that it is necessary to justify their continuation. Let us take up some of the factors which are often said to favor a topping out or even a downturn of Japanese growth:

1. "Cream has been skimmed" off European and U.S. technology
2. Size of Japanese work force no longer increasing rapidly
3. Lagging infrastructure
4. Greater defense expenditure
5. Hedonistic tendencies of younger generation
6. Younger generation resents system in general and in particular "escalator system"
7. Domestic demands for amenities and social investment and expenditure
8. Likely difficulties with foreign trade
9. Economy may become overheated by excessive equipment investments, which might eventually lead to oversupply when the expansion of exports levels off
10. Rising barriers to American and other foreign investments will introduce managerial techniques that will revolutionize firms still adhering to vertical organizations
11. Japan is becoming a service economy—soon will be post-industrial
12. Serious political strains within the existing system
13. Serious American recession

Most of these are overstated, assumed to have too great effectiveness, assumed to affect growth rates too rapidly, are subject to counteraction (or at least can be limited through proper policies and/or likely events), and in some cases are more positive than negative in ultimate effect. We will discuss some aspects of this that are of more general interest. Some say that Japanese growth has been heavily dependent on technology "borrowed" from the West, that the "cream has been skimmed," but the Japanese have also made many important improvements on the original technology. Furthermore, Japan is rapidly improving its R&D capability, is now investing as much in research and development as West Germany or France, and appears to be more efficient in its investments than most countries. The government portion of this investment is also lower than that of the major European countries or the United States. In fact, Japanese research and development actually supports the argument for continued high growth rates, rather than the reverse.

Japan obviously does have a labor shortage but it also has two ways of overcoming it: bring the work to the workers or bring the workers to the work. A classic example of the first approach is the United States at the time of the great immigrations around the turn of the century. The recent immigration of labor from Greece and Southern Italy into Northern Italy and West Germany provides another good example. For a number of reasons the Japanese probably will not choose this approach. They will prefer to "send the work to the laborer" by establishing industries in other countries, particularly the areas which we call Non-Communist Pacific Asia (NOCPA). In fact, Japanese presence is already evident throughout this Non-Communist Pacific Asian region, in some cases painfully so. Whether or not the Japanese can increase their operations and presence in this area is still debatable. In the past few years there has been mounting opposition to the Japanese in this region, even in some countries, such as Indonesia, that have not been traditionally hostile to Japan. If Japan does not solve its mounting problems with fellow Asian nations, it is hard to imagine that the increased economic ties that we are suggesting will be feasible. If they are successful, as we expect, both Japan and the NOCPA will benefit. We might add here that one of the most important factors is whether or not the United States will maintain an active presence in this area, to act in effect as a balance to Japanese economic power.

The Japanese save and invest almost forty percent of the gross national product, which is growing ten to twelve percent a year. Over the next decade the Japanese will be able to afford to correct obvious inadequacies in their infrastructure without seriously slowing their growth and have money to spare.

They also have plenty of money to rearm. Japan is a special case in terms of its potential military might. Whether or not Japan decides to obtain nuclear weapons in the next decade will certainly depend largely upon its relationship with the United States. If the United States physically withdraws its presence from the Pacific (e.g., after a very dramatic, disastrous ending to the Vietnam conflict), Japan must seriously consider rearming and obtaining nuclear weapons. Whether or not Japan does rearm is strictly up to the Japanese themselves. We would suggest, however, that if they do rearm they have an obligation to do so in a way that does not touch off a general arms race. A superstate should be responsible. But, again, it is an open issue and represents a decision that the Japanese alone will have to make.

Many Westerners are amazed to hear that Japan's continuous favorable balance of trade is a *problem* to them. But there has been concern that this might slow exports and growth. A short-term solution is to upgrade the yen, but we feel that long-term solutions can be found in more tourism (Japanese tourism abroad grew from 265,000 in 1965 to 1.3 million in 1971) and overseas investment through long-term purchases of necessary resources, private investment in goods-producing industries, and foreign aid.

Because such a large and growing percentage of Japanese production (currently ten percent) is exported, foreign protectionism could have serious restricting effects on the Japanese economy; however, Japan is not as dependent on trade with the developed world as is often believed. While it is dependent on raw materials (about fifteen billion dollars per year), these are available from a number of sources and it is hard to see how Japan could be put in a situation where it could not fill its requirements. Its trade with the developed world is important, of course, but if it were largely cut off today there would be little effect on Japan's overall growth rates. The problem here is that this situation *may* change, depending upon Japan's course in the next few years. If the trend is toward increasing concentrations of energies in established industries directly competitive with the West, it may find itself much more dependent. If it shifts its focus to high technology and service areas, among others, Japan should be able to maintain its traditional relatively independent stance with regard to specific markets or suppliers.

Perhaps most important is the belief among many Japanese that their national élan is ebbing. Maybe so, but this is a slow process. By most historians' judgment our traditional values in the West have been "eroding" since the Victorian age. Japan's are just beginning to "erode." The Japanese are said to be going soft like Europeans and Americans. Yes, they are, but a recent anecdote by a Japanese participant at an international business meeting nicely demonstrates the degree to which they're going soft: our visitor, a high official of a major Japanese company, a man of the generation of World War II, bitterly complained about the current slackness of the younger generation in Japan. "Why," he said, "you can no longer expect young executives to work late *every* night." This will have very serious ramifications for Japan over the next twenty or thirty years, but compared to the change going on in the United States, the change in Japan is very limited. If you are an older Japanese observing the change, the younger generation looks more like Americans than Japanese, but if you are an American, the younger Japanese still look very Japanese indeed.

More important, if we are correct in concluding that Japanese national character is the "engine" of Japanese economic potential, is that the specificity of a nation is a lasting stubborn quality that changes little and very, very slowly. We do not think national characteristics are genetic. They are generally formed before puberty and reinforced from that point on by the milieu. The Japanese culture is a firm mould and the leaders of 1985 and even the year 2000 have already been shaped.

On the basis of this analysis, it seems to us that the burden of proof is now on those who argue that Japan's economic growth will slow, that Japan's economic power will not be translated into political power, and that the rise of Japan will not require major changes in the world environment.

XI

The Ideology of Tomorrow

AT various places in this book, some readers may have asked themselves: "Do the authors think this potential development is good or bad?" Other readers may feel that our judgments of the desirability of future events were all too explicit, especially if they were offended by our perceptions or manner of presenting them. Just as we suggested the possibility of a technological index, others may consider a sociological index equally desirable. However, we have tried to take a "value-free" perspective, indulging in attempts to achieve what Marxists sneeringly call "bourgeois objectivity."

Two different perspectives can be used in future studies; these sometimes overlap and are hard to distinguish, but in most policy research projects we can draw a line between them. The two perspectives can be labeled *descriptive* (or *predictive*) and *normative.* In the descriptive perspective we try to understand what the future situation will be for the purpose of adapting to it—possibly taking into account various uncertainties in facts, theories, and values by hedging our policies. If we do this hedging we would talk about a *preferred system* rather than an *optimal system.* A preferred system is one where a good deal of attention is paid to reliability, toughness, flexibility, and various compromises so that favorable events can be exploited if they occur and unfavorable events can be avoided or their consequences mitigated. However, descriptive forecasting is basically passive, merely attempting to record what the world will be like so that we may react to it.

The normative perspective emphasizes changing the future in a desired fashion, making more likely the good and/or less likely the bad. Like descriptive forecasting, it often employs a preferred system. In other words, normative forecasting means the setting of reasonable goals—what things should be like, what we should strive for, how we should shape the world. When an individual says, "In seven years I will be sales manager," he is making a normative forecast, which may be quite wrong. But he has some influence upon the outcome of that forecast; insofar as he strives toward that goal he will achieve the forecast situation, thus creating what is commonly called the "self-fulfilling prophecy." From the point of view of descriptive forecasting, this is cheating —our ambitious young man can directly affect the outcome. However, although descriptive forecasting may be useful in many fields where the outcome cannot be affected by choices today, decision makers are primarily concerned with normative forecasting.

In practice, it is not possible to separate the two types completely. There are obvious constraints and limits on the ambition of any individual or institution that must be descriptively forecast before any normative forecast can be made. When working on individual projects for agencies or organizations we put our primary emphasis on the "normative" approach, trying to delineate what options are open to decision makers and what can be the implications of their decisions; but when addressing a more general audience, as in this book, we emphasize the "descriptive" face of futurology, although normative aspects are certainly present.

It may be impossible to completely separate descriptive from normative futurology; nevertheless, we feel it is extremely important and rewarding to make a serious attempt. Unfortunately, the field of future studies is thick with normative forecasting masquerading as descriptive. Many prognostications of many distinguished American thinkers are statements of what the author wants to happen, not necessarily what he thinks will happen, and frequently they are a bald pitch for some express policy or program. If done openly and honestly this is a perfectly valid method of political advocacy, with many honorable precedents (such as Bellamy's *Looking Backward*), but it tells us very little about what the future *will* be, except insofar as it is influenced by the ideas and desires of important men today. Similarly, a great deal of impetus behind the prophecy that humanist left values will quickly spread throughout our society is based upon the hope for their diffusion held by people sympathetic to those values. We cannot live without dreams, but we should not permit our fantasies to substitute for the real and concrete future.

But no matter how objective one may try to be (and some of us try very hard) most views of the future are almost necessarily founded upon some ideological preconceptions about the nature of man, the place of man in the universe, the inevitability or desirability of progress, national or class bias, or even ordinary optimism or pessimism. For example, in our attempts to elucidate even relatively simple and straightforward policy issues, we have been struck by the fundamental importance of the persistence of an ancient dispute between the Augustinian and Pelagian views of man. The dichotomy results from a theological squabble of the fifth century. The African bishop Augustine, author of the macro-history *The City of God*, vigorously accused the British theologian Pelagius of the heresy of believing that man could achieve salvation through his own efforts; that is, man was basically the master of his fate and through his unaided efforts could be good. St. Augustine took the opposing view, which came to be the orthodox Christian point of view, that man was fundamentally sinful and could achieve salvation only through God's Grace. In the modern world, Augustinians tend to be conservatives. The liberal tradition (including Marxism) is Pelagian. To the best of our knowledge, neither of these positions can be proved. To some extent, one position or the other is taken on faith.

The present disputes over the relative importance of heredity

versus environment in determining intelligence and performance in school reflect these two perspectives. If you are Pelagian,
believing that man can achieve self-improvement, then you cannot accept data which purport to prove that there are hereditary
differences between ethnic groups. There must be another explanation. Conversely, an Augustinian cannot accept the view
that any secular program is going to change people's fundamental weaknesses. Attempts to do so must necessarily fail.
Whether we are Augustinians or Pelagians strongly affects our
view of the future. The Augustinian cannot admit that things are
going to get much better in this world and certainly they are not
going to be improved by the efforts of professors, governments, or
policy analysts. And the Pelagian must necessarily believe that
the future will be affected by such changes.

The same issues are raised by less fundamental presupposi-
tions. A person who accepts the radical critique of industrial
society as corrupt, dehumanizing, and self-destructive might not
accept projections of its steady improvement; in fact, he could
even reject unimpeachable historical data showing past improvement. The Marxist, of course, has a detailed scenario of the future worked out, and will shut his eyes to alternatives.* Happily,
such extreme positions are rare. But less striking differences have
their effects on future perceptions. In the Hudson Institute's studies of national security policy, it was useful to identify thirty
different foreign/military policies presently being advocated. In
presenting these to people involved in policy and program formulation and effectation, we found that most could comfortably
classify themselves under one of these labels: *Austere Pragmatic
Interventionist, Prudential Internationalist*, or *Aggressive Democrat*. These labels were carefully chosen to be descriptive, acceptable to their proponents, and value-free; the purpose of such an
exercise is to promote rational discussion of basic issues without
cat-calls or fist-fights. Briefly, the Prudential Internationalist policy
is the policy that dominated U.S. national security policy from
1940 to 1970; the Austere Pragmatic Interventionist policy is a
much more cautious position about intervention, sometimes called
neo-isolationist. Versions of this policy are gaining ground on the
Prudential Internationalist policy. The Aggressive Democrat

* Igor Bestuzhev-Lada, "Utopias of Bourgeois Futurology," *New Times*,
12 August 1970.

policy advocates a "forward" policy by the United States. This policy, held by much of the Right and other strong anti-Communists and neo-Machiavellians, is currently experiencing lean days. This display of policy positions was invaluable in discussions of national policy issues. But we found something else as well— we expected adherents of different policy positions to have different views of the present and different interpretations of the past, but these differences extended to the future as well. To a remarkable degree expectations and even predictions are flavored by such ideologies. Generally, the Internationalists have expected and predicted convergence and detente between the United States and the Soviet Union (many were shattered by the Czechoslovak intervention) while the Aggressive Democrats emphasize the fundamental ideological unity of the Communists and their basic differences with the West and are constantly looking for a revival of "pure" Stalinism in the East.

We should not be surprised by the reflection of present ideology in future studies because the reflection of present ideology on *past* studies is well known. And when we are talking about the future, we are talking about history, not just the past but the totality of man living in time. Previously, ideologies could be defined in terms of their views of the past. *The Year 2000* used the following classification:

Macro-historical Perspectives on Change

1. Static, traditional, and/or repetitive
2. Progressive: the multifold trend, progress, revolution of rising expectations, utopian, chiliastic, culminating point
3. Decay: not competitive, "hubris," lost golden age, nostalgia, conservatism
4. Cyclic: rise and fall, growth and decay, fluctuation, "regular" ebb and flow
5. Patternless, unpredictable, and incomprehensible
6. Typical (empirical) patterns: the multifold trend, irregular ebb and flow, empirical and analytic trend analysis, typical or phenomenological scenarios
7. Eclectic and syncretic: the multifold trend, other trend analyses, other typical patterns, metaphors and analogies, some current speculations on decline and/or rebirth

But the study and the belief in the relevance of past history may be fading.* Modern industrial society may not have the same need of the past; we are increasingly rooted in innovation and change, not in authority and stability. Perhaps so. Perhaps the present interest in futurology portends the substitution of the future for the past in the center of our historical consciousness, of our perception of our place in time. Each of the macro-historical perspectives above is reflected in future studies. Of course, those who see history as static are not much interested in the field—if the world is unchanging there is no point in thinking about the future—it will be the same as today.

We still have many people in the world who see progress as inevitable. These include orthodox Marxists and classic liberals. Technological utopians, prophesying sweeping changes in the quality of life and even of man, are rampant in the futures field. Good nineteenth century ideas of progress are very strong in American technical and middle management milieus, as well as among dynamic bourgeois elements in Japan and other rapidly growing economies. The Positivist slogan, "Order and Progress," emblazoned on the Brazilian flag reflects the world view of the industrial elements of Rio and São Paulo. Moral utopians also are very much on the scene—judging from the enthusiastic reception given to Charles Reich's *The Greening of America*, a chiliastic vision of man's immediate secular redemption.

Those who see inevitable decay—"catastrophists" we call them—are rare—the spectre of things to come becomes too painful to study. But as discussed in Chapter VIII, many modern intellectuals are losing their faith in material progress, seeing the future not as shining cities of man, but as nightmares of over-population, pollution, nuclear war, and/or programmed Skin-nerite tyranny. And it may be that the reactionary analysis of modern culture as necessarily declining is spreading to one-time liberals. Growing crime, cynicism, drugs, and pornography cast the old liberalism in doubt. Some intellectuals have cultivated their despair to the degree of seeing all human affairs as pattern-less, incoherent, and without meaning, holding with the poet Robert Lowell that "the world is absolutely out of control and is not going to be saved by reason or unreason."

Nevertheless, most contemporary Cassandras do not believe

* See, for example, J. H. Plumb, *The Death of the Past* (Boston, 1969).

in the prospect of irreparable decay. Even those who mournfully forecast "decline and fall" or ecological disaster do so for didactic purposes. They wish to provoke us into taking steps to prevent the impending disaster. Almost all of these people share with most modern men, including ourselves, a view of the future as following typical patterns, resembling the contemporary view of scientific "laws," and as an eclectic and syncretic combination of all the perspectives. Even if there is an equation of history, as some who would model the future hope, man and even an individual man is an important term in that equation. Vary him and you change the outcome. We believe it is possible to alter the future normatively. In any event we can react to the future positively, even if mankind faces the worst possible "worst-case" scenarios— of thermonuclear holocaust, ecological catastrophe, or the Vandals without (or within) the gates—in any case such horrors should not materialize before 1985, we believe and hope.

Index

Abortion, 208–09
Affluence, 9, 21–22, 226
  see also Leisure
Afro-Asia
  black states, 13, 147–48
  nationalism, 73
  possible territorial changes, 128
  poverty, 147
Aggressive democrat, 247–28
Agricultural Revolution, 221, 222
Agriculture
  decline, 25, 26
  "green revolution," 41, 58, 134, 154,
    168
  primary industry, 9, 25–26, 223, 224
Allende, Salvador, 21
Ancien regime morale, 142–44
Anglo-Japanese Naval Treaties, 34, 239
Anti-Semitism, 110–12
Anti-submarine warfare (ASW), 192
Arabs, 135–36, 158, 201
Aristotle, 225–26
Armbruster, Frank, 95n., 179n.
Armed force, 122–23, 125
Arms controls, 133
Aron, Raymond, 119
Austere pragmatic interventionist, 247
Authority, 67–68
Ayres, Robert W., 187n.

Backlash movements, 80, 96, 97–98,
    109
Baden-Powell, Lord, 236
Balance of power system, 151
Balance of terror, 192, 198
Ballistic Missile Defense (BMD), 191,
    192–93, 196, 202
Ballistic missiles
  defense against (BMD), 191, 192–
    93, 196, 202

ICBMs, 191, 195, 200
MIRVs, 191
  on ocean floor, 202
  "Safeguard" ABM system, 191
  SLBM, 192, 195
  spread of, 197
  SRAM, 193
Barrier technology, 196
Bell, Daniel, 68, 82, 92, 223
Bellamy, Edward, 246
Belle Epoque, La
  characteristics, 32–33, 44
  and "La Deuxième Belle Epoque,"
    32, 35–36
  fin de siècle feelings, 33, 35
  Great Britain, 33–34, 234–36,
    238–39
  Japan, 239
  violence, 69, 70
Benedict, Ruth, 234n.
Bengal, 115
Berlin blockade, 194
Berrigan group, 97
Bestuzhev-Lada, Igor, 247n.
Bethe, Hans, 189
Bipolar system, 122, 151
Birth rate, 22–23
Bismarck, Otto von, 235
Black Muslims, 86
Black Panthers, 94, 100
Bogue, Donald, 23n.
Boredom in post-industrial society,
    226–27
Borlaug, Dr. Norman, 58
Bourgeoisie
  in La Belle Epoque, 33
  and counterculture, 95–96
  elite, 11
  in government bureaucracy, 12
  life style, 44

Branch points, 176–77
Brazil, 57, 64, 65
Brummel, Beau, 98
Bureaucracy
    educated incapacity, 81
    effect of intellectuals on, 28
    elite, 11
    embourgeoisment, 12
    in quaternary economy, 224–25

Cable television, 16, 171–72
Can We Win in Vietnam?, 179n.
Canada, 49, 62–63
Carlyle, Thomas, 218
Castro, Fidel, 19, 21, 115, 136, 159
CBW, 193–94, 198, 202
Census Bureau "D" projection, 23
Central nuclear war, 194, 195
C-5 transport aircraft 194, 203
Chamberlain, Neville 160
Chemical and biological weapons
    (CBW), 193–94, 198, 202
Chile, 21
China
    aggressive ambitions, 127
    attitude to Western culture, 21
    bourgeoisie, 11
    industrialization, 18
    in multipolar world, 46
    newly integrated nation, 125
    nuclear weapons, 198
    puritanism, 19, 21
    Sino-German collaboration, 153–54,
        159
    Sino-Japanese confrontation, 71–73
    Sino-Soviet split, 135, 136, 159
    and Third World, 157
    and United States, 131
Christianity, 79, 110, 126, 246
Chrysanthemum and the Sword, The,
    234n.
City of God, The, 246
Clergy, 100–01
Cohen, Sam, 189–90
Cold War, 130–31, 144, 151
Colonialism, 147–48
Comecon, 50–51
Command and control systems, 194–95,
    197–98
Common Market, *see* European Eco-
    nomic Community
Communes, 85–86
Communications, 65, 66, 141, 208

Concorde, 197
Condemned to Freedom, 70n.
Conflicts
    chronic, 71–73
    law and order issues, 69
    separatism, 50–56
    in surprise-free projection, 42
Conglomerates, 14–15
Congo, 19, 75, 86
Conservative movements, 80
    see also Ideological renewal gov-
        ernments
Conurbations, 24
Counterculture
    backlash, 96, 97–98
    chart, 90, 91
    counterreformation, 37, 95–98, 99
    decline, 92–99
    drugs, 92, 93, 94, 95, 96, 98, 112
    and ecology, 218
    effects, 21–22, 91, 95, 96, 112
    hippie communes, 85–86
    influence on Third World, 20–21
    and religion, 100–02
    in Soviet Union, 151–52
    in surprise-free projection, 42, 83
Counter-insurgency techniques, 196–97,
    199
Counterreformation
    anti-Semitism, 110–12
    and counterculture, 37, 95–98, 99
    effects, 100–13
    fascism, 98, 104, 105–06
    ideological renewal governments,
        104–07, 112
    and late sensate society, 11, 89, 90,
        105
    neo-racism, 107–09
    polarization, 96
    populism, 102–04, 105
    Protestant parochial schools, 101–02
    religion and, 100–02
    in surprise-free projection, 40–41, 42
    synthesis, 96–97, 112–13
Countervailing forces, *see* Counter-
    reformation
Crime, 69–70, 109
Cuba, 19, 21, 75, 135, 136–37, 159
Culture
    ideational, 9–10
    mass culture, 227–28
    Middle Ages, 10
    post-industrial, 42, 227–28

in surprise-free projection, 42
world, 19–20
    see also Sensate culture, Western
        culture
Czechoslovakia, 115, 127, 131, 138,
    139, 155–56, 158, 176, 248

Death of the Past, The, 249n.
De Gaulle, Charles, 153
Delphi forecasting, 187–88
Depression, 154–55
Descriptive forecasting, 244, 245
D'Holbach, Baron de, 143
"Deuxième Belle Epoque, La," 32, 35–
    36, 37–38, 40, 43–45
Disasters as branch points, 176, 177
Discretionary behavior, 68
Disillusionment with progress, 210–13,
    214, 215
Dropouts
    in mosaic culture, 85–86, 164, 170,
        225
    scientists, 16–17
    underdeveloped nations, 20–21
    upper-middle-class, 78
Drugs, 92, 93, 94, 95, 96, 98, 112, 152,
    166, 173

Eastern Europe
    Comecon, 50–51
    economic development, 64
    Germany, 47–48, 124
    Poland, 156
    rise of nationalism, 138
    Soviet control, 124, 127, 130, 155–56
    stability, 155–56
    trade with Western Europe, 64
    see also Czechoslovakia, Soviet Union
Ecology, 218–19, 237, 250
    see also Pollution
Economic debacle as branch point, 176,
    177
Economic development
    centralization, 13, 14
    conglomerates, 14–15
    five dynamic areas, 60, 63–65
    "gap ideology," 56–58
    limits, 214, 215
    long-term trend, 8, 13–15, 37, 56–58
    multinational corporations, 41, 58–63
    socialist nations, 15
    in surprise-free projection, 41
    see also "Green revolution"

Educated incapacity, 28, 69–70, 80–82
Education
    Japan, 233
    long-term trend, 9, 26–28
    multinational corporations, 59
    in post-industrial society, 228–29
    scenario, 184
    see also Educated incapacity
E-folding rate, 217, 218
Eisenhower, Dwight D., 35
Elites
    cultural, 15
    educated, 27–28, 34, 59
    and mass movements, 103
    meritocratic, 11, 12–13
    multinational corporations, 59
    search for meaning and purpose in
        life, 78–79
    types, 11
    underdeveloped nations, 18
    Western society, 8, 11
Embourgeoisment, 12, 227
Emerging Japanese Superstate, The,
    232n., 234n., 239–40
Ennui in post-industrial society, 226–28
Envelope forecasting, 187, 188
*Environment and Change: The Next
    Fifty Years*, 209n.
Europe
    La Belle Epoque, 32–36
    fractionalization, 55–56
    ideological renewal governments, 105
    in multipolar world, 45–46
    separatism, 50–56
    stability, 51–52
    see also Eastern Europe, Western
        Europe, Specific countries
European Economic Community
    (EEC)
    effect on nation-states, 52
    enlargement, 48–50
    France in, 41, 48–49
    Great Britain in, 14, 48
    long-term goal, 14
    separatism and, 54, 55–56
Ewald, William P., Jr., 209n.
"Expatriate" communities, 66
Exponential process, 217, 218

Fanon, Franz, 75
Fascism, 98, 104, 105–06, 144
Fast deployment logistics (FDL), 194
Ferdinand, Archduke Franz, 69

Fin de siècle feeling, 33, 35
Five dynamic areas, 60, 63–65
Five Stages of Greek Religion, 168n.
Food deficit, 154
Forecasting, 39, 43, 176, 244–46
  see also Technological forecasting
Forgotten Americans, The, 95n.
Fractionalization, 55–56, 121
France
  ancien regime, 143, 200–01
  in European Economic Community,
    41, 48–49
  French Revolution, 220–21
  multinational corporations, 61
  after World War II, 45, 46
Futurology, *see* Forecasting, Ideolo-
  gies, Macro-historical perspectives,
  Multifold trend, Perspectives, Sce-
  narios, Surprise-free projections,
  Technological forecasting

Galbraith, John Kenneth, 26
"Gang society," 70, 173
"Gap ideology," 56–58
Gentlemanly society, 229–30, 231
George, Lloyd, 239
Germany
  La Belle Epoque, 34, 35–36
  East Germany, 47–48, 124
  Imperial Germany, 34, 35–36, 234–
    36, 238, 239
  Sino-German collaboration, 153–54,
    159
  in surprise-free projection, 41
  after World War II, 45, 46, 47–48
Ghibellines, 85
Gini curves, 21
Global metropolis, 44–45, 65
Global village, 44
Gordon, T. J., 187n.
Graham, Billy, 228
Great Britain
  Anglo-Japanese Naval Treaties, 34,
    239
  La Belle Epoque, 33–34, 234–36,
    238–39
  Boer War, 33
  economic development, 56, 222
  in European Economic Community,
    14, 48
  and Japan, 238–39
  racial problem, 110n.

Regency England, 98–99
  separatism, 53, 54–55
  Ulster, 34, 55, 70, 115
  World War I, 34
  after World War II, 45, 46
Great Depression, 154, 177, 182
"Great Society" programs, 29
Greece, 87, 105–06, 168, 230–31
"Green revolution," 41, 58, 134, 154,
  168
Greening of America, The, 93–94, 249
Gross national product (GNP)
  France, 49
  Great Britain, 49
  Japan, 47, 49, 232–33, 240, 242
  in surprise-free projection, 41
  United States, 164, 171, 173
Gross world product (GWP), 43, 63
Guelfs, 85

Hellenistic Greece, 87, 168, 230–31
Helmer, Olaf, 187n.
Heredity-environment conflict, 246–47
Heuristic device, 89
Hippie communes, 85–86
Historical analogies
  La Belle Epoque, 32–36, 234–36,
    238–39
  dangers, 30–31, 36n.
  "La Deuxième Belle Epoque," 32,
    35–38, 40, 43–45
  Japan today and Japan in early
    twentieth century, 238–39
  sources, 31–32
  uses, 31
  pre-World War I Great Britain and
    Germany, 234–36
Historical scheme, 222
Hitler, Adolf, 107, 110
Hudson Institute, 57, 115, 118–19n.,
  176, 177, 232, 233, 247
Humanist left, 82–85, 89, 91, 94, 97,
  102, 141, 246
  see also Counterculture

Ideational culture, 9–10
Identification techniques, 196
Ideological renewal governments, 104–
  07, 112, 178–79
Ideologies
  and futurology, 246–50
  new, 70–71

revisionist communism, capitalism, and Christianity, 79–80
social and political (chart), 90
India, 125–26, 128
Indian Ocean, 157, 160
Indonesia, 19, 65, 122, 241
Industrial development, 9, 18–19, 41, 74
see also Technology
Industrial Revolution, 18, 25, 221, 222, 229
Industry, 9, 25–26, 223, 224–25
see also Post-industrial society
Instability (sources)
ancien regime morale, 142–44
chart, 116, 149
deliberate nuclear war, 145
domestic violence, 146
irredentism, 140–41, 148
nationalism, 140
neo-anarchism, 70, 139–40, 142, 163
remnants of colonialism, 147–48
revenge against ex-imperialists, 147
revolutionary acts by youth, 146–47
"spiritual constriction," 141
technological changes, 141–42
terrorism, 142
underdeveloped nations, 18–19
unintentional war, 146
violent ideologies, 144–47
see also Turning points
Institutionalization of technological change, 16
Intellectuals, 27–28, 73, 182–83
Intercontinental ballistic missiles (ICBMs), 191, 195, 200
International law, 128
Irish Republic, 55
Irrational governments
Allende's Chile, 21
Caribbean area, 75
Castro's Cuba, 19, 21, 75–76, 136–37
Irredentism, 127, 140–41, 148
Israel, 110, 111, 112, 125, 128, 135, 158, 198, 200–01
Italian-American Civil Rights League, 86
Italy, 54

Japan
Anglo-Japanese Naval Treaties, 34, 239

and Asia, 241
birth rate, 23
conglomerates, 15
early twentieth century, 238–39
economic growth, 46–47, 49, 64, 132, 232–34, 237, 240, 241, 242–43
and Great Britain, 238–39
gross national product, 47, 49, 232–33, 240, 242
labor shortage, 240, 241
multinational corporations, 65
in multipolar world, 46
national character, 234, 243
rearming of, 242
recovery after World War II, 131–32
research and development, 241
Sino-Japanese confrontation, 71–73
Soka, Gakkai, 105
as superstate, 41, 46–47, 233–43
trade, 242–43
and United States, 200, 233, 236–38, 239, 242, 243
Jefferson, Thomas, 224
Jensen, Arthur, 108
"Jesus freaks," 228
Jewish Defense League, 68, 86
Jews, 101, 110–12, 138, 171
Johnson, Lyndon B., 29

Kennedy, John F., 35
Knowledge industries, 9, 27

Language-minority groups, 121
Laser technology, 16, 195–96, 197, 204
Late sensate culture, 10–11, 54, 89, 90, 105, 163–64
Latin America, 56–57, 64–65, 73
Law and order issues
authority, 67–68
conservative movements, 80
discretionary behavior, 68–69
global metropolis, 45
in surprise-free projection, 41–42, 67–70, 184
worldwide, 67–70
see also Crime, Terrorism, Violence
Learning in post-industrial society, 228–29
Leisure, 9, 225–26, 230
see also Affluence
Life styles, 44, 85–86, 169–70, 226

Literacy, 9, 26, 27
Looking Backward, 246
Louis XIV, 207–08
Lowell, Robert, 249
Luther, Martin, 98

MacDonald, Dwight, 239n.
Machiavelli, Niccolo, 29
Macro-historical perspectives, 7–8, 246, 248–49
Mandarinism, 13
Marijuana, 95, 96
Marshall Plan, 172
Marx, Karl, 7, 218, 221
Marxism, 151–52, 244, 246, 247, 249
McCarthy, Joseph, 92, 181
McLuhan, Marshall, 44
Megalopoli, 9, 24, 69
Melbourne, Lord, 98
Memoirs of a Revolutionist, 239
Meritocratic trends, 11–13
Mexico, 64–65, 66
Middle Ages, 10, 18, 26, 98
Military capability, 8, 12, 17
Military force, 123, 125, 131
Military-industrial complex, 173
MIRVs, 191
Missiles (*see* Ballistic missiles)
Modernization, 9, 18–21
Monarchies, 11–12
Mosaic cultures, 43, 85–86, 87, 101, 163, 172, 226
Moslem world, 11, 126
Multifold trend
  affluence, 9, 21–22, 226
  economic development, 8, 13–15, 37, 41, 56–65, 214, 215
  education, 9, 26–28, 59, 184, 228–29
  "green revolution," 41, 58, 134, 154, 168
  industrial development, 9, 18–19, 41, 74
  industry, 9, 25–26, 223, 224–25
  leisure, 9, 225–26, 230
  literacy, 9, 26, 27
  modernization, 9, 18–21
  political power, 8, 13–14
  population growth, 9, 22–23
  science, 8, 10, 15–16
  social engineering, 9, 28–29, 208–09, 213

surprise-free projection, 42
  urbanization, 9, 18, 23–25, 165
  see also Sensate culture, Technology
Multinational corporation (MNC), 41, 58–63, 65
Multipolar world
  and bipolar world, 122, 151
  Europe, 45–46
  European Economic Community, 48–50
  Germany, 47–48
  Japan, 46–47
  multinational corporations, 58–63
  pentapolar world, 46
  in surprise-free projection, 41, 67
Murray, Gilbert, 168n.

Nasser, Gamal Abdel, 115
Nationalism, 73, 120–23, 140
Nation-state system, 120–21, 123, 140, 151
NATO, 52, 167
Natural calamity as branch point, 176, 177
Nazis, 144
Negroes, 107–09, 110, 162, 165–66, 170–71, 174, 183, 184
Neo-anarchism, 70, 139–40, 142, 163
Neo-epicurean, 169, 171, 231
Neo-fascism, 71
Neo-gentleman, 169, 171
Neo-isolationism, 17, 151, 159–60, 167, 175, 185, 200
Neo-materialist, 169
Neo-nationalism, 70–71
Neo-racism, 107–09
Neo-stoic, 169, 170, 231
Neumann, John von, 76, 189, 215–16
New Industrial State, The, 26
New Left, 70, 78, 94
Nixon Doctrine, 151
Nixon, Richard, 185, 194, 207, 208, 217-18, 239n.
Non-Communist Pacific Asia (NOCPA), 241
Normative forecasting, 245, 250
Northern Ireland, *see* Ulster
Northwestern Europe, 10–11, 20, 42, 88–89
Nuclear weapons
  forecasting, 188

orbiting, 202
proliferation, 198, 199–201, 242
Nuclear-powered aircraft, 202–03

Optimal system, 245
Organization of American States
    (OAS), 128
Orwell, George, 97

Pacific Asia, 65, 241
Pacifist propaganda, 128–29
Pakistan, 19, 86
Paradigm, 89
Patton, George S., 239
Pelagius, 246–47
"Pentagon Papers," 177
Perspectives of future studies, 244–45,
    248–49, 250
Pfaff, William, 70n.
Plumb, J. H., 249n.
Poland, 156
Polaris/Poseidon force, 192, 195
Polarization, 96, 174
Police politicalization, 107
Political debacle as branch point, 176,
    177–82
Political power, 8, 13–14, 116, 173,
    174, 182–83
Politics, 225–26
Pollution, 166, 168, 172, 173, 216,
    217–18, 219
Pompidou, Georges, 226
Population growth, 9, 22–23
Populism, 102–04, 105, 178, 184
Post-economic society, 225
Post-industrial society
    boredom, 226–27
    ennui, 226–28
    evolution or revolution, 220–21
    gentlemanly society, 229–30, 231
    Japan, 240
    learning, 228–29
    leisure, 225–26, 229
    post-economic society, 225
    post-manufacturing economy, 223–24
    quaternary economy, 9, 26, 224–25
    religiosity, 228
    travel, 227, 230
    unemployment, 227
    Westernistic society, 230–31
Post-manufacturing society, 223
Predictions, 39, 43, 176

Predictive forecasting, 244, 245
Preferred system, 245
Primary industry, 9, 25–26, 223, 224
Progress, 206–07, 210–13, 214, 215,
    218, 249
Projections, 39–43
Protectionism, 237–38, 242
Prudential internationalist, 247, 248

Quaternary industry, 9, 26, 224–25

Racism, 103, 104, 107–09
RAND Corporation, 118n., 187, 188,
    189
Reformation, 98
Reich, Charles, 93–94, 249
Religion
    and birth control, 23
    clergy, 100–01, 171
    counterreformation, 100–02
    "Jesus freaks," 228
    in post-industrial society, 228
    Protestant parochial schools, 101–02
    Western culture, 10, 226
Research and Development (R&D),
    204, 233, 241
Responsible center, 82–85
Reversal of alliances, 153–54, 158–59,
    160, 200
"Reverse discrimination policies," 17c
Rhodes, Cecil, 235
Rhodesia, 122, 147

"Safeguard" ABM system, 191
St. Augustine, 7, 246–47
SALT talks, 17
Satellites, 195
Scenarios
    defined, 176–77, 182
    nuclear proliferation, 200–01
    responsible (or humanistic) center
        reestablishes itself, 182–85
    United States-Soviet war, 192
    Vietnam "debacle," 177–82, 183
    "worst case," 200–01, 250
Schlesinger, Arthur, Jr., 182
Science
    long-term trend, 8, 15–16
    in United States, 164, 173
    Western culture, 10
    see also Technology
Science Advisory Committee, 218

Scientific Advisory Board, 189–90
Search for meaning and purpose in life, 77–79, 84
Secondary industry, 9, 26, 223, 224
Self-fulfilling prophecy, 245
Sensate culture
late sensate, 10, 54, 89, 90, 163–64
and mosaic culture, 86, 101, 163
multifold trend, 8, 9, 10, 113
Northwestern Europe, 10–11, 54
Separatism, 50–56
Service industries, 9, 26, 223
Sino-German collaboration, 153–54, 159
Sino-Soviet split, 135, 136, 159
Six Day War (1967), 111
Skinner, B. F., 249
Snow, Sir Charles P., 50
"Soccer War," 128
Social engineering
long-term trend, 9, 28–29
and technological advance, 208–09, 213
in United States, 164
Socialist nations, 11, 13, 15, 20, 23, 24
Societal levers, 67, 77–78, 84
Socrates, 99
Soka Gakkai, 105
Sombart, Werner, 53
Sorokin, Pitirim, 9–10
South African Republic, 22, 147
Southern Europe, 65
Soviet Union
and Communist parties, 138, 139
and counterrevolutionary elements, 124
and Cuba, 135, 136–37, 159
disappointing foreign and domestic policy, 135–39
and Eastern Europe, 50–51, 124, 127, 130
in multipolar world, 46
research and development, 204
Salyud "space station" program, 195n.
Sino-Soviet split, 135, 136, 159
Soviet thermidor, 133, 134–39
Josef Stalin, 99, 134, 144
United States-Soviet conflict, 115, 130
weapons systems, 191–97, 198, 200–01, 202
see also Czechoslovakia

Spain, 54
Spengler, Oswald, 7, 36n.
Spiritual constriction, 141
Stability (sources)
agricultural developments, 134
arms controls, 133
chart, 117–18, 149
climate of apathy, 130
crisis management, 133
economic and social recovery of Europe and Japan, 131–32
end of Communist/non-Communist confrontation, 130–31
fear of extremism, 128
fear of nuclear war, 129, 130
few "power vacuums," 133
great powers, 123, 126, 127
high cost of sophisticated strategic weapons, 134
high standards of international behavior, 130
internal development, 124–25
international economic development, 130
international law, 128, 131
invulnerability of United States and Soviet forces, 133–34
lack of irredentism, 127
military weakness, 132
nation-state system, 120–23
pacifist propaganda, 128–29
sense of world community, 124
Soviet thermidor, 133, 134–39
spheres of influence, 127
technology, 118, 125
United Nations, 121, 123, 126, 127
United States military superiority, 132–33, 150, 151
weakened ideology, 126
"world public opinion," 122
see also Turning points
Stalin, Josef, 99, 134, 144
Straight-line projections, 39
Strategic air defense systems, 193
Strategic command and control systems, 194–95, 197–98
Student activism, 94
Submarine launched ballistic missiles (SLBM), 192, 195
Suburbanization, 9, 24–25
Sukarno, Achmed, 19

Supersonic transport (SST) aircraft, 197, 203
Supreme Court of the United States, 101
Surprise-free projection
chronic confrontations, 71–73
Comecon, 50–51
communications, 65
conservative and backlash movements, 80
counterculture, 42, 83
defined, 39–40
La Deuxième Belle Epoque, 43–45
economic development, 56–63
educated incapacity, 80–82
European Economic Community, 48–50
five dynamic areas, 60, 63–65
"gap ideology," 57, 58
Germany, 47–48
global metropolis, 44, 45, 65
"green revolution," 58
humanist left-responsible center confrontation, 82–85
Japan, 46–47
law and order issues, 67–70, 80
modestly optimistic for U.S., 169–72
modestly pessimistic for U. S., 172–75
mosaic culture, 43, 85–86, 87
multinational corporations, 58–63
multipolar world, 45–46, 67
nation-states, 51–53, 67
neutral for U.S., 163–69, 182–85
new ideologies, 70–71, 79–80
1985 technological crisis, 42, 76, 205–19
outline, 40–43
problems of numbers, size and bigness, 76–77
relatively unlikely events, 149
revisionist ideologies, 79–80
search for meaning and purpose in life, 77–79, 85
sectionalism, 51–56
societal levers, 78, 84
synthesis between old and new, 87
terrorism, 69–70
Third World, 73–75
trade, 63–64, 65–66
travel, 65–66, 75
for United States, 163–85

violence, 69–70
violent movements, 75–76, 80
Sweden, 125, 197
Syndicalism, 70, 173
Synthesis, 87, 96–97, 112–13

Technocrats, 229
Technological forecasting
automobile, 205–06
ballistic missiles, 191–92, 195
barrier technology, 196
chemical and biological weapons (CBW), 193–94, 198, 202
command and control systems, 194–95, 197–98
counter-insurgency techniques, 196–97, 199
delphi, 187–88
envelope, 187, 188
fast deployment logistics (FDL), 194
fusion weapons, 202
helicopters, 196, 197
identification techniques, 196
intuition, 187–88, 190
lasers, 195–96, 197, 204
methods, 186–90
military aircraft, 193, 194, 196, 197, 203, 204
nuclear weapons proliferation, 198, 199–201
nuclear-powered aircraft, 202–03
orbiting nuclear weapons, 202
possibilities for the 1980s, 201–04
possibilities for the 1970s, 191–97
satellites, 195
SST, 197, 203
strategic air defense system, 193
"technological surprise," 204
transport aircraft, 194
V/STOL aircraft, 196, 197
weapons systems, 188–97
Technological Forecasting and Long-Range Planning, 187n.
"Technological surprise," 204
Technology
disadvantages, 207–08, 211, 213, 214, 215, 216
and ecology, 218–19
educated incapacity, 81
effect on society, 205–19
exponential process, 217, 218

idea of progress, 206–07, 210–13
institutionalization, 16
Japan, 233
long-term trend, 8, 15–16, 205–19
loss of control, 216
1985 technological crisis, 42, 76, 205–19
post-industrial society, 227
sabotage, 69
and social engineering, 208–09, 213
source of instability, 141–42
source of stability, 118, 125
in surprise-free projection, 41, 42
in United States, 164
Western culture, 10
see also Science, Technological forecasting
Television, 16, 171–72
Teller, Edward, 189
Terrorism, 69–70, 92, 98, 142, 152, 162, 196
Tertiary industry, 9, 26, 223
Third World
anti-colonialism, 111–12, 120
in bipolar world, 122
China and, 157
fractionalization, 121
industrialization, 18
lack of importance, 73–75
language-minority groups, 121
law and order issue, 69
multinational corporations, 59–60
nationalism in, 120–21
revolutionary movements, 157
turmoil and violence, 73–74
violent ideologies, 144–46, 147
and Western culture, 19–20, 73, 74
see also Underdeveloped nations
Tocqueville, Alexis de, 220
Tourism, 66, 67, 75, 227
Toynbee, Arnold J., 7
Trade, 63, 64, 175
Trade unions, 173–74
Transport aircraft, 194, 203
Transportation, 25, 141
Travel, 65–67, 227, 230, 242
Trotsky, Leon, 97
Tupamaros, 70
Turning points
chart, 149
Communist regime in Latin America, 159
counterculture, 151–52
depression, 154–55
dynamic Communist leadership, 156–57
food deficit, 154
loss of American strategic advantage, 150–51
Middle East confrontation, 158
new ideology, 153
nuclear weapons proliferation, 160–61
reversal of alliances, 153–54, 158–59, 160
rise of a Third World power, 160–61
shift in moral balance, 151
Sino-Soviet tension, 159
Soviet intervention, 155–56
threat to Third World area, 157–58, 160
U. S. neo-isolationism, 151, 159–60
Vietnam War, 155
Two Cultures and the Scientific Revolution, The, 50

Ulster, 34, 55, 70, 115
Underdeveloped nations
and counterculture, 20–21
elites, 18
"green revolution," 58
industrialization, 18–19
instability, 18–19
literacy, 27
military weakness, 132
multinational corporations, 59–60, 62
poverty, 147
in surprise-free projection, 43–44
urbanization, 18, 23–24
Westernistic trend, 19–20
see also Third World
Underground churches, 101
Underground press, 11
Unemployment in post-industrial society, 227
United Kingdom, see Great Britain
United Nations
aid to poor nations, 142
long-term trend, 14
membership, 120, 123
and nation-states, 121
source of instability, 140
source of stability, 126, 127

United States
  anti-Semitism, 110–12
  birth rate, 23
  and Canada, 49, 62–63
  and China, 131
  counterculture, 88–89, 94–99, 100–02, 151–52
  counterreformation, 11, 95–98, 99, 100–13
  crime, 69–70, 109, 163, 166, 173, 183
  and Cuba, 136–37, 159
  culture, 20
  "La Deuxième Belle Epoque," 32, 35–36, 37–38
  dropouts, 16–17, 78, 85–86
  ecology movement, 218–19
  educated incapacity, 81–82
  education, 26, 27
  fascism, 98, 104, 106
  Great Depression, 154, 182
  "Great Society" programs, 29
  ideological renewal governments, 104–07, 112, 178–79
  intellectuals, 27–28
  and Japan, 200, 233, 236–38, 239, 242, 243
  knowledge industries, 27
  labor force, 165, 237
  law and order issue, 69, 70, 80
  lower-class movements, 102–04, 105
  military establishment, 167
  military power, 132–33, 150, 151
  modestly optimistic surprise-free projection, 169–72
  modestly pessimistic surprise-free projection, 172–75
  mosaic culture, 43, 163, 172
  multinational corporations, 59, 60, 65
  in multipolar world, 46
  neo-racism, 107–09
  neutral surprise-free projection, 163–69, 182–85
  pollution, 166, 168, 172, 173
  populism, 102–04, 105, 178, 184
  protectionism, 237–38
  racism, 103, 104, 107–09
  research and development, 204
  social and political ideologies, 90, 96
  social engineering, 29, 164
  suburbanization, 24–25
  surprise-free projections, 163–85
  urbanization, 165
  U.S.-Soviet conflict, 115
  weapons systems, 191–97, 198, 200–01, 202
  and Westernistic world, 19–20
  world policeman, 126, 200
  see also Negroes, Neo-isolationism, Vietnam War
Untermenschen, 124
Urban guerrillas, 70, 199
Urbanization, 9, 18, 23–25, 165
Uruguay, 70

Vietnam War, 32, 35, 115, 126, 131, 138, 155, 160, 163, 177–82, 183, 184, 185, 195, 196, 197, 199
Vietnamization policy, 181
Violence, 69–70, 75–76, 80, 116, 144–46
V/STOL aircraft, 196, 197

Wallace, George, 82, 103, 109, 176
Wallace, Henry, 92
Weapons systems, see Technological forecasting
Weathermen, 94, 97
Weltanschauungen, 89, 90
Western culture
  cable television, 16, 171–72
  idea of progress, 206
  ideational, 9–10
  long-term trend, 8–9, 19–20, 85–86
  newspapers and periodicals, 122
  religion, 10, 79–80, 86
  societal levers, 78
  technological advance, 206
  Third World, 20–21, 73, 74
  see also Hellenistic Greece, Mosaic culture, Sensate culture, Westernistic world
Western Europe
  anti-Semitism, 110
  La Belle Epoque, 32–36, 44
  and Eastern Europe, 51, 64
  law and order issues, 67
  multifold trends, 8–9, 10–29
  nation-states, 51–52, 53
  separatism, 51–56
  see also Specific countries
Westernistic world, 19–21, 38, 230–31
Wiener, Anthony J., 90, 209n.

Wilhelm II, Kaiser, 235
Women in labor force, 165
Work discipline, 21–22
"World public opinion," 122
World War I, 34, 35, 36
World War II, 144
"Worst case" scenario, 200–01, 250

Year 2000, The, 8, 89n., 169n., 230, 248
Youth, 146–47
    see also Counterculture
Yugoslavia, 127

Zero population growth, 23